As Parents Age

As Parents Age

A PSYCHOLOGICAL AND PRACTICAL GUIDE

Joseph A. Ilardo, Ph.D., L.C.S.W.

VanderWyk & Burnham

Acton, Massachusetts

Published by VanderWyk & Burnham
A Division of Publicom, Inc.
P.O. Box 2789, Acton, Massachusetts 01720

This publication is sold with the understanding that the publisher is not engaged in rendering legal, psychiatric, or other professional services. If expert assistance is required, the services of a competent professional person should be sought.

This book is available for quantity purchases. For information on bulk discounts, call (800) 789-7916 or write to Special Sales at the above address.

Library of Congress Cataloging-in-Publication Data

Ilardo, Joseph A.
    As parents age: a psychological and practical guide/Joseph A. Ilardo
        p.   cm.
    Includes bibliographical references and index.
    ISBN 1-889242-04-7 (hc.). — ISBN 1-889242-05-5 (pbk.)
    1. Aging parents—United States—Psychology. 2. Aging parents—Care—United States. 3. Aging parents—United States—Family relationships. 4. Adult children—United States—Family relationships.   I. Title.
HQ1064.U5I47   1998
306.874—dc21   98-20874
                                                                              CIP

Interior book design by Cory Design
Cover design by Joyce C. Weston
Cover photograph by Randy Wells, Courtesy Tony Stone Images

FIRST PRINTING
Manufactured in the United States of America
10 9 8 7 6 5 4 3 2 1

This book is dedicated to Roberta Ilardo, my wife of more than thirty years, who has been an inspiration as a woman, as a wife and mother, as a professional educator, and of late, as a caregiver whose earnestness and love have helped both her aging parents and mine immeasurably.

ACKNOWLEDGMENTS

I am deeply grateful to the readers who so generously gave of their time to critique various chapters in the book. Thanks to Ann Leiss, chief patient representative at Danbury (Connecticut) Hospital, for her helpful reading and critique of early drafts of several chapters. I am also grateful to Suzanne Murdock, LCSW of Homecare, Inc., for her thoughtful review of Chapter Five. She offered many valuable suggestions that made for a much better chapter. Carole Rothman, Ph.D., clinical psychologist and colleague at Lehman College, offered useful suggestions on the fourth chapter, especially in distinguishing between cognitive and emotional components of mental disorders among the elderly. Julia MacMillan, RN, BSN, a critical care nurse for twenty-three years, offered a careful critique of Chapter Seven. Her participation in a task force on ethics of the American Association of Critical Care Nurses enabled her to bring invaluable insights to her reading. Her comments improved the chapter immeasurably. Attorney Mark Pancrazio and Judge Peter Larkin offered valuable commentary on sections of the book dealing with Conservatorships; I am grateful for their assistance. The suggestions and criticisms of these professionals added much to what you are about to read.

Meredith Rutter, Katy Allen, and Sheila Boyle of VanderWyk & Burnham have been helpful and delightful partners in the process of bringing this book to completion. Their enthusiasm and insights, their editorial suggestions and contributions have shaped the book in important ways and improved it substantially.

My daughter Karen Leigh Ilardo provided invaluable assistance by bringing her computer experience to the various formatting tasks, most importantly the creation of an index.

Literature provided by Kelly Assisted Living, the Lutheran Home of Southbury, Mediplex., Inc., Patient Care, Inc., and other institutions has been a valuable source of help, as have materials provided by the professionals in the Connecticut Elderly Services Division of the

Department of Social Services, especially Pamela Giannini. I also owe a special debt of gratitude to the social workers, nurses, librarians, and other professionals, too numerous to name, who have taken the time to answer questions, verify information, and otherwise improve this book.

As always, my wife, Roberta, has been an invaluable source of support and understanding. Without her wisdom, sensitivity, practical suggestions, patience, and insight, this book would never have been written.

CONTENTS

Contents

"You got me, doctor!" the elderly gentleman said politely, a pleasant smile on his face. He had been stumped again by a question from the young physician.

The doctor was unruffled. "That's okay," he responded affably. "Now tell me," his voice was soft. "Do you know what year it is?" The man paused, a frown furrowing his brow. The pause grew embarrassingly long.

"1988!" he finally blurted. He was off by four years.

The doctor was calm. None of this was extraordinary for him—clinically interesting, perhaps, and useful for purposes of diagnosis, but not extraordinary.

Sure. This wasn't *his* father.

The ritual of the routine physical exam that followed was reassuring. As I struggled to absorb what I had just witnessed, the thought occurred to me that the same scene is undoubtedly repeated many times every day, in physicians' offices from coast to coast. An elderly family member is brought in for a check-up. An examination reveals that he or she is seriously ill, or as in my father's case that he is losing his grip on life. The family reacts with stunned sadness. They are challenged to accept the unsettling reality that things will never again be what they once were.

I learned in a very visceral way that day that aging has a profound impact not only on seniors themselves but also on their adult children. In some cases, as in mine, the impact is both personal and professional. In addition to redefining my relationship with my father and reevaluating my relationships with my mother, wife, and children, I began reading widely to understand professionally all I could about aging and its effects. I attended seminars, consulted with geriatricians and gerontologists, and became an active member of several national associations created to help caregivers. I befriended attorneys and critical-care nurses and otherwise deepened and broadened my appreciation of aging and its impact on the family.

All this began changing my then fifteen-year-old practice as a psychotherapist. Within several months of that visit to the doctor's office, I began offering workshops on eldercare at my local hospital, organizing caregivers' support groups, and writing a column for a local newspaper.

Each activity sparked an avalanche of responses. It became clear that caregivers' needs are largely unmet. As a consequence, I formed an organization devoted exclusively to meeting those needs. Under that umbrella, I now see many seniors as well as adult children struggling with the practical and emotional demands of caregiving.

The more time I have spent helping these clients, the deeper my understanding of their needs has grown. In a very real sense, this book is an outgrowth of my personal and professional journey over the past six years.

Experience has taught me that one of the things adult children need most is information. Chapter One is a response. There, as elsewhere, I have summarized as accurately as I could the increasing body of data on the subject of aging and its effects. I have tried doing it in a way that is both informative and engaging. Throughout, I have presented my ideas in as "reader friendly" a manner as I could, addressing my readers in the second person and inviting *your* participation in the learning process.

I have learned many important lessons from my clients over the past six years. One lesson was brought home when I conducted a brief survey during my very first workshop. Though the workshop had been advertised as designed for adult children of the elderly, several attendees reported that they were not providing care for parents. One woman was the primary caregiver for an aunt of the husband she had divorced many years ago. One man came to the meeting because he had assumed responsibility for the care of an elderly neighbor. A third person looked after a family friend.

The word "parents" had been interpreted loosely by these people, and it should be defined loosely by you, too. For convenience, I will use the word "parents" throughout this book. However, much of what I impart will be relevant regardless of whether the person cared for is a parent. You are invited, therefore, to replace *parents* with whatever label more accurately describes your elderly care recipient.

Throughout this book, you will learn from the experiences of other adult children. For the most part, these examples are composites of actual families and individuals with whom I have worked. In all cases, details have been changed in order to respect the privacy of clients and to ensure confidentiality. Any resemblance to identifiable individuals and families is strictly coincidental.

I am always interested in hearing from readers. If you would like to share an experience, offer a suggestion, or pose a question, please write me care of VanderWyk and Burnham, P.O. Box 2789, Acton, MA 01720.

JOSEPH A. ILARDO
MAY 1998

As Parents Age

CHAPTER 1

*W*hat Happens as a Person Ages?

A certain degree of decline in physiological and psychological functioning is normal as a person ages. However, many caregivers are not sure what should be cause for concern and what does not need to be.

What is considered "normal" aging? What is "abnormal"? When is it advisable to start an elderly care recipient in an age-appropriate exercise program? When should exercise be avoided? Does a lapse of memory always mean the elderly person has Alzheimer's or some form of dementia, or is some memory loss benign?

These and similar questions have occurred to every conscientious caregiver. The more you know about the changes that occur as a person grows older, the better able you are to help your aging parents and to cope with your own feelings and reactions. Accordingly, this chapter is intended to serve as an introduction to aging and its consequences.

Part One will provide a brief summary of what happens physically as a person ages. Why, for example, do older people become frail? Why are certain diseases, such as cancer and heart disease, so common among the elderly? What happens to the brain as we age? In the second part of the chapter you will learn how growing old affects the aging person emotionally. You will see why, for example, depression and anxiety are common among the elderly. (In later chapters you will learn why the same feelings are also common among the children of the elderly, and why long-dormant family problems sometimes reemerge under the stress of watching a parent age.)

The chapter ends with an inventory that offers you the opportunity to gauge your sensitivity to the needs of the elderly. You will choose among alternative solutions to real problems faced by actual adult children with whom I have worked. You will be able to estimate your sensitivity and apply some of what you will have learned in this chapter.

PART ONE: What Happens Physically as a Person Ages?

The news about aging is not all bad. On the contrary, there is much that is both positive and encouraging. Not only are more people living longer than ever before, but recent research reveals that a great deal can be done to improve the quality of life among the elderly. It is likely that your parents' day-to-day life can be drastically improved, often simply and inexpensively. Following are four basic truths about aging.

1. Although predictable changes occur in people as they grow older, there are many variations in the rates at which people age.

It is therefore inaccurate to speak of "the elderly" in a monolithic way, except for purposes of convenience. Just as children grow at different rates and develop capacities at different times, so, too, do the elderly vary in the ways they age. Anyone who deals with elderly people needs to be sufficiently flexible to see beyond a person's years and to think instead of the unique strengths, capacities, and weaknesses of the individual in question.

2. Even with the same individual, there are significant variations in the rates at which age-related changes occur.

According to Leonard Hayflick, Ph.D., one of the nation's foremost authorities on aging and author of *How and Why We Age* (New York: Ballantine Books, 1994), all bodily systems do not age at the same rate. Changes occur in different parts of the body at different times, and the annual rate of change varies among different tissues, cells, organs, and systems.

Thus, chronological age does not equate with functional age. A person may be 80 years old chronologically, but her cardiovascular system may be only 50 years old functionally. Hayflick compares the body to a clock shop, with tissues and organs behaving independently, each ticking at its own rate.

3. In order to distinguish among elderly individuals, different ways of classifying elderly people are widely used.

While no one way is entirely satisfactory, each way affords a slightly different perspective on the needs and problems of older people. Each way can help you prepare for your parents' aging and can help you discuss your parents' needs with health-care professionals.

One way of classifying elderly people is by age alone. As Figure 1.1 shows, people between the ages of 65 and 74 are considered the *young old*. People between 75 and 84 are considered the *middle old*. The *old old* are above age 84. Different capacities are typically lost in a more-or-less predictable order as a person moves from the *young old* to the *old old* category. For example, a person who is *young old* may be quite self-sufficient, whereas the *old old* require greater levels of assistance. Reference to this classification system will be made throughout this book. Although this system is crude, it provides rough guidelines that

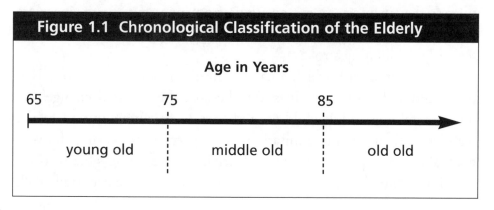

Figure 1.1 Chronological Classification of the Elderly

are helpful in preparing yourself for changes likely to occur as your parents age.

Another way of categorizing elderly people is according to their ability to manage self-care and the activities of daily living. *Self-care* includes actions like bathing and dressing oneself; *activities of daily living* include homemaking, shopping, bill paying, and similar tasks. As represented in Figure 1.2, at one end are people who can manage their own affairs with little or no assistance, and at the other extreme are people who require total supervision and custodial care—they are entirely dependent on others for the most elemental tasks, such as dressing and using the toilet. In between are people who require regular help in managing their lives (for example, an elderly widow who needs to be visited three times a week by a home-health aide for assistance with shopping and homemaking).

Figure 1.2 Life Management Classification of the Elderly

those who can manage their lives with little or no assistance	those who require regular help in managing their lives	those who are entirely dependent on others

Note that in both systems of classification, a continuum is used to suggest that in most cases transitions from one stage to the next are gradual. Exceptions include a sudden and unexpected event such as a seriously debilitating stroke.

The slowness with which a parent's need for care usually grows is at once kind and pernicious. It is kind because the fact that changes are incremental gives adult children a chance to become adjusted to the realities of their parents' limitations. It is pernicious because the very gradualness of a person's functional decline makes it possible to overlook important changes and even to deny that they have occurred at all.

4. Aging can no longer be equated with inevitable decline and disease.

Systematic research conducted over recent decades has begun to yield impressive data suggesting that many of the impairments that were once thought to be inevitably associated with aging simply are not. We now know that many of these conditions are under the control of the person to a much greater degree than formerly known. Senility, for example, is not inevitable. Neither is cancer. Neither is heart disease.

PRIMARY AND SECONDARY AGING

Gerontologists have determined that there are two parallel processes involved in aging. In this book I use the terms *primary aging* and *secondary aging* to differentiate between those aspects of aging that are inevitable and those that are in varying degrees under the control of the individual.

Primary Aging

Primary aging refers to genetically based, unavoidable changes that are built into the organism. These "hard-wired" changes are not yet subject to much significant influence, although some progress is being made in this direction. Eventually, it will be possible to alter primary aging factors profoundly by the use of such tools as genetic engineering, but for the time being, we may be said to have "good genes" or "bad genes."

Among the most significant changes that occur during primary aging is the decline in levels of something gerontologists call *trophic factors.* This is the name given to hormones and hormonelike substances produced by the body, including estrogen, testosterone, human growth factor, and insulinlike growth factor. The decline in these substances results in the frailty so characteristic of people who are middle old and old old. By that point in life, there is a measurable decline in the thickness of the skin, in bone mass, and in the number of muscle fibers.

These changes account for an elderly "look" that is reflected in the skin, posture, gait, and other features.

Even though the decline in trophic factors is currently considered inevitable, scientific developments are already making it possible to reduce and even reverse the impact of this decline. One obvious instance is hormone replacement therapy. Long available for post-menopausal women, hormone replacement therapy is now beginning to become available to men. The results are often dramatic, with patients receiving hormone replacements reporting a marked increase in youthful vigor.

The course of primary aging can also be slowed somewhat by making the most of what you have left. In the January 1994 issue of the *Journal of Gerontology*, interesting research was reported. The authors studied the effects of a year-long course of resistance training, or "weight training," on eleven people with an average age of 68.2 years (young old). By examining muscle strength and size at the outset of the study and periodically thereafter, the researchers concluded that while resistance training could do nothing to recover lost muscle fiber, it did result in increased strength of remaining fibers. A moderate program of exercise, the researchers concluded, leads to sustained increases in strength. Whether these same changes apply to the middle old and the old old remains to be seen, but it is very likely they do.

Primary aging also involves a decline in the acuity of the senses. Vision, hearing, touch, taste, and smell all decline in their efficiency. Thus, for example, older people often report difficulty seeing at night, seeing straight ahead, and doing close work. Regular visits to an ophthalmologist, and an immediate visit at any indication of a rapid change in vision, are the best ways to understand the causes and to ensure that necessary remedial steps are taken.

An ongoing study of the elderly conducted under the auspices of the National Institutes of Health has determined that, for reasons not yet understood, hearing loss occurs more rapidly in men than in women.

Among the most common consequences of the loss of auditory acuity is the inability to distinguish between closely related sounds such as *f* and *s*. Unfortunately for many seniors, hearing loss often becomes more general and extensive than mixing up a few sounds. When extensive hearing loss occurs, the consequences are devastating. Inability to hear well deprives victims of a major means by which people relate. It inhibits communication, turns the person more inward, and increases the probability of misunderstandings. Elderly people who suffer from significant hearing impairment report feeling left out and suspicious of others.

Once again, however, careful monitoring of an aging parent's hearing can point to remedies that are often simple and dramatic in their effect. In one case, for example, Mr. M struggled for years with difficulty hearing. My client and her family presumed nothing could be done about it. When they took him to a geriatric health center for the first time (for an unrelated problem), they learned they were wrong. Immediately upon meeting Mr. M and realizing he was hard of hearing, a nurse practitioner reached for a simple amplifying device that made it possible for the elderly man to hear everything she said when she spoke in a normal voice. The family learned that same day that the device is available in any local electronic gadgets chain store for under $25.

As a person grows older, he or she experiences a decrease in the efficiency of the mechanisms by which sensations register on the skin and of those neural pathways by which sensations travel to the brain. For example, an elderly person will not feel or react quickly to a stimulus that a younger person would find painful. In her eighties and still living on her own, Mrs. R occasionally reported "discovering" small burns on her hands. She did not recall burning herself at the stove. Although Mrs. R didn't recall feeling painful sensations, her skin tissue showed damage. Her experience is not unusual.

When older people talk of food losing its taste, they are really commenting on the decrease in their body's ability to respond to flavors and to discriminate among them. This often results in a tendency to over-season food. The consequences may be simply inconvenient, as when overseasoning causes gastrointestinal distress, but they can also be downright dangerous, as when the excessive use of salt contributes to high blood pressure.

The decline in the ability to smell robs the elderly both of pleasure and of necessary warning signs. Recently, a patient told me about an experience her elderly mother had had not long before. Mrs. P was alone at home on a cold winter day, with the house all shut up. As was her habit, after breakfast she sat in the kitchen for about two hours reading her daily newspaper at the table. Mrs. P noticed nothing amiss until her home-health aide arrived and immediately began opening windows and doors. Shocked, for it was cold outside, Mrs. P asked what was going on. "This house smells like a gas leak!" the aide explained. Sure enough, the elderly woman had failed to notice an open, unlit jet on her gas stove.

It has been argued that the single most important event in the aging process is the decline in the efficiency of the immune system. For reasons not yet fully understood, the immune system becomes weaker with age, making elderly people more susceptible to influenza, pneumonia, and other infections. Aggressive steps taken to protect the elderly from infection can yield benefits. This is why it is so common and important for the elderly to get flu shots.

Secondary Aging

Secondary aging refers to changes directly and measurably affected by lifestyle, disease, and trauma. Whether these age-related changes occur at all, and how quickly they come about, are affected by both a person's behavior and his experience. We cannot control accidents and injuries, but we do make lifestyle choices. It is now well known that a person's health in old age is directly and dramatically influenced by the diet, exercise patterns, and use of tobacco, alcohol, and other substances carried on throughout life. In other words, what one does in her twenties and thirties carried on throughout life makes a difference when she reaches her seventies.

It is more difficult to control whether or not one contracts a disease or suffers a traumatic injury. Nevertheless, an individual's personal habits can affect the likelihood of disease or injury. For example, a furniture mover, dancer, or football player might expect to suffer physical ailments in old age as a consequence of his or her profession. Similarly, a missionary or a person in the medical field runs the risk of contracting a disease that might have long-term consequences.

It is clear that choices made in one's youth affect how well and how rapidly a person ages, but it is also true that choices made in one's golden years have a similar impact. Seniors who remain active and whose lives serve a purpose often do better than those who are timid and reclusive. We have all heard of people who were healthy and productive until they sold their business or retired from a satisfying career. Afterward, their health declined; they did less well both emotionally and physically. Their stories clearly have a lesson to teach.

Later, you will learn more about specific steps your parents can take to remain healthy and active and to retard or prevent altogether many of the declines we associate with secondary aging. Right now, we will look more closely at some of the declines that can occur.

In general, as people age, their physical systems gradually slow down, most becoming markedly less efficient over time. For example, according to research undertaken by the National Institute on Aging, 40 percent of lung capacity is lost between the ages of 20 and 80 years.

Similarly, the circulatory system declines in efficiency as the heart weakens and obstructions accumulate in the blood vessels. The digestive system, too, loses some of its former efficiency, making certain foods difficult or impossible to digest. Declines in the strength and efficiency of the components of the muscular-skeletal system result in stiffness, muscle weakness, and balance problems. General muscle atrophy causes bladder control problems, which affect nearly 10 percent of all people over age 65.

All the declines mentioned in the previous paragraph are subject to influence by a combination of exercise, adequate nutrition, and a positive mental attitude. These may not prevent the declines altogether, but each can certainly slow down the rate at which the declines occur. Thus, a vigorous program of exercise, along with a healthy diet and attention to one's mental attitude, can have profound effects on the quality of an elderly person's life. Encouraged by her physician and the friends in her seniors club, one 83-year-old client undertook a program of aerobic exercise that corrected shortness of breath and balance problems that had threatened to make her housebound.

As a person ages, there is a drop in the efficiency with which the brain assimilates and processes information, a subject of special complexity and interest. Brain function is one of the body's most complex processes. Recent technological developments have begun to shed light on brain activities which previously had been beyond our understanding. One such development is the brain scan. Better than an MRI, positron-emission tomography (known as a PET-scan) enables us to watch the brain in action.

Before going further, several critical distinctions about brain processes need to be made.

1. *Brain is not mind.* The physical organ of the brain is not the same as one's mind; the latter concept is broader and includes skills such as abstract reasoning and individual factors such as personality. Thus, a person's mind may remain sharp, although the speed with which his or her brain functions may decline.

2. *Processing time, the rate at which information is manipulated by the brain, is not equivalent to thought quality.* Processing time is purely physical and can be measured by watching the brain in action. For example, using a PET-scan, it is possible to count the

nanoseconds required for a person to read and solve a math problem. Decline in brain speed explains why older people become confused during rapid-fire conversations. There is no doubt that reaction time slows as we age. This fact argues in favor of road-testing older drivers, but there are wide variations in the rate at which reaction time slows, so each person should be evaluated individually. Later I will discuss the strong emotions that accompany decisions about driving. In our automobile-oriented society, taking away a senior's right to drive is equivalent to depriving an impoverished person of economic opportunity, then wondering why that person is upset.

Thought quality refers to such characteristics as the sophistication of one's judgments and the accuracy of one's interpretations of reality. When we describe older people as "wise," our words reflect an awareness of the qualitative dimension of thought. An old person may be slow to process information yet simultaneously more sophisticated in his or her understanding of what is being processed.

3. *Learning and cognitive function involve both brain and mind.* Learning theorists and researchers have established beyond a doubt that mental abilities are subject to conditioning throughout the life span. By keeping one's mind active, a person can achieve a sort of mental fitness equivalent to the physical fitness that results from exercise.

Contrary to the popular myth, people can learn at any age. Mental abilities can be maintained and improved with training, regardless of age. Research conducted over forty years has debunked the myth that old people experience a decline in intelligence.

Again, a distinction is in order. There are two kinds of intelligence, fluid and crystallized. *Fluid intelligence* is what we think of as mental dexterity. It is measured by studying a person's ability to solve unanticipated problems and to abandon traditional ways of viewing problems in favor of new ways. While fluid intelligence does respond to training, recent evidence suggests it does decline slightly with age unless put to use regularly.

Crystallized intelligence, on the other hand, which includes such things as reading comprehension, the ability to express oneself in speech and writing, and the ability to understand information, does not decline and may actually *improve* with age. One of my clients, who is 79, regularly writes for a major Connecticut newspaper. His articles are invariably thoughtful, provocative, and full of insight.

You may be thinking, "What about dementia?" We have all heard of people who are unable to recognize members of their family or who cannot remember a conversation only a few moments afterward. We know, too, that some aged people cannot recall the most basic information about themselves and their past.

Dementia is an illness. Sometimes it is a direct symptom of a disease such as Alzheimer's; other times, dementia occurs as a result of some other disease process. For example, dementia can be caused by one or more mini-strokes that deprive the brain of needed oxygen and result in the death of cells. The result is called *vascular dementia*. Regardless of its origins, however, dementia is decidedly *not* a normal part of the aging process. Only about 10 percent of the population over age 65 show signs of true dementia. Many more show some memory loss, but that is a different phenomenon altogether; memory loss is not equivalent to dementia, although it is one component of the disorder.

Formally defined, *dementia* is a gross intellectual impairment resulting in a loss of memory, inability to concentrate, and increased difficulty with numbers. In addition, the person with dementia experiences restlessness, depression, and loss of time and space orientation. Sometimes the demented person experiences delusions (clinging to false beliefs) and hallucinations (seeing, hearing, or otherwise sensing things that are not there). Sometimes he or she undergoes personality changes: A formerly light-hearted person may become ponderous and depressed; an easy-going person may become irritable and violent. Later you will learn more about dementia and how to help an elderly parent who suffers from its effects.

Thus far we have looked at the physical processes involved in aging. We will now turn to the impact these and other age-related changes have on the emotions of the elderly person.

PART TWO: Emotional Effects of Aging on the Elderly

It is difficult to generalize about the emotional changes that affect elderly people, because the nature and direction of those changes depend on many factors. Key among them is the level of emotional adjustment each person reached during his or her younger years. In the absence of disease or other physiological causes, it can safely be said that a well-adjusted, self-realizing person will remain generally content and optimistic well into old age, although, as we shall see, experiences of loss and disappointment do take their toll. A less well-adjusted person, however, will tend to experience anxiety, depression, paranoia, or other psychological symptoms. Emotional changes among the elderly stem from two sources. Some are the result of life experience. Others are the consequences of the physical changes that occur as people age.

EMOTIONAL CHANGES STEMMING FROM LIFE EXPERIENCE

As a result of many years of life experience, seniors perceive themselves and the world around them differently than younger people do. No less a master observer than the Greek philosopher Aristotle commented on the differences between the characters of the young and the old. Here are a few of his observations:

- The young love and hate passionately. They have strong desires and are inclined to act on them. By contrast, the elderly have often been deceived and have made their share of mistakes. They have few strong loves or hates. They tend to desire little and to be contented quite easily. They err on the side of extreme caution, weighing everything carefully, much to the dismay of the young.

- The young live in anticipation; the elderly live in memory.

- The young are brave but lack self-control; the elderly tend toward temperance and sometimes become afraid.

Whatever you may think of Aristotle's observations, it is a fact that life exacts a toll on all of us. In the words of a depressed elderly client, "I feel as though I've been run over by life and left on the road for dead." While this view is decidedly negative, it does contain a germ of truth.

Think, for a moment, of the experiences of the elderly, and decide for yourself whether these are likely to have an impact on their emotions.

- The elderly lose their day-to-day importance as parents as their children leave the nest and establish lives of their own, sometimes far away. There may be few opportunities for significant interaction between elderly parents and their offspring.

- The elderly lose important relationships as spouses, friends, and siblings die.

- The elderly often experience a loss of a sense of the future. Many elderly people are reluctant to look forward to a future that they doubt they will see.

- Many elderly people lose their physical attractiveness. As they do, their self-esteem suffers.

- In general, people lose their authority, power, and status as they age. They lose their ability to work and to play useful roles. This robs them of their sense of purpose. One retired physician with whom I worked typified this kind of loss. Once a respected and well-known professional, by the time I came to know him, this man felt as though he was now valueless. "I'm just waiting to die," he told me one day.

EMOTIONAL CHANGES STEMMING FROM DIMINISHED CAPACITIES

There is no doubt that as people age, they become aware of their diminished capacities. How often have you heard people comment on the fact that they do not see as well as they used to? Or that the mile they could once walk in fifteen minutes now takes them twenty-five minutes? The fact that you and I are aware of ourselves means that we will observe the changes that occur as we age. To expect that we will not react emotionally is unrealistic.

How people react affects not only their mood but the aging process itself. For example, a person seeing himself becoming more frail may become frightened and therefore limit his physical activity. Due to lack of use, his muscles weaken and he becomes even more frail. A vicious cycle develops, as frailty leads to inactivity, which in turn leads to increased frailty.

An interesting study conducted recently at the Washington University School of Medicine and published in the *American Journal of Public Health* (September 1995) underscores this point. The researchers identified 900 people in the middle-old and old-old groups and studied their attitudes toward the act of falling. They concluded that the fear of falling is as devastating as falling itself. Those who described themselves as "very fearful of falling" reported that they curtailed their social activities to prevent an accident. Thus, their fear limited their lives and actually increased their risk of falling!

A realistic respect for one's limitations and impairments is, of course, healthy. However, so is a sense of humor about them. One elderly woman, Mrs. A, told me she realized she could no longer climb on kitchen chairs to clean her windows the way she used to. She gracefully accepted the help of a home-health aide. But Mrs. A joked that she could not look too closely at the windows, because nobody did them as well as she.

Diminishing capacities may have more serious and direct consequences, however. For example, decreased blood flow to the brain may result in confusion, frustration, impatience, and other adverse consequences. In other cases, diminished capacities may have indirect effects. For example, they may make it necessary to leave home. One middle-aged client, Mrs. T, told me recently that it breaks her heart to hear her elderly mother complain about her living arrangements. Some months earlier, Mrs. T, seeing that her mother could no longer live alone safely, brought her to live nearby. At considerable expense, Mrs. T arranged for housing for her mother in a lovely senior community, where she might make friends and where her health and day-to-day life could be simplified and monitored by professionals. However, her mother never adjusted to her new living arrangements. She became reclusive and made few attempts to develop friends. She felt lonely and displaced, and so she complained. Her experiences and reactions, and those of Mrs. T—who felt terribly guilty and sad—are not unusual.

Increased dependence on others, another indirect consequence of diminished capacities, may be humiliating. When elderly people lose their privacy, they often lose their freedom, and in some cases their dignity. It is a truism in psychology that loss of control over one's life leads to depression. Thus, as a person's ability to exercise control diminishes as a result of aging, depression is a frequent consequence.

Recent initiatives in eldercare, detailed in a book by William H. Thomas, M.D., *Life Worth Living: How Someone You Love Can Still Enjoy Life in a Nursing Home* (Acton, MA: VanderWyk & Burnham 1996), are centered around providing the elderly not only with more control over their lives, but with responsibilities and opportunities to interact with people of all ages. The Eden Alternative, Dr. Thomas's program, holds the promise that life for seniors can be simultaneously more responsible and more fulfilling.

POSITIVE EFFECTS OF AGING

While many of the emotional changes so far discussed are negative, there is another perspective that needs to be kept in mind. There are definitely positive emotional changes that occur as a consequence of aging. They include deeper understanding and insight, increased compassion, an affirmation of one's life, and a concern for the welfare of future generations.

Erik Erikson, the psychoanalyst who has written so wisely about aging, observes that one of the characteristics of the well-adjusted elderly person is something he calls "generativity," a deep concern about the welfare of the next generation. Rather than being absorbed in one's own emotional, financial, and physical needs, high-functioning seniors focus on sharing the wisdom acquired during their lives. They dedicate themselves to helping in whatever ways possible to make the world a better place for the next generation.

For many people, old age is a time of peace and contentment, a true ripening that carries with it the fulfilling sense of a life well-lived.

INVENTORY: NEEDS OF THE ELDERLY

Following is an inventory designed to gauge your sensitivity to the needs of the elderly. Each item consists of a brief description of a problematical situation involving an elderly parent. Following each description, you are asked to say how you would respond. Read each item and select the choice that comes closest to your natural response. At the end of the inventory, you will have a chance to see which principles were illustrated in each situation and to uncover the sometimes hidden meanings in the way we respond to the needs of elderly parents.

1. When an elderly widow complains of running short of day-to-day necessities at home, an adult child's most appropriate response would be:
   a. to begin doing the shopping for her.
   b. to encourage her to learn to do without and to substitute less familiar foods for more familiar ones.
   c. to buy a memo pad and encourage her to write a shopping list, take it to the store with her, and check off items as she buys them.

2. When an elderly widower, living alone in a small, one family home, complains that he can no longer see well enough to go down to the basement to do his laundry, an adult child's most appropriate response would be:
   a. to begin doing his laundry for him.
   b. to install a bright light on the stairwell going to the basement.
   c. to discuss his increasing tendency to make demands on his children.
   d. to look into relocating the washer and dryer upstairs.

3. When an elderly father expresses feelings of loneliness and despair, an adult child's most appropriate response would be:
   a. to discourage him from feeling or talking about such things, perhaps suggesting that he ought to get a grip and stop feeling sorry for himself.
   b. to ignore the comments.
   c. to listen empathically and give the parent an opportunity to vent.

4. When a widow of small stature must continue to climb on a kitchen step-stool to reach her kitchen cabinets in order to access dishes and canned goods required for everyday use, an adult child's most appropriate response would be:

a. to rearrange the cabinets, placing items used frequently within easy reach.

b. to scold her for taking the risks she takes.

c. to begin preparing her for entering a nursing home by deliberately showing little sympathy.

5. An elderly parent whose ability to cook is fading expresses a desire to contribute a dish to a family dinner celebration. Her adult child's most appropriate response would be:

a. to tell her candidly that she doesn't cook well anymore and that her dish would ruin the meal.

b. to accept the contributions but deliberately "forget" to serve it.

c. to select a dish she cooks adequately and serve it with pride.

6. When an elderly parent, living alone in a private home, can no longer manage the task of taking heavy, metal garbage cans out to the sidewalk for trash pick-up, an adult child's most appropriate response would be:

a. to make it a point to visit his or her parent on trash day and carry out the trash for her.

b. to replace the metal garbage can with a light-weight, plastic one.

c. to contact the trash haulers and see whether alternate pick-up arrangements might be made.

7. An elderly raconteur begins repeating the same stories of his or her youth with increasing frequency, much to the consternation of the children and grandchildren. An adult child's most appropriate response would be:

a. to remind the parent that everyone has heard that story before.

b. to pretend the story is new each time it is told.

c. to impatiently criticize the person for repeating the story yet again.

8. An elderly parent who enjoys helping out in a family business has a mishap—one day he trips and falls in the office. An adult child's most appropriate response would be:

   a. to discourage the parent from coming to the place of business, for his own safety.

   b. to ignore the incident and hope it does not happen again.

   c. to reduce the likelihood of another mishap by rearranging and "senior-proofing" the office.

9. An elderly widow, living alone in a private home, proudly but casually comments that she is saving money by not turning on the heat on cold mornings. An adult child's most appropriate response would be:

   a. to admonish her for her lack of good sense.

   b. to applaud her efforts and encourage her to save in other ways as well.

   c. to discuss her behavior and your concerns about it, providing reassurance that the family will see that she has enough money to heat her home.

10. An elderly parent engages in odd behavior, perhaps speaking with people who are not present in the room. An adult child's most appropriate response would be:

    a. to argue with the parent, insisting that such crazy behavior is unacceptable.

    b. to ignore the behavior and try to distract the parent.

    c. to draw the parent out but arrange for an evaluation by a physician, preferably a psychiatrist, at the earliest opportunity.

Answer Key

1. The preferred answer is *c* because by providing Mom with a shopping list and instructions, you enable her to help herself rather than taking responsibility from her *(a)* or indicating a lack of concern *(b)*.

2. If the problem is simply that of lighting, as it appears to be, then alternative *b* would be the right answer. Of course, if someone in the family were handy enough or well off enough to arrange to have the washer and dryer relocated to the first floor of the home *(d)*, that would be an acceptable response. Both of these options share a common characteristic: they make it possible for the widower to care for himself. Option *a* smacks of overfunctioning on the child's part, while item *c* serves little purpose other than to induce guilt and shame needlessly.

3. When an elderly parent conveys feelings of loneliness and despair, he needs to be listened to with empathy *(c)*. To invalidate the feelings expressed *(a)* is certainly not helpful and can increase one's feeling of not being understood or appreciated. To ignore the feelings *(b)* is, at best, insensitive, and perhaps even cruel.

4. It serves little purpose to scold the widow for taking risks *(b)*. Rearranging the cabinets so daily necessities are within easy reach *(a)* makes a great deal of sense. Needless to say, the woman herself should be involved in deciding which items should go where.

5. The parent's wanting to contribute to the meal helps make her feel useful and valuable as a family member. To deny her that opportunity, whether cruelly *(a)* or deceitfully *(b)*, exacts a tremendous toll. Unless family members are boorish, serving the dish *(c)* makes the most sense.

6. If replacing the trash can *(b)* would solve the problem, then it is clearly the preferred response, since it enables the elderly parent to maintain her independence and self-sufficiency simply. Sometimes

special arrangements can be made with the trash haulers *(c)*, and that is perfectly acceptable, too. The least desirable response would be for the child to take on responsibility for hauling out the trash can *(a)*. This not only burdens the child, it robs the parent of a sense of self-sufficiency.

7. Pretending the story is new each time it is repeated *(b)* is neither honest nor helpful, though in some cases one has little choice. Criticizing the raconteur *(c)* serves no purpose. Depending on the mental status of the raconteur, a polite reminder that everyone has heard the story before *(a)*, offered in private if possible, seems the most tactful way of handling the situation.

8. Clearly, this person's participation in the family business is important to him. Forbidding him to return *(a)* is cruel and can be destructive. Moreover, it may not be necessary. Ignoring the incident *(b)* is foolish and potentially dangerous. However, ensuring that walkways are clear and well lit *(c)* reduces the likelihood of another accident, not just for the elderly person but also for everyone else who works in the office.

9. There is no reason for anyone to avoid heating a home in order to save money. Therefore, applauding her efforts *(b)* is unacceptable. However, admonishing the widow for doing what she thinks is commendable *(a)* would likely be perceived as confusing and offensive. (It might also cause her to withhold such information in the future.) Sharing your concern and offering reassurance that she does not need to be cold to save money *(c)* is clearly the most reasoned response. Taking it one step further—for example, by looking into state assistance programs—may make the most sense of all. Many states offer such programs for the elderly, often paying a substantial portion of the cost of heating a home or condominium.

10. It is almost always impossible to argue someone out of the reality of a hallucination *(a);* attempting to do so may actually heighten the

conviction of the ill person while triggering other reactions such as suspicion. Frequently, ignoring the behavior and distracting the person *(b)* is an appropriate response. However, if the elderly person can be drawn out, perhaps the meaning of the behavior can be ferreted out and the underlying problem addressed. If the elderly person has not seen a psychiatrist or other mental health professional, that might be a good idea *(c)*.

As this inventory shows, it is often not enough simply to "help" aging people or to "protect" them from themselves. Sensitivity to feelings, your own and those of the elderly, is essential as well. Without all of these facets, you cannot consider yourself as having done all that was needed.

SUMMARY

Both physical and emotional changes occur as people age. Some basic truths about aging include that people age at different rates and that there are a number of ways to classify seniors. Some of the effects of aging are primary (genetically based or "hard-wired") and some are secondary (mostly controllable to varying degrees). There are also the emotional consequences typically experienced by people as they age. Whether the result of life experiences or the deterioration of abilities once taken for granted, these physical and emotional consequences exert a great deal of influence on the attitudes and day-to-day existence of the elderly. Finally, completing an inventory helped you to apply the information in this chapter

In the next chapter, you will learn about the emotional reactions you are likely to have in the course of coming to terms with your parents' aging.

CHAPTER 2

Coming to Terms with Your Parents' Aging

No matter how much adult children know about the biology of aging and its psychological impact on the aging person, we still react emotionally. How could it be otherwise? Knowledge is no buffer when the aging senior is such an important person in our lives.

When we are growing up, our parents are all-powerful, all-knowing figures on whom we rely for almost everything. They see and understand the world in depth—or at least they seem to—and they make judgments far beyond our abilities. Eventually, we come to see our parents as imperfect, even as inadequate in some areas, yet they remain very special people in our eyes.

As parents age and begin losing their edge on life, it is understandable that adult children will respond emotionally. Many reactions are predictable. Anxiety and sadness, for example, are entirely typical, though their intensity levels may not be.

Other reactions are atypical. For example, when the parent-child relationship has been poor, feelings such as resentment and anger sometimes arise. This can be very unsettling, because such feelings may not be expected and because they may be considered "wrong" or unacceptable.

When no real love or even loyalty exists, adult children have mixed feelings. As they watch remote, abusive, or otherwise inadequate parents age, adult children may experience anger, guilt, relief, and satisfaction all at the same time. Such reactions often make it particularly difficult for the adult child to find peace.

One client of mine visited her dying father in the hospital. She watched as her once robust and hot-tempered father struggled to breathe. Recalling the many times he had treated her cruelly and insensitively, she felt a surge of mixed feelings. "I was crying tears of sadness, rage, and guilt, all at the same time," she told me. "It was so awful knowing he would die without ever acknowledging, let alone apologizing for, what a lousy father he'd been!"

It is important to note that physical or emotional distance from the parent does not change one's responses. Nor does it reduce their intensity. It may even strengthen the intensity, since either type of separation often makes it more difficult to manage the feelings constructively.

No feeling is completely unreasonable or blameworthy. They are all ways of protecting oneself. Short of acting out one's anger or fear by abusing the parent, no response is reprehensible.

In Part One of this chapter, we will first look at how adult children respond when they see a formerly vigorous parent grow increasingly frail and intellectually tentative. Next, we will turn to their concerns about their own future, for as they observe their parents deteriorate, adult children invariably project into the future and wonder about themselves and their own aging. Under specific circumstances, even the most predictable reaction can become problematic. In the second part of the chapter, you will learn how to distinguish between reactions that fall within normal limits and those that do not.

PART ONE: A Range of Understandable Individual Reactions

Whether or not an adult child's feelings are predictable, whether their intensity falls within appropriate limits, and whether they are complicated by a history of a poor relationship, they must be confronted and worked through. If not, they will interfere with the healthy process by which we prepare to say good-bye.

Emotions cannot be observed directly, but they can be inferred from a person's behavior. Therefore, in attempting to uncover an adult child's feelings in response to a parent's aging, it is often necessary to observe how he or she actually behaves. There are a number of typical behavioral responses.

RESPONSES TO AGING PARENTS

Shock and Surprise

"Mother never used to go out looking unkempt!" remarked a client of mine, Mrs. C, about her retired attorney mom. "She always took such pride in her appearance. And she wasn't above making cutting remarks about women who went around the way she does now!"

My client had arranged to take her mother to lunch at a restaurant near her senior residence. When she went to pick up her mother, Mrs. C was shocked to discover that she was wearing a soiled blouse and a skirt that did not match. Rather than make a scene, Mrs. C elected to go ahead with the lunch plans, but all the while she found herself embarrassed for her elderly charge.

The daughter's reaction is altogether understandable and normal. It is difficult to adjust to the fact that one's parent is not as self-aware or as meticulous as he or she once had been. Elderly people sometimes lose the ability to choose appropriate clothing. Often they do not see a problem that seems obvious to others. In this case, for example, Mrs. C wondered whether her mother was aware of the dirty spots on her blouse. Sometimes lack of care about personal appearance is a sign of depression. My client wondered about that, too.

Gentle exploration can yield valuable results. If Mrs. C's mother had been unaware of the problem, for example, then tolerance of her loss of judgment might well have been in order. On the other hand, if she had been aware of the problem and simply did not care, another course of action might have been better. If her lack of self-care had gone beyond simply failing to make herself presentable when going out in public, then a psychiatric evaluation might have been called for. Important questions might have included: Does this person maintain adequate standards of personal hygiene? Does she eat properly? Does she socialize? Does she still take pleasure in formerly enjoyable pastimes?

My client's mother *was* quite aware of her unkempt appearance and simply did not care because she had begun to give up on life. Mrs. C probed for other signs of depression and concluded that her mother might require evaluation by a mental health expert. In the end, her mother was given antidepressant medication. As a result, her self-care improved; so did her mood and outlook on life.

Denial

Some adult children choose to ignore signs of aging, both obvious and subtle. One of my "young old" clients told me one Thanksgiving season that she was planning a holiday dinner party at her home. While she did not mind entertaining eighteen people, she did have a problem with her two adult daughters bringing their dogs with them for the holiday weekend. Between the daughters, they owned three dogs, one of which was an aggressive and hyperactive puppy. Together with my client's own dog, this meant there would be four of man's best friends underfoot during Thanksgiving dinner!

My client wanted to satisfy her children, but she doubted she could manage eighteen people and four dogs at once. She and I discussed the problem, and in the end, she decided to ask her daughters not to bring the pets.

The example illustrates an important truth about adult children of aging parents. Both of my client's daughters failed to appreciate the fact that their mother was aging. They felt that "Mom" could serve dinner for eighteen people with four dogs underfoot. They remembered her as she had been years ago, not as she was now.

In an even more extreme case of denial, a son heard that his father had been hospitalized with cancer and was dying. He insisted it was not true. "Dad's a tough old horse," he said. "He'll be fine!" The son's denial was so complete, he never allowed himself to visit his father in the hospital, insisting that he would see him again when his father returned home.

This young man's response gave rise to obvious avoidance. However, avoidance also takes other forms. Sometimes a child moves farther and farther away as parents age. Such behavior amounts to a refusal to acknowledge the decline of one's parents and the responsibility that goes along with it. In such cases, one sibling is typically left behind to assume primary responsibility for the parents. You will learn more about family dynamics of this sort in the next chapter.

Distrust and Disbelief

Closely related to denial is a tendency on the part of some adult children to distrust the honest reports of their parents. "Does he really not hear me?" a client asked about his father, in whom a progressive but very real loss of hearing had occurred. The son misinterpreted his father's inability to hear as an attention-getting device, a form of passive-aggression.

The same thing occurred when a daughter asked me, "Does she really not understand?" Her mother, always intellectually sharp, had begun to display signs of being unable to follow a conversation. It was difficult for my client to believe what she was observing. She, too, doubted the legitimacy of her mother's confusion.

Like denial, disbelief is more likely to occur during the early stages of adjusting to a parent's diminished capacities. It takes time to accept the reality that one's parents are no longer the same vigorous, alert, and intelligent people they may have been when they were younger.

Resentment

As noted previously, it is not uncommon for an adult child to resent the demands placed on him or her by an aging parent. This is especially true when the two have not had a good relationship or when the parent has failed the child in important ways.

In one case, a father who had been cold and rather selfish throughout his life made it clear that he expected to be cared for by a son whom he had ignored. "I'll do it because he's my father," the son told me. "But I must confess, I resent everything I do for the old man!"

In another case, a client's long-widowed mother, Mrs. X, had tacitly collaborated with a profligate son to rob my client of her fair share of a small family inheritance. Feigning distress the entire time, Mrs. X nevertheless allowed her son to write checks on her personal checking account, take possession of real estate intended for my client, and otherwise plunder the family assets. Yet, as Mrs. X grew more infirm, the son, having gotten what he wanted from his mother, neglected her. My client felt it her duty to help her mother in whatever ways she could. Although this meant long trips to Mrs. X's residence, some two hours away, my client could not bring herself to allow her mother to go uncared for. Thus, despite her justifiable resentment, she fulfilled her duties as a daughter.

Disappointment

Along with sadness, real disappointment sometimes accompanies the infirmity of a parent. For example, I recall one professional woman who had postponed child-rearing in order to devote herself to her career. When she became pregnant, she began looking forward to sharing the excitement of the birth with the mother she loved so much. Then her mother had a stroke that left her seriously impaired. My client reacted with both sadness for her mother and profound disappointment for herself. Her mother's incapacity meant she was simply no longer present to enjoy the birth of her grandchild.

Impatience

Dealing with the elderly can be taxing. Elderly people often repeat themselves, occasionally become uncooperative, and may require the kind of constant care a child needs. Many adult children lose their patience with parents. "At least my children will become self-sufficient," said one client when talking about her custodial responsibilities. "But when I care for Mom, I know it's just the opposite. She'll never be back to what she once was. Hers is a one-way street downhill."

Frustration

Even under the best of circumstances, dealing with elderly parents can be extremely frustrating. Depending on their condition, at times they may not understand or retain information conveyed to them. They need to be told the same thing repeatedly. Even then there is no guarantee that it will sink in. In extreme cases, they lose control—sometimes more or less deliberately—of even the most primitive bodily functions. One woman told me her mother had begun soiling as a way of getting even each time my client made demands on her.

Sometimes the elderly become stubborn and inflexible. Perfectly capable of understanding what they are told or what they are asked to do, they nevertheless go along their merry way, ignoring their adult children's desires and requests.

Because there is such a fine line between frustration and anger, it is often important for frustrated adult children to get help, from a professional or from the support of others in their situation. An informal network of friends or an organized, professionally run support group can be very valuable in helping adult children cope with their frustration.

Projection

Sometimes, adult children cannot admit their feelings to themselves. They project them onto others. In one family, the father was suffering with dementia. The daughter was devastated by her father's deterioration. However, rather than accept her own feelings, she projected them onto her mother. She continually prodded her father, at times even scolding him with the words, "Cut that out, Dad! You're upsetting Mommy!"

Passive-Aggression

One resentful son professed great concern for his father's health. Yet he consistently "forgot" arrangements he had made to pick up his father to take him to doctors' appointments or to help out in other ways. His forgetfulness is a classic example of what happens when angry feelings are not acknowledged or worked through.

Intellectualization

Instead of feeling their pain, some adult children remove themselves emotionally by resorting to extreme intellectual reactions. One man read everything he could about his father's illness. He attended seminars on the condition, spoke with his physician, and so on. However, what he did not do was allow himself to feel the anxiety and pain that his father's illness triggered.

Guilt and Shame

It is not uncommon for adult children to feel guilt and shame about past behaviors as they observe a parent age. These mixed reactions often stem from a sense of having failed the parent in one or more important ways. One client had declined to become the rabbi his parents wanted him to become. He had lived with guilt over his decision for many years. As his father lay dying, he felt that reaction even more strongly.

Guilt and shame can also result from having formed an alliance with one parent against the other. Mr. E had had a very close relationship with his father. The parents had not had a good marriage, and the mother was guilty of having wounded both father and son by her almost constant criticizing and nagging. Nevertheless, instead of working to improve his relationship with his wife, the father had responded by drawing Mr. E to him; the two had become enmeshed. They formed a silent alliance against the mother and unconsciously set out to exclude her in many ways. Mr. E and his father shared warm and close feelings with each other. They did many things together. But they never invited the mother along. In response to feeling isolated and ignored, Mr. E's mother became even more shrewish. In the end, the father died and Mr. E was left with the care of his aging mother. He felt real guilt as a result of his having aligned himself with his father at her expense.

Many adult children feel guilt and shame about their current behavior. "I should be doing more," said one client about the care he was providing and arranging for his mother, who was dying of cancer. A good and devoted son who was doing a great deal for his parent, he nevertheless struggled with the question "How much help is enough?" His question is not unique. Many adult children struggle with this same question. I urged my client to ask himself what would constitute the "norm" in providing care, given the fact that he had a job and family to maintain. This is a good, commonsense question for any adult child to ask. (I will discuss this issue in more detail in a later chapter.)

REACTIONS THAT SUGGEST CONCERN ABOUT ONE'S OWN FUTURE WELL-BEING

In response to the aging of a parent, adult children may begin worrying about their own future. They may begin looking at themselves and wondering about their own health and old age. Such reactions are neither inappropriate nor selfish, only human. Here are a few of them.

Fear

Sometimes adult children become frightened for themselves when they see their parents age. "Will I be likely to get Alzheimer's if my father has it?" asked a client recently. His reaction is far from blameworthy.

One gerontologist I know sometimes recommends autopsies when his elderly patients die. The autopsies serve the important purpose of alerting offspring to risk factors that might dictate changes in their own behavior and lifestyle. In light of impressive research indicating that steps can be taken to minimize many of the adverse effects of aging (see Chapter One), his advice is sound.

Self-oriented Grief

The realization that one's own life is limited hits home as an adult child watches a parent age. One client, his father's namesake, witnessed his father's death. He recalled that at the moment his father died, he glanced at the nameplate above the hospital bed, and found himself thinking, "The next time someone dies in a bed with that nameplate above it, it'll be me."

Disappointment with One's Life

It is not uncommon for adult children to begin reevaluating their own lives in the course of watching their parents age. Many report feeling dissatisfied because their own lives are not what they had hoped or expected.

The reordering of priorities, summed up in the question, "What is really important, anyway?" has long been characteristic of midlife. Little wonder, given the truly ultimate nature of the concerns triggered by the aging of a parent.

One case comes to mind. Mrs. F, a very hard-working and fiscally conservative woman and the mother of two teens, had long fought her older adolescent daughter's desire to train as a fashion model. The child was an adequate student, but both parents had hoped she would go to college. For years, they had pushed the child to achieve in school. Their efforts had been unsuccessful.

Not until Mrs. F's mother became seriously ill did her thinking change. Only then did she relent and convince her husband to allow their daughter to pursue her dream. They agreed to spend well over $1200, a lot of money for them, to enroll the child in a modeling course and hire a photographer to begin building a portfolio of portraits.

"Why fight it?" my client asked. "If this is where her heart is, why shouldn't we support her?"

Not surprisingly, after making this decision, Mrs. F began reordering the priorities in her own life. She gave herself permission to travel more and to spend money on things that gave her pleasure. Disciplined to the end, she kept this newfound "hedonism" within reasonable limits and reported that her life and that of her family were richer for it.

These examples of adult children's reactions to a parent's aging are quite typical. They pose no special problems. None are blameworthy, none beyond comprehension.

PART TWO: Appropriate versus Extreme Emotional Reactions

Any therapist who has worked with young children knows that they often accept the most horrible living conditions at home. They may live in a squalid environment or put up with neglect and abuse. They do so simply because they have no frame of reference with which to judge such conditions as unacceptable.

In many ways, the same is true of adult children. Because most people consider the aging of a parent a private family matter, they cope with the problems and feelings alone. Their own reactions are the only ones they know. They, too, lack a frame of reference with which to judge the appropriateness of their reactions.

How, then, can you monitor your own emotional reactions? When are they healthy and when not?

In extreme cases, it is easy to determine whether one's feelings are problematic. If an adult child finds himself abusing or neglecting an elderly parent, clearly something is wrong. A problem also exists if he or she experiences barely controllable depression or rage after each visit with the parent.

But what about less extreme situations? What of the husband who finds himself arguing with a spouse more often? How about the wife who finds herself having headaches she had not suffered from before, or whose headaches become more frequent or more severe? What about the person who begins feeling anxious and sullen for no apparent reason? Or the executive who begins having problems concentrating on her job? In all these cases, making the connection between the aging of a parent and current symptomology can be difficult.

REACTIONS CHECKLIST

Below is a set of criteria that can be used to assess your reactions. Each criterion is framed as a *yes* or *no* question. Any *yes* answer suggests a problem. Several point to the need for prompt action. In a few moments, you will learn how to cope with both typical and extreme reactions.

☐ *Do your reactions cause you to lose your sense of priorities?* For example, do you find yourself giving up more and more of your life in order to care for an elderly parent? Have you moved in with them or allowed them to move in with you for no compelling reason? Have you stopped asking, "How much help am I willing and able to provide?"

☐ *Do you find yourself experiencing unexplained or atypical physical ailments?* The emergence of unfamiliar symptoms is often a warning sign. So is any change in the frequency, severity, or duration of familiar ailments. Such unexplained or atypical physical ailments may be related to your involvement with your elderly parents. A competent therapist can help you make the connections and control your symptoms.

☐ *Do you find yourself experiencing more conflict at home or on the job than is typical for you?* In mild forms, feelings such as anxiety, anger, depression, and resentment can make you irritable. In more extreme cases, they can affect you more profoundly and for longer periods of time.

It is not unusual for a depressed or an angry person to redirect or displace feelings. You may become increasingly intolerant of the age-appropriate behavior of your children, for example. The same is true if the predictable behavior of coworkers begins eliciting angry responses that seem uncharacteristic of you.

Unacknowledged emotional reactions to a parent's aging can cause you to overreact to things. If you find others urging you to calm down, or if people are commenting that your reactions are disproportionate to the events that trigger them, then it is likely that your responses are being colored by unacknowledged feelings inside you.

☐ *Are there changes in your personality or your ways of behaving?* One usually responsible teacher began taking many days off shortly after his father became terminally ill. Examination revealed that he was in the early stages of a depression prompted by his father's looming death.

One woman who had been very outgoing became distressed by the rapidly declining health of a dearly loved father. She found herself losing interest in social activities and ignoring the company of people she enjoyed. Before long, she was unable to get out of bed in the morning. Fortunately, she had the good sense to call her family physician, who saw her promptly and made a referral to a clinician who was able to help her.

> ☐ *Do you find that the your feelings don't ease with time, but remain intense and unremitting, perhaps even grow?* It is not at all unusual to have strong, immediate reactions to the realization that one's parent is declining dramatically and approaching death. In most people, however, these reactions subside gradually, and a quiet acceptance sets in. If this does not happen, you may be coping with reactions that are in the atypical or extreme range.
>
> Mr. E, who had colluded with his father to isolate and exclude his mother from their close relationship, continued to feel guilt long after his father died. In fact, I saw him several years later. At that time, not only had Mr. E not forgiven himself for colluding with his father, he had still not gotten over his father's passing. Nor had he resolved the guilt he felt toward his mother.

HOW TO COPE WITH NORMAL EMOTIONAL REACTIONS

Feelings that are predictable and within normal limits usually can be dealt with by using common sense. For example, it is always important to acknowledge and accept feelings, whether you approve of the feelings or not. Anger at a parent who was inattentive to you is perfectly understandable. Even when the cause of the anger is less clear, it is important to accept it as valid, for only then can you begin to explore its origins and come to grips with it.

Talk them out.

The best way to deal with any feeling, especially one with which you are uncomfortable, is to admit it to yourself. Avoid denying the feeling or judging yourself harshly for feeling the way you do. Try talking out the feeling with a spouse, family member, friend, or mental health professional. Often, that is all that is needed to put the feeling in its proper place as you set about the task of living your life normally. If for any reason more help is needed, look into a support group for caregivers. (See the Selected Resources appendix for information on locating such a group.)

Gather information.

If you experience uncertainty or apprehension about what will happen next in the course of a parent's decline, it makes sense to gather information. Your parent's physician is a good source of guidance. So are professional associations. For example, the Alzheimer's Association offers information for those who must deal with or care for victims of the disorder. Many informative books are available on a variety of illnesses and their effects. Often, knowing what is likely to happen is extremely reassuring. (See the Selected Resources appendix for guidance on locating sources of information.)

Arrange for assistance.

Sometimes guilty feelings can be alleviated by arranging for practical assistance for an aging parent. One woman felt she needed to spend more time with her ailing mother. However, family and job responsibilities made that impossible. By arranging for help, she felt satisfied that her mother was being adequately cared for, while she spared herself the need to be in more than one place at a time.

Geriatric care managers represent a useful resource for many people. These professionals serve as advocates and coordinators of care for the elderly. While they are often hired by adult children who live far from their parents, they can be useful even to those who live nearby but lack the skill or time to coordinate care or advocate on behalf of their parents. Care needs to be taken in hiring a care manager, since the field is relatively new. However, professional associations and accrediting organizations have begun to spring up, and they can be relied on to provide guidance in finding qualified individuals who adhere to strict ethical standards. (See the Selected Resources appendix for information on locating a qualified geriatric care manager.)

HOW TO COPE WITH EXTREME EMOTIONAL REACTIONS

If you determine that your reactions are outside normal limits, it is advisable to take immediate and aggressive steps to get them under control. If you do not, they are very likely to have adverse effects on you, your elderly parent, your spouse and children, your family of origin, or your career. Below are several specific suggestions of where to go to get help.

Talk with your own or your parent's physician.

He or she will likely understand your reactions, having seen many people in your situation over the years. Sometimes, the doctor will prescribe a simple anxiolytic (antianxiety) medication or a mild antidepressant. Other times, he or she will make a referral to a trusted therapist. The most psychologically sensitive physicians will typically do both.

See an EAP (Employee Assistance Program) counselor on the job.

Many employers provide crisis assessment services for employees. Turning to your EAP representative will give you a chance to verbalize your distress while simultaneously gaining the insights and judgment of an experienced mental health professional.

Seek out your minister, rabbi, or parish priest.

As training of clergy improves, many are able to provide short-term counseling. Most members of the clergy know when the client's needs are beyond their ability to satisfy. They often know of experienced professionals whom they can recommend.

In urgent cases (if, for example, you are feeling suicidal or fear your feelings may erupt violently), call or visit the crisis intervention unit or the emergency room of your local hospital.

You will be seen almost immediately, and your condition will be evaluated by a person well-trained in handling acute crises.

It should be obvious that all my recommendations fall under one broad piece of advice: Do not go it alone. The informed assistance of a trained professional is worth every penny you pay for it. Given the seriousness of your reactions and their potential to do you harm, seeking out help is the only sensible thing to do.

SUMMARY

There are reasons why adult children often experience strong reactions to the aging of a parent. This chapter described some of the many reactions that do occur, and a checklist helped you to determine whether your reactions fall within an appropriate category or not. There are strategies for coping with your reactions.

In addition to individual reactions, there are also collective reactions that affect the entire family. These will be discussed in the next chapter.

CHAPTER 3

The Impact on the Family

In addition to the reactions of each individual within the family, aging evokes collective, familial responses. In this chapter, you will learn what happens within the family as a whole as parents age.

In Part One, you will learn how to look at the family as a system— a unit constantly striving to maintain a balance among its members in order to ensure its survival and to do its work, much as the human body automatically maintains a certain temperature in order to ensure good health. You will read about the typical systemic family responses to a parent's aging, both healthy and unhealthy. Each of these efforts to maintain balance is played out in a predictable manner, and there are steps you can take to change your family's responses when they are dysfunctional.

Just as individuals pass through phases as they mature, so do families. Part Two traces the stages in the family life cycle, explaining that transitions from one stage to the next are always difficult. The failing health of parents, presaging their ultimate death, signals a new phase in the family's life cycle. Under this stress, symptoms (for example, arguments among siblings) may develop in the family. The emergence of symptoms of *any* sort is a clear indication that the family is stuck in its attempts to negotiate its way through this difficult stage in the family life cycle. Finally, you will learn the factors that affect the quality of the solutions arrived at by a family in the face of parents' aging and death.

In the event that *your* family is struggling, specific suggestions are provided in Part Three that stress the importance of recognizing symptoms for what they are. For instance, rather than seeing a caregiver's overinvolvement as an indication that he or she is "neurotic," or another person's lack of involvement as an indication that he or she is "uncaring," family members should view such behaviors as symptoms of a *family* problem. Part Three offers specific suggestions for talking about a problem and explains methods you can follow to solve the problem logically and systematically.

PART ONE: The Family as a System

Systems are complex units made up of parts that work together to accomplish a purpose. The word *system* is applied to many things, from a car's electrical system to the human body's cardiovascular system.

Systems of all kinds possess certain characteristics. Key among these is a tendency to maintain a balance or harmony that ensures the system's effective functioning. Like a well-oiled machine, a properly operating system has many complicated and independent components that work together to achieve an objective. When something threatens that harmony, whether from within or without, the system works to ward off the danger. When the balance is upset, the system works to restore it. If such steps are not taken, the entire system may cease to function.

For example, when bacteria—a threat from without—invade your body, your immune system goes to work to ward off the invasion. Certain cells that recognize and kill invaders are produced in greater numbers; your blood chemistry changes as the amount of gamma interferon increases to promote the growth of the cells needed to ward off the invasion; and so on.

Now consider a different example—a threat from within. Instead of looking at a biological or physical system, consider a human group.

When an organization of any kind (a community group, a business organization, or even a group of friends) is threatened from within by dissension among its members, the group begins pulling together to restore the balance that used to make it effective.

As a family member ages and undergoes changes in physical or mental condition, the entire family system experiences a number of threats. The first is internal: Because that person can no longer play the role he or she used to play, someone must "fill in," and that can be a difficult task. Perhaps there is no one in the family with the same constellation of talents and insights. Other family members might not accept a substitute player.

The second threat is external: Unfamiliar professionals begin intruding in the family's life and draining energy, time, finances, and other resources. They may even make decisions or recommendations inconsistent with the family's way of doing things.

The stress occasioned by the aging of a parent triggers an automatic survival response in the family. Members engage in many balance-maintaining strategies. One of these may be to reinforce old patterns. For example, a responsible adult child, thought of as the most "together" family member, may be looked at by his or her siblings as the *only* child capable of handling the crisis. Such a response is not entirely healthy. Often, the challenge of being on the threshold of a new stage in the family life cycle may require that old balance-maintaining strategies be replaced by new strategies that are more appropriate. In other words, the roles people play and any long-standing dominance-submission patterns may need to abandoned.

Take the example of the N family. Mrs. N, who was 85 years old when I came to know her, had been a professional woman in very good health for most of her life, and she prided herself on her independence and self-sufficiency. She had two children—a daughter, Janice, and a son, Mark. Mark was married to Pam, and they had one daughter, age 19. Janice had stayed unmarried into midlife, and Mrs. N had been living with her for many years, when Janice surprised everyone by getting married.

This was several years before the family came to see me. The marriage was extremely rewarding for Janice. Her husband, Dennis, was a most understanding man and loved her very much. He had welcomed his mother-in-law into their home, and for several years the situation was stable. Janice and Dennis cared for Mrs. N. Mark and Pam made reasonable and consistent efforts to help out to some degree. Since the two siblings and their spouses lived nearby, it was easy to share many of the responsibilities.

The situation destabilized when Mrs. N's health began failing. As a result of a serious illness, she placed many more demands on Janice and Dennis. Furthermore, her "independence" began turning to obstinacy; she proved to be a very difficult patient. She did not listen to instructions and did not cooperate in her care. For instance, she "forgot" to do the simple chores she had been assigned; she refused to take medications as prescribed; sometimes she refused to bathe or to do much to help herself.

Janice and Dennis ran a small business out of their home. Increasingly, they found it very difficult to meet Mrs. N's needs, run their business, and have any sort of life for themselves. They felt unfairly burdened.

Mark and Pam were sensitive to this, but both of them worked, and their daughter was in college, which carried its own demands. Because they were one step removed from the immediate situation with Mrs. N, Mark and Pam managed to socialize and take vacations, neither of which Janice and Dennis could do.

As Mrs. N's demands increased, the two siblings, who had gotten along well for many years, began bickering. Janice complained that she was tired of hearing about her brother and sister-in-law's good times. Mark reminded Janice that her many years of caregiving for their mother had enabled her to live rent-free for decades. As a result, she had been able to build a successful home business of her own, even before marrying Dennis.

Both in-laws became involved as well. Pam felt her many efforts to help her mother-in-law were unacknowledged and unappreciated. Dennis felt that Mark was taking advantage of Janice's good nature. Strife and hurt feelings abounded. All these behaviors were attempts to maintain the pre-existing balance in the family. Here is how:

- Janice was telling her brother and sister-in-law that she was barely able to cope with Mrs. N's demands. Hearing about their good times made it more difficult. If the current balance was to be maintained—that is, if they expected her to play the familiar role of martyr/caregiver—they could at least not rub salt in her wound.

- By "reminding" Janice of the benefits of her having lived with her mother, Mark was unknowingly coercing her into silence. "Play your role as you always have," he was saying, "and don't complain, for you've gotten a great deal out of that role."

- Pam's hurt feelings were her way of letting her husband and sister-in-law know that she was prepared to continue doing her part to maintain the existing balance, but she wanted an acknowledgement of her contributions.

- Dennis's complaint about his wife's being exploited was an invitation to Mark to help out. He wanted Mark to provide just enough help so that nothing would have to change radically. Dennis did not object outright to being involved in caring for his mother-in-law, nor was he insensitive to the financial advantages of being caregiver.

It was at this point that the family sought help. Their story is not at all unusual. It illustrates how a stable family situation can be thrown into chaos by the stress of an aging parent. It also shows that the first line of defense against such a threat is to try to maintain the old balance and to reinforce it.

The Ns were an intelligent family. When the bickering began they knew they needed help. They realized, without having the words for it, that theirs was a *family* problem, a systemic response to stress that required professional intervention. Unfortunately, not all families recognize their problems for what they are, nor do they seek help when they should.

HEALTHY AND UNHEALTHY SYSTEMIC RESPONSES

What constitutes a healthy response to stress? Which responses are unhealthy?

Healthy Systemic Responses

In general, a response is healthy when it takes advantage of the strengths of family members in such a way as to meet the challenge, without distributing responsibilities unfairly or arriving at "solutions" that breed new problems. For example, one healthy systemic reaction is sharing responsibility based on the strengths and expertise of family members. If one adult child is good at organizing things, that person might take on the task of scheduling appointments with doctors, physical therapists, and other health-care providers. If another adult child is able to help with personal care such as bathing and dressing, he or she might take on that task.

Another healthy response occurs when the family unites in the face of an adversary. For example, when a health-care provider fails to respond appropriately to the needs of an aging parent, the family often bands together to prevail upon that person to change his or her behavior. Their doing so is healthy and appropriate.

I recall one instance in which a particularly insensitive physician chided an elderly woman for becoming upset when he reported that testing had revealed she had cancer. "Tears won't help a thing," he said unsympathetically and impatiently, before rushing off to his next patient. In response to this insensitive comment, made in the presence of one of the woman's children, the entire family united, fired the physician, and found another who was more skilled.

A third example of a functional systemic response occurs when the family works together to place limits on how much work any one member does on behalf of the aging parent. "You can't do it all!" I recall one man saying to his exhausted sister. "You've got to let Donna and me help take care of Mom!"

Unhealthy Systemic Responses

Unfortunately, unhealthy systemic responses are at least as common as healthy ones. For example, a family consisting of three siblings may always have relied heavily on one child to take on the disagreeable tasks. As parents age, that family member would be likely to assume the bulk of the caregiving responsibilities. Moreover, her siblings, despite their being able to help out, would probably not do so, simply out of habit.

Another dysfunctional systemic response occurs when long-dormant sibling rivalries reemerge. Take the case of two sisters with whom I worked. When their elderly mother had a disabling stroke, these two professional women rallied to her side. Before long, however, they began bickering about who was doing more for Mother and who was slacking off. When they came for help, questioning revealed that this kind of bickering had characterized their relationship as little girls. The bickering now was a replay of the past.

Another unhealthy systemic response occurs when parents "play favorites" among their children as they may have done when the children were young. Sometimes a parent will keep one sibling informed of her condition while not informing others. Such a parent will often accept help and comfort from one child while not accepting it from another. This behavior is an attempt to ensure that the "pecking order" within the family remains clear, even in these extreme situations.

Family members may also unthinkingly fall back on old, familiar roles and play them with more intensity than ever before, and thus act out another dysfunctional systemic response. Take the situation in which one child has always been the "good" child while the other has been the "bad" one. These "good child/bad child" roles are replayed when the "good" child takes on the role of caregiver while unconsciously elbowing out his sibling, often with the silent consent of the elderly parent. He may "forget" to inform his sibling about upcoming doctor's appointments or about the result of testing. It may never occur to him to allow his sibling to become involved in caregiving. With such oversights, he says, in effect, "I am the good child! I am the one my father can count on." The other sibling, feeling rejected and pushed aside, distances himself and becomes less involved, thereby confirming his place as the "bad child."

Sibling alliances that were evident years before may reemerge, and rival alliances may engage in struggles everyone thought had been long since put to rest. Two sisters, for example, might be drawn together in the face of their mother's illness while engaging in a silent conspiracy to paint another sibling as uncaring or selfish.

PART TWO: The Life Cycle of the Family System

Every parent knows that children go through phases as they grow. Parents speak casually of the "terrible twos," for example, to suggest there is a period when every child begins asserting herself. The same is true of adults. The "midlife crisis" is, for most people, a period of reassessment. Youth is gone and old age is not yet upon us. We reevaluate our lives and think of the changes we might want to make before it is too late to make them.

Every family can be viewed as a dynamic, living entity. It, too, passes through phases and predictable crises as it matures. By the phrase *predictable crises*, I mean the change and stress that occur with each new and normal phase in the life cycle of the family (such as the birth of children). Each new phase challenges the family to adapt to the stress, to negotiate the troubled waters caused by growth, and still to maintain its identity.

It is also true, of course, that certain crises are unpredictable. The death of one or both parents, for instance, may shatter a family completely. The impact of such a tragedy often depends on the ages of the children, the willingness of relatives to work to keep the family intact, and other factors. For my purposes in this chapter, I will emphasize predictable crises.

PHASES IN THE FAMILY LIFE CYCLE

Researchers and theorists have identified several stages through which a normal family passes. While not all authorities agree on what to name these phases, all *do* agree that there are discrete periods through which every family passes.

In this brief discussion, I have taken the liberty of assigning my own labels and identifying in my own words the challenges or tasks the family must negotiate in order to survive. I have assumed for the purposes of discussion that the family's life begins when a heterosexual couple, each with living parents, marries. I have also assumed the couple has children. (I realize that not every couple is heterosexual, has four living parents, or has children.) I also have not sought to identify every single challenge a family must negotiate as it passes through each phase, only the most obvious challenges. I have phrased the challenges I do identify in the form of questions to be answered by the couple. In the interests of brevity and intelligibility, I have simplified the complexities of family evolution. You may think of other ways of describing the family and its phases. Such active thinking will enhance your understanding of this material; I encourage it!

Look over the scheme that follows. Think about your own experiences, and see whether they jibe with this formulation.

Table 3.1 Family Phases and Challenges

PHASE	CHALLENGES
I. Marriage: Launching the Family	How will our relationship be defined? What will our roles be? Who will be responsible for *what* in our relationship? How will we manage conflict and disagreement? How close to or distant from our families of origin will we be?
II. Birth of Children	What parenting philosophy or style will we adopt? How will we manage our children? How will we allocate responsibilities for child rearing? How will we keep our own relationship alive and healthy while accommodating children into our lives?
III. Schooling of Children (K–12 and beyond)	How will we work together to negotiate the outside world of school, religious instructors, and so on for the benefit of the children? To what degree should we help our children with their school assignments? Who will do it? Will our children attend college? How much financial responsibility will we assume for our children's college educations?

Table 3.1 Family Phases and Challenges (continued)

PHASE	CHALLENGES
IV. Empty Nest: Children Leave Home	How will we redefine our relationship now that the children are gone? If our child marries, how will we incorporate the new in-law into our lives? If our child has a child, how will we incorporate a grandchild into our lives? What roles will each of us assume as grandparents?
V. Declining Health of the Couple's Parents	How will we allocate responsibilities to care for our aging parents? How will we balance the needs of our parents with those of our children while still satisfying our own needs? How will we cope with our emotional losses and unresolved conflicts with our parents? How will each of us manage relationships with our siblings and in-laws?
VI. Death of Parents	How will we cope with the death of our parents? How will we manage the distribution of parental assets and debts?

continued

Table 3.1 Family Phases and Challenges (continued)

PHASE	CHALLENGES
VII. Couple's Own Declining Health	How will we prepare for our own aging and declining health? What will our old age be like? What financial and practical living arrangements will best meet our needs?
VIII. Death of Spouse	How will I create a new life without my spouse? How will my relationship with our children change now that only I survive?
IX. Remaining Spouse's Death	Children are likely to be in the middle phase of their own lives, a time when they must make decisions about *their* life without a parent.

Such a delineation of the phases in the family life cycle is useful for understanding how and why families stray off the mark as they attempt to grow. Simply put, when a family has trouble meeting the challenges posed by each life phase and by moving from one phase into another, problems develop and symptoms emerge.

For example, when a child is born, a transition period begins. Mother's attention is necessarily and appropriately directed to the infant's needs. Many men, accustomed to having their wife's undivided attention, react badly to this development, despite the fact that they understand it is inevitable. They may feel rejected. If they are also feeling burdened financially, they may feel more isolated than ever. Also, some women become very depressed after they have children. Some reject the child, feeling they are not yet ready to become a mother; some reject their husband, blaming him for having gotten them pregnant. Some men become distant. Some become depressed. Others are so upset they seek the gratifications of an intimate sexual relationship outside the marriage. Such behavior is less a moral failure on the husband's part than it is a measure of the *couple's* failure to negotiate the challenges of this transitional life phase.

Another example is the phase that begins when the child reaches adolescence. During this tumultuous time in a family's life, parents and children struggle over how to redefine the parent-child relationship. Parents may themselves disagree on how strict or lenient they should be in dealing with the adolescent. The child, in turn, is struggling with his or her own ambivalent feelings about separating from the parents. It is not at all unusual for symptoms to emerge under these circumstances. An adolescent may act out angrily and recklessly. From the perspective of the system, such symptoms are not evidence of "inadequate parenting" or that the child is "bad." Rather, they are indications that the family is having difficulty moving through this transitional life phase.

Similarly, the decline of a parent's health marks the beginning of another transitional phase in the family life cycle. The once-strong father, for example, becomes a dependent man, necessitating the shifting of roles and responsibilities. A day is envisioned when Father is no longer around; that, too, requires emotional, financial, and other adjustments.

THE TENDENCY TOWARD INCREASING COMPLEXITY

Speaking practically, when a parent ages, the demands he or she makes on his adult children increase, often at the same time as the adult child's own progeny increase *their* demands. The middle-aged couple feels all the stresses of the classic "sandwich generation." If the couple cannot find a way to manage all these demands, either one or both members may become depressed, angry, remote, or worse. The results can vary widely, from mild distress to infidelity, separation, and divorce. In extreme cases, suicide may occur.

Despite the difficulties, the family *must* resolve the crisis posed by a parent's aging. If the parent had more than one child, then many families are affected and are drawn into the negotiations that must occur. Most families manage the negotiations and resolve the crisis, although the quality of the solutions arrived at varies widely. Later, I will discuss solutions in more depth, and the variables that affect their quality, but consider some of the possibilities:

- Siblings who get along with each other may or may not continue to get along under the stress of a parent's declining health. As parents age, adult children necessarily become involved with their siblings. If the family is not close, they need to become reinvolved, if only for a limited time.

- Siblings who are estranged may continue to be estranged. Their relationship may worsen under the stress. It may also improve, although this is not typical.

- Siblings who have simply drifted apart from one another may rediscover each other. This can have positive or negative consequences.

- Siblings may have spouses. The spouses may or may not get along with each other.

As these possibilities suggest, involvement among siblings adds many layers of complexity to an already stressful and complex situation.

How do families negotiate the stress occasioned by an elderly parent's declining health and reduced self-sufficiency? While the process can be described in different ways, one makes the most sense. I call it the *dialectical model.*

The process is one that begins with stability, passes through a period of crisis and instability, and then goes in one of two directions. Either (1) the family successfully resolves the conflict, in which case a new, creative, and adaptive resolution is arrived at, or (2) the family fails to resolve the conflict and either becomes more rigid or breaks down altogether. The dialectical model is depicted in diagram form below.

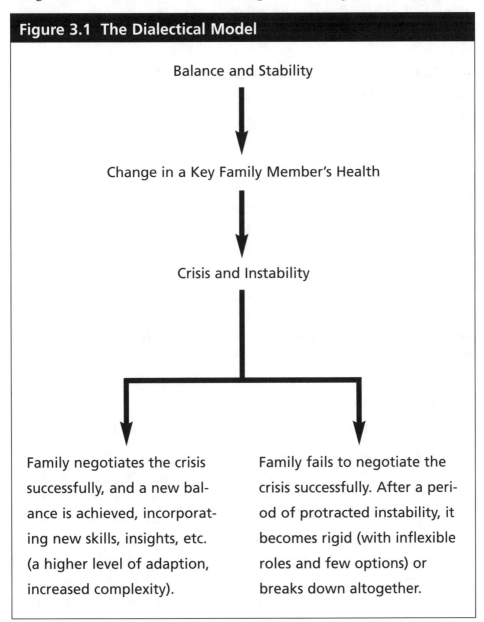

Figure 3.1 The Dialectical Model

Balance and Stability

Change in a Key Family Member's Health

Crisis and Instability

Family negotiates the crisis successfully, and a new balance is achieved, incorporating new skills, insights, etc. (a higher level of adaption, increased complexity).

Family fails to negotiate the crisis successfully. After a period of protracted instability, it becomes rigid (with inflexible roles and few options) or breaks down altogether.

The dialectical model takes into account the fact that destabilization of an existing balance always creates conflict and distress. Destabilization also *requires* a response. Confronted with the challenge of destabilization, the family will always be called upon to arrive at some resolution of the crisis. Not all resolutions are equally good.

FACTORS INFLUENCING THE QUALITY OF THE FAMILY'S SOLUTIONS

What factors determine whether a family successfully adapts to the stress of an aging parent? Even more specifically, what variables affect the *quality* of the family's solution? There are many variables, but four are most important: (1) the informal rules that govern behavior within the family, (2) the role and importance of the aging person, (3) the extent to which problems can be directly addressed within the family, and (4) past experiences within the family and the quality of relationships over the years. Because the family is a human system, it is possible for us to know what these variables are and to appreciate their potential influence. Knowledge of these variables can prevent families from being victimized and stymied by them. With the help of books like this one and the intervention of skilled mental health professionals, families can arrive at better solutions, solutions that might otherwise not have been possible.

Informal Rules That Govern Behavior within the Family

Families, like other dynamic, human systems, are governed by informal rules. Often, these rules are completely outside the awareness of family members. Unless they are brought to the attention of the family, members simply follow the rules and assume "this is just the way it is." For example, in some families, people are discouraged from expressing feelings. Stoicism and self-containment are highly valued, and the free expression of feelings is discouraged, perhaps considered gauche or embarrassing. In some other families, people who *do not* express their feelings are viewed with suspicion and are perhaps even disliked as being too quiet and hard to read.

One of my clients came from a family in which the expression of feelings was discouraged. She told me that when her mother grew ill and ultimately died, the family's way of dealing with feelings compounded the loss and panic she felt. She was a young girl at the time, and she recalls only that a sort of "shroud" seemed to overcome everyone when her mother became ill. No one talked about what was going on, yet she knew something was dreadfully wrong. Her mother was isolated in the bedroom, and my client was given very limited access to her. Her questions about her mother's health were either avoided or answered with platitudes and empty reassurance. There were no demonstrations of grief, no frank discussions of what was going on. In fact, so far as my client knew, there were no family discussions of any sort. When at last the mother died, the family remained stoic. My client recalled standing next to the casket in tears for what seemed like an eternity at her mother's wake. At last, a caring adult came and wrapped her arms around the little girl, who was finally able to cry some of the tears she needed to shed. Ironically, the adult was not a family member, but a neighbor.

The point of the story is that unspoken family rules almost always dictate what can and cannot happen among members, even in times of crisis. If important emotional topics cannot be discussed, then only inferior adjustments and adaptations are possible.

The Role and Importance of the Aging Person

In the ideal human group, whether a family or not, roles are evenly distributed among members. Perhaps you have observed this. Among friends who are seeking something to do on the weekend, there may be six roles at work—one person initiates ideas; another person jokes around to relieve tension; a third makes encouraging comments and reinforces the group's good work; another sees to the details of the plan; a fifth gathers needed information; a sixth smooths over ruffled feelings. These are all different group roles (the initiator, the tension-reliever, the encourager, the organizer, the information-provider, and the peacemaker); in this example, different roles are being played by different people.

Sometimes, however, roles are not evenly distributed. One or a very few persons play most of the roles, while others go along for the ride. In some families, for example, parents remain in the "problem-solver" role long after their children are capable of assuming responsibility for their own lives. In these families, one or both parents continue to make decisions for the children long after they need to do so. Thus, the parent's role remains pivotal. As a result, children fail to acquire the skills they need to cope with life. When this parent ages, becomes ill, and dies, the family may be at a loss about how to cope.

I recall one family of four, composed of a high-functioning man, an obese and emotionally unstable wife, a female child with personality traits much like the mother's, and an aloof son. As long as the father was alive, most of what needed doing in the family got done. Father did the shopping and household tasks. He arranged outings, drove his wife and child wherever they needed to go, and so on. As he aged and his health failed, this family slowly but inexorably fell apart. Because a pathological pattern of dependency had developed, no one was available to pick up the slack.

When the father died, everything unravelled. His son moved away. His wife was admitted to a nursing home shortly thereafter, and his little girl—intelligent though she was—grew up to be a lonely and sickly woman. Eventually, all the family finances were drained. The daughter was too ill to work, and she lived out the remainder of her life a ward of the state.

Such families reveal what happens when one key person occupies too pivotal a position. Again, the quality of the adaptations arrived at when that key person grows old or becomes ill is almost always inferior. In the absence of aggressive and competent professional help, which the family you just read about did not get, the ending is almost always unhappy.

The Extent to Which Problems Can Be Directly Addressed within the Family

In some families, expectations of self and others run high. In such cases, problems that need to be discussed are often avoided, for fear that someone will be disappointed or will think less of themselves. The L family was a case in point. Mrs. L was 81 years old and in good health. Nevertheless, concern for her safety, along with other factors, caused Karen and Jake, her daughter and son-in-law, to invite her to live with them and their two children. In return, Mrs. L happily agreed to do the cooking and ironing, two jobs she enjoyed. For a few years, the arrangement worked well. However, as Mrs. L aged, she began to become exhausted by the work. In many families, the problem could have been discussed, but in this one, it was not possible.

On one side of the problem, Mrs. L dreaded becoming a burden to her daughter and son-in-law. Furthermore, she feared losing her status as a contributing member of the family. Thus, she decided to "protect" the family by not telling them about her exhaustion and increasing fragility.

On the other side, her children felt equally constrained. They realized she was having a difficult time keeping up with the tasks she had agreed to perform. However, they were uncomfortable depriving her of her role. So they "protected" her by pretending she was able to do what she had always done. This meant that sometimes Karen would get up in the early morning to iron clothing her mother had ironed poorly the night before—all in an effort to spare her mother's feelings.

It took a crisis to bring the situation to an end. After this charade of mutual protection had gone on for several months, Mrs. L suffered a serious burn when she attempted to lift a heavy pot from the stove. A trip to the emergency room and a few tense days made it possible for this family to discuss openly, at long last, the problem of her increasing incapacity. Her children willingly accepted her playing a diminished role, and she willingly stayed on in their home, performing lighter tasks.

Past Experiences within the Family and the Quality of Relationships over the Years

For countless reasons, in some families people bond and experience a long-standing and profound sense of unity. Such families are fortunate. Siblings who truly do get along have a much easier time coping with a parent's aging and death. In other families, however, no such bonding occurs. For many reasons, siblings may never really feel connected emotionally. Often, in such families, siblings who marry choose as mates partners who do not really fit into the family and may draw the married sibling away. When in-laws enter the picture, the situation becomes even more complex.

Contrary to what we all might wish, no magical transformations occur within families as parents age. Siblings who have had a poor relationship in the past are likely to continue to have a poor relationship. In-laws who do not like each other will rarely start to discover likable qualities in each other. A history of conflict is unlikely to be washed away under the stress of a parent's aging. Unfortunately, many families with whom I have worked demonstrate this only too clearly.

PART THREE: Rearranging the Family Portrait

On the following pages, you will learn the most productive way to correct problems that arise if your family responds in an unhealthy or a nonproductive way to the problems occasioned by the aging of one or more parents. I offer several suggestions and illustrate how each can be implemented, using a typical problem for purposes of illustration. To correct a family's unhealthy responses to the aging of a parent, three steps are required: Identify the problem, talk about the problem, and create a plan for solving it. Then it is important to periodically evaluate your family's progress in moving toward its goal.

IDENTIFY THE PROBLEM

Families of aging parents face many practical difficulties, among them deciding about financial responsibilities, choosing medical treatments, and deciding how to respect a parent's wishes about end-of-life matters. These tasks are frequently compounded by systemic reactions. For example, if one member becomes detached, her contributions are lost to the family and her attitude may undermine its efforts. Rather than seeing her lack of involvement as a moral failure or proof of her indifference, the family needs to view it as an indication that the *entire* family is failing to respond adequately to the crisis.

In my experience, families face these *system-related* problems most frequently:

- One or more family members may become overinvolved. As they do so, others will become detached.

- A struggle may emerge between siblings about how best to deal with the problems of an aging parent. For example, some children may advocate institutionalization while others may see that as a course of last resort.

- An aging parent who is capable of helping herself may not take responsibility for doing so.

To illustrate how to use the problem-solving methods I am recommending, I will take the first systemic problem, overinvolvement and uneven distribution of responsibility. You will see how this problem, which is often intimately bound up with the other two, can be addressed. The method illustrated here can be applied to any problem faced by your family.

The first step in solving this or any other problem is to determine whether a problem exists. Here are some questions that can help you to step outside your immediate situation and look at the big picture.

1. *Am I, or is someone else in the family, taking on too much responsibility?* One woman reported that whenever a crisis arose in the care of her elderly father, her siblings invariably turned to her, despite the fact that they were no less able than she to provide help. Understandably, she felt resentful. She buried that resentment for a time, but that took its toll: she was short-tempered with her children and her spouse. She knew she had to do something. Rather than swallowing her anger, she brought the matter to the attention of her siblings.

2. *Am I, or is another family member, doing things for my elderly parent that are not essential?* Sometimes, in an adult child's desire to help an aging parent, he or she does more than is necessary. For example, one son was determined to accompany his elderly but robust mother to every doctor's appointment she had. While this, in itself, might be considered a bit extreme (after all, not every appointment is crucial), he also felt constrained to pick up his mother at home and drive her to and from the doctor's office. This added to his burden. It was only when he stepped back and reevaluated his behavior that he realized his mother was perfectly able—financially and otherwise—to arrange a ride for herself. When he began backing off, his mother happily hired a taxi or asked a willing neighbor to drive her.

3. *Am I, or is another member of the family, doing more for our care-recipients than they are willing to do for themselves?* One client told me that her parents—both ill and in need of help—bickered constantly and failed to help each other, when they could have behaved more rationally and been more mutually supportive. The most conscientious caregiver in the world cannot rescue people who will not make an effort to help themselves. When she tries to do so, she does them and herself a disservice. They become increasingly dependent and noncooperative, and she becomes resentful. Everybody loses.

4. *Am I suffering, or are my spouse and children suffering, while others in the family are barely affected by the demands of caregiving?* One client, an educational administrator with a busy professional life and a family of her own, lived two hours from her elderly mother. Once or twice a week she drove from her home in Connecticut to provide care; the trips became more frequent as her mother's health deteriorated. Meanwhile, her brother and sister-in-law, who lived only twenty minutes away from the elderly woman, saw her once a year, if that. Pressed for his help, my client's sibling's response was, "Take Mom to Connecticut, and let me know when she dies." (In this case, efforts to discuss the desirability of sharing responsibility seemed pointless. Consequently, it became necessary for my client to convince her mother to accept help from neighbors and professionals. Reluctantly, the elderly woman agreed.)

5. *Am I entering into a silent conspiracy with my parent to "elbow out" other family members who could help?* One man was very wedded to his long-time role of the good son. In caring for his elderly father, he consistently took on the primary burden of caregiving. Simultaneously, he made certain his two siblings (one male, one female) were not encouraged to share the burdens of caregiving. Only in therapy was it possible for him to recognize that his overinvolvement served *his* psychological needs at the expense of the psychological well-being of his siblings and the welfare of his father.

It may seem odd that I speak of the undesirable behavior of family members as *symptoms* of the fact that the entire family is failing to respond appropriately to the problem. It is often convenient for a family to think of such undesirable behavior in other terms: The overinvolved daughter is often seen as "a goody two-shoes." The uninvolved son is seen as "uncaring, cold, and selfish." The adolescent who acts out his or her distress is labeled a "deviant" or a "brat."

Such harsh and judgmental labels do little to facilitate problem solving. Specifically, they prevent the family from looking at the *family* problems at the root of such behavior. "Goody two-shoes" may feel she has no choice but to do what others are not inclined to do. The "uncaring, cold, and unselfish" son may feel deeply hurt that he is being pushed away once again, while the "good" sibling is allowed to maintain closeness and provide care. The "deviant brat" may be bringing the wrath of the family on himself deliberately (though unconsciously) in order to maintain the existing hierarchy and rules governing the dysfunctional family system.

Looking at families from the perspective of family systems requires that all individual behavior be seen in the broad context of the entire family's way of functioning. When this perspective is maintained, and when undesirable behavior is seen as symptomatic of a family problem (rather than as a personal quirk or a moral failure), it is possible to look at the issues that give rise to the behavior. This is far and away the most constructive approach to take.

Sometimes the help of a professional therapist is required to recognize symptoms for what they are and to examine what needs to change. Competent help can expedite the corrective steps that must be taken so that nonproductive patterns of caring for aging parents do not become deeply rooted. A well-trained therapist will take into account the many factors contributing to the family's collective difficulty.

TALK ABOUT THE PROBLEM

A family's systemic difficulties rarely go away unless discussed. For that reason, one or more family meetings should be arranged to discuss what is wrong openly. A family problem-solving discussion often decreases unnecessary strife while increasing the odds that an elderly parent will receive optimum care in a healthy and caring emotional setting. Often it is a good idea to hire a professional therapist to serve as a mediator and to run the meeting, especially if feelings run deep.

FAMILY MEETING GUIDELINES

Whether you hire a therapist or not, these guidelines can be helpful in assuring that the issues requiring discussion are addressed in the family meeting. These guidelines are adapted from a handout I distribute to family members before a meeting takes place. The guidelines reflect the assumption that only one meeting will be arranged; however, several may be required.

1. Plan an agenda.

Before the meeting, each person attending should write down and set priorities for three or four topics he or she wants to discuss. If a therapist is involved, it might be desirable to send or fax this information to the therapist a few days before the meeting. If this is done, be certain that written materials are clear and easy to read. If possible, type.

2. Gather key information.

If a therapist is involved, bring to the meeting the following items and data:

- Your aging parent's full name, social security number, date of birth, address, and phone number. Bring his or her Medicare card and any other insurance data. For example, if your parent has any supplementary (medi-gap) insurance, bring that information along, too.
- A brief history of your parent's illness and a description of his or her current condition.
- Your parent's diagnosis and prognosis.
- A list of all medications your parent is taking. For each, include dosage and frequency, as well as the name of the prescribing physician and the date on which your parent began

taking the medication. Include any regularly taken over-the-counter medications and "natural" remedies such as herbs, herbal teas, vitamins, and so on.

☐ Name, address, and phone number of your aging parent's primary physician(s).

☐ If other health-care professionals or formal caregivers are closely involved with your parent or have been involved within the past six months, bring their names, addresses, and phone numbers as well. This includes medical specialists (including psychiatrists), counselors, home-care nurses, home-health aides, physical therapists, nutritionists, and so forth.

☐ A copy of a release form authorizing the therapist to contact other professionals and to exchange information with them. (Most therapists can provide such a form on request.) It should be signed by your parent. If your parent is not capable of understanding or signing a release form, the family member who is responsible for legal decisions pertaining to your parent should sign. (Note: Only your parent can sign a release. Someone else may sign in the event of incompetence. If you are uncertain about your parent's competence to sign a release, you need to contact an attorney for advice.)

☐ A copy of all your parents' current advance directives: living will, health-care proxy, durable power of attorney for health care. If these are not available, the therapist can direct you to the appropriate community resource for the forms and guidance on completing them.

☐ Copies of any other relevant documents that will help the therapist understand your parent's condition or the problem that caused you to contact him or her.

3. Set goals.

For a family meeting to succeed, everyone must agree on the goals they want to achieve. Before the meeting, each person attending should answer the following questions. Although there is no real need to write the answers down, you may find that you benefit from doing so.

  a. What is the current problem? Why is there a need for this meeting? If a therapist is involved, what brings you to him or her?

  b. What do you hope will happen as a result of the meeting? When the meeting is over, how will you know it has been a success? What will a success "look like"?

  c. In your view, why has your family been unable to solve the problem?

  d. What are you personally willing to do to ensure the success of the meeting?

  e. Where are your limits—that is, what are you *not* willing to do?

4. Set communication guidelines.

During the meeting, the following rules of communication may prove helpful, especially when there is conflict. If a therapist is involved, he or she should take responsibility for articulating and enforcing these rules.

- No one should dominate the meeting. If necessary, someone should be appointed to set time limits.
- All family members should listen to one another, without interrupting, in order to understand each other's perspectives. If necessary, people can restate each other's messages, in order to ensure understanding before any response is made.
- All attendees should speak for themselves and not for anyone else. You should use "I-messages" rather than "you-messages."

> Preaching, judging, blaming, and giving advice should not be allowed. Neither should telling someone else how he or she needs to change in order for the situation to improve.
>
> **5. Avoid private communications.**
>
> Any communication with any member of the family should also be exchanged with everyone else. To ensure the success of the meeting, there can be no "silent" agreements or secret exchanges between any family members.

When a family faces any challenge, some degree of discomfort usually exists. However, the potential for growth is also present. A well-run family meeting will not only help your family solve the problem but will also help you grow collectively.

CREATE A PLAN FOR SOLVING THE PROBLEM

To solve any problem, a disciplined approach works best. When a family sets out to solve a systemic problem, it's best to formulate a plan. In doing so, two models of problem solving are particularly helpful. The first model, called the Creative Problem-Solving Sequence, originated with the turn-of-the-century educational philosopher John Dewey, whose book *How We Think* is still useful. The second model, called the Criterion Method, is more detailed and comprehensive; accordingly, it is a bit more time consuming to use. While each model has its strengths, as you shall soon see, neither is ideal. You may find it desirable to combine the best features of each method.

The Creative Problem-Solving Sequence

Dewey's problem-solving model is composed of eight stages, or steps.

Step One: Ventilation Before any rational problem solving can take place, pent-up emotions must be vented. This means giving family members an opportunity to vent feelings by airing their grievances, discussing their fears and uncertainties, or unburdening themselves of any guilt they may carry. Whatever feelings the family members may have, they need to be expressed constructively as a prerequisite to problem solving.

Step Two: Clarification The issues being discussed must be made clear to all parties. This means understanding what the real problem is, tracing its origins, understanding its effects, and seeing how the problem manifests itself.

For example, it is not enough to say, "We're here to discuss how Mom and Dad can be better cared for," when the real problem is the fact that only two of five siblings are bearing the brunt of the responsibility. The real problem may be more accurately formulated by saying, "We're here to talk about how the burdens of caring for Mom and Dad can be more evenly distributed among all of us."

Step Three: Fact Finding Before the problem can be solved, family members must know the pertinent facts. The guidelines for the family meeting summarized in the previous section identify most of the factual data you need to know. You must be familiar with your aging parent's diagnosis and prognosis, current health-care providers, medications, and so on. It is also important to provide facts such as the nature and extent of care required by your parent, the number of hours spent on caregiving by each family member during a typical week, expenses incurred, and the adequacy of your parent's current living arrangements in terms of safety and comfort.

Step Four: Discovery Having identified the problem and gathered the pertinent facts, family members are encouraged during the next phase of the problem-solving process to begin formulating possible solutions. This is brainstorming. No real evaluation of proposals is made during this phase. (That happens next.) Instead, every possible feasible solution is proposed, and captured in writing when necessary to remember them all for subsequent evaluation.

Step Five: Evaluation This is when proposed ideas are evaluated one by one, to see which seem most practicable, workable, and effective. To do this, you need to establish criteria by which to judge the worth of the various solutions that have been proposed. (Later you will see that the Criterion Method of problem solving provides excellent guidelines for formulating criteria.)

Step Six: Decision Making Once your family decides on the best solution (there may be more than one, depending on the complexity of the problem), you should all begin thinking about what needs to happen to put the solution into effect. Who will do what? Whose cooperation is essential? What might go wrong? What can be done to solve, or at least reduce the impact of, anticipated problems associated with implementation?

Step Seven: Implementation Your family's plan is put into effect. Responsibilities are allocated. Plans are made for ensuring that the required tasks are completed in a timely way.

Step Eight: Follow-up In this final stage, your family agrees to review the outcomes. After implementation of the plan, you all look back and ask, Has the plan worked? Can it be improved? Can it be made more efficient or more fair?

The Creative Problem-Solving Sequence provides a good set of guidelines for systematic problem solving. While it is rather nonspecific, it is a good tool in helping you to focus on the problems at hand and to understand and monitor your family's progress toward a solution.

The Criterion Method

The Criterion Method is quite a bit more detailed. It, too, consists of eight steps, but many of these are broken into substeps. In Chapter Five, I will show how this method can be used to decide among options for living arrangements when a parent can no longer live alone. Here, I will illustrate how it can be used when confronting problems that arise within a family's collective responses to the aging of a parent.

Step One: Define the Problem As during the Clarification stage in Dewey's scheme, at this point in the problem-solving process you and your family should explicitly state the problem you are setting out to solve. Ask yourself these questions:

- Why does the problem exist?
- What are the problem's origins?
- What will happen if the problem is not solved?

A crucial question that must be answered when defining a problem is, What *kind* of problem is it? It is difficult to overstate how important addressing this question is, because your family's view of a problem dictates the kind of solutions you will find. For example, consider these four different ways of looking at the problem of an underinvolved sibling. Notice that each formulation of the problem implies or lends itself to a different kind of solution.

- "My brother won't help out in caring for our mother" implies that the brother is individually to blame: If he were a better person, he would help out. Period.

- "I can't get my brother to help out more" implies that the problem is the speaker's: If the person with the complaint were more persuasive, the problem would be solved.

- "My brother and I can't work it out so that we can share responsibilities for our mother's care" implies that the problem is in the relationship between the siblings: If they had the tools to work out their differences, they would be able to get unstuck.

- "My mother will only accept help from me, so my brother and I are unable to work out a care plan" implies that all three people involved have the problem: If their collective difficulty could be addressed and solved, then the sharing of responsibility would occur naturally.

As this simple example shows, the way a problem is defined often determines automatically the nature of the solution that will be proposed.

The following questions are a useful tool for analyzing the problem your family is confronting:

- What *should* be happening now that is *not?*
- What *is* happening now that should *not* be?
- What *could* be happening now? In other words, if the situation were ideal, what *would* be happening?

To illustrate how this method is used, I will consider the steps taken by an actual family with whom I worked a few years ago. The family consisted of two adult sisters, one married with two teens, the other a single parent of an 8-year-old. Faced with a decision about admitting their 85-year-old mother, Mrs. B, to a nursing home, the family used the Criterion Method very successfully.

They began by defining the problem, as required by this method. Here is what emerged:

Why does the problem exist? Mrs. B had lived alone after her husband's death for many years. Until about six months ago, she had managed very well. After injuring herself slightly in a minor fall, she began having trouble getting around. She was having difficulty preparing meals and caring for herself. She had begun to become forgetful. On several occasions she left an empty pot on the stove above a lit burner, almost starting a fire in the kitchen. Home-health assistance had been tried but for a variety of reasons had not worked out. Hence, admission to a long-term care facility was the only care option available.

What are the problem's origins? No single event had caused Mrs. B's rapid deterioration. Instead, the inevitable consequences of aging had begun to occur. Mrs. B made excuses for the lapses she could not ignore. She also made it quite clear that she wanted to stay in her home. When pressed about the issue, she became quite upset. "I'm in charge of my life!" she said angrily. She was adamant about not being admitted to a home.

What will happen if the problem is not solved? In other words, why not do absolutely nothing? If the situation were allowed to go on, certain outcomes were predictable: Mrs. B would continue to practice inadequate self-care. Her nutrition and personal hygiene would deteriorate. Her mild dementia would likely progress, exacerbated by isolation and lack of stimulation. She might fall again, perhaps injuring herself more severely. She might cause a fire, resulting in injury or death.

What *kind* of problem is it? As I showed on page 73, there are various ways of framing such problems. Here are three possibilities:

- "Mother doesn't want to leave her home and is refusing our efforts to place her in a nursing facility." The implication is that the problem here is Mother's obstinacy.

- "We cannot convince Mother to leave her home and enter a nursing facility." The implication is that finding more convincing arguments would bring Mrs. B around.

- "We cannot agree on how to convince Mother to enter a nursing home." The implication is that this is a *family* problem.

The B family decided the problem wasn't just mother's obstinacy. It was also lack of knowledge on her part and that of all the family. No one had visited nursing homes. Mrs. B had never even seen the inside of one.

What <u>should</u> be happening now that is <u>not</u>? Preparations should be underway for Mother to enter a long-term care facility. This was the only way her safety and well-being could be protected. Visits—with Mother along—should be arranged. Discussions should be held with intake residents; perhaps Mother should even spend a few days in a facility to experience it first hand (the hope being she just might find it less dreadful than she feared).

What is happening now that should not be? Mother continues to live under increasingly unacceptable conditions. Tension between us is growing, as our levels of anxiety over Mother's safety have heightened. We have begun faulting each other for "not doing enough for Mom."

What could be happening now? In other words, if the situation were ideal, what would be happening? The B family was clear about this. In the best of all possible worlds, they agreed, Mother would willingly accept their recommendation that she enter a nursing facility. She would then be in a safe place, living out her last years or months in a dignified way, with proper care, good hygiene, adequate nutrition, and so on.

Step Two: State the Purpose of the Decision Using the Criterion Method of problem-solving to its best advantage, the B family stated precisely what they wanted to decide. Their purpose was stated as an infinitive phrase: "to identify and learn about possible long-term care facilities in our area and to determine which one best meets Mother's needs." Note that the assumption in this statement was that the B family had already decided to do *something*. Hence, the task at hand was to choose among alternatives, not to decide whether to do anything at all.

Step Three: Formulate Your Criteria The B family arrived at several criteria for choosing among nursing homes. Not all criteria weighed equally in their decision making. In Chapter Five, I speak in more depth about choosing a nursing home. For the moment, however, let me share an abbreviated list of criteria used by the B family.

Does the facility provide the level of care Mother needs? By taking an inventory of what Mrs. B could do for herself (always a good starting point in any decision about the level of care an elderly parent might need), the B family easily ruled out some facilities simply because they did not provide the appropriate level of care required. (See the Glossary or Chapter Five for information on levels of care.)

Does the facility meet licensing and accreditation requirements? The B family checked to be sure the facilities they were considering were state-licensed and accredited by the Joint Commission of the Accreditation of Hospitals. They also made certain that the facilities were Medicare and Medicaid approved.

Can we afford this facility? For the B family, cost was an important criterion. They made a careful survey of all costs associated with Mother's taking up residence. They also looked into Mrs. B's ability to meet copayments and to pay for care after her insurance benefits had expired. They contacted an attorney to learn about the rules that would operate in determining which family assets could be protected from the government and which could not.

Does the facility provide the nonrequired services we want? After narrowing their choices to facilities that met their first three criteria, they moved on to preferences. They looked into opportunities for socialization and the observance of religious practices. They found out the cost of extras such as laundry service and a private television.

Are staff well qualified and attentive? In evaluating each facility, the B family considered such factors as staff credentials, caring, and attentiveness. They looked at the ratio of staff to patients. They found out the rate of turnover among the staff. They asked about night coverage and about the presence of a pharmacist on staff to make it easier to monitor medications.

Other? Then they moved on to consider many other criteria, including safety (smoke detectors, hand rails in the bathrooms, adequate lighting, etc.), cleanliness (of the facility and of residents), and quality of life concerns (privacy, cheeriness of surroundings, tastiness and nutritional value of food, and such).

Step Four: Weight the Criteria The B family placed their criteria into two categories: *musts* and *wants*. Their *must* criteria were inflexible. An institution had to meet these criteria to be considered by them. For example, they knew that the nursing facility must be state-licensed and Medicare approved. It *must* also be located in a place that made it relatively easy for both daughters to visit.

The B family's *want* criteria were desirable but not mandatory. They assigned a weight to each criterion, reflecting its importance; hence, some of their *wants* weighed more heavily than others. For example, because Mrs. B placed a great deal of importance on religious practice but had little interest in reading, the presence of a chapel was more highly valued (that is, given more weight) than an on-site library.

Step Five: Identify Alternatives At this point in the decision-making process, the B family listed and briefly described each of the four institutions they were considering.

Step Six: Arrive at a Score for Each Option You Are Considering After ruling out all facilities that did not meet their *must* criteria, the B family began choosing among remaining alternatives by considering the degree to which each one met their *want* criteria. They used a numerical approach to arrive at a score for each facility by calculating the degree to which it met each *want* criterion. (Numbers aren't always needed; in many cases, just common sense is enough.) For example, a facility earned fewer or more points depending on its convenience to visitors. The more conveniently located the facility, the more points it earned.

Step Seven: Consider What Can Go Wrong This is sometimes referred to as "conducting a *Murphy's Law* analysis." Murphy's Law states that anything that *can* go wrong *will* go wrong. The B family thought about possible problems, and they found ways to avoid most of them and to cope with problems that *could not* be avoided. For example, they anticipated that Mother would be upset if she could not take some personal possessions from home and use them to decorate her room and to give it a "homey" feel. They ensured that Mother could do so.

Step Eight: Implement the Plan and Monitor Progress Once Mrs. B was admitted to the nursing facility with which all members felt comfortable, the two girls kept watch to see that their desired goals were being achieved. (As in the Creative Problem-Solving Sequence discussed earlier, monitoring makes it possible to determine whether the plan is having the desired result. If not, it becomes necessary to think about what might be done to revise the plan so it works even better.) After an initial period of adjustment, mother showed signs of being well fed and well cared for. She was more alert mentally and enjoyed socializing with other residents. She was safer, happier, and more engaged in life than she had been at home. The B family's decision making had been a success.

Summary

There is great value in looking at the family as a system—a unit constantly striving to maintain a balance among its members in order to ensure its survival and to do its work. In addition to individual responses to a parent's aging, there are *systemic* family responses as well. These can be either healthy or unhealthy. Actions can be taken to change your family's responses when they are unhealthy.

Normal stages exist in the family life cycle, and the failing health of parents, and their ultimate death, signals a new phase in that cycle. Family problems are best viewed as *symptoms* that the family is stuck in its attempts to make its way through this difficult phase, and specific factors affect the quality of the solutions arrived at by a family. After identifying a family problem, you can talk about it and create a logical and systematic plan for solving the problem.

The responsibilities of caregiving are compounded when an elderly parent suffers from a mental disorder. In the next chapter, two broad classes of mental disorders are discussed, and advice is offered on recognizing, verifying, and overseeing treatment for a mental disorder.

CHAPTER 4

*W*hat to Do If Your Aging Parent Has a Mental Problem

When 71-year-old Sheryl Q entered the doctor's office, the waiting room erupted. She was in a rage, accusing the distressed daughter who accompanied her of trying to have her "put away." With no sense of propriety or shame, she shouted whatever thoughts came to mind. Most of them were disjointed and her words were garbled and usually made little sense. She loudly refused to sit down and wait her turn. Her conversation shifted rapidly from topic to topic. Her mood swung just as rapidly, from belligerent and hostile to pleading and pathetic. She wrung her hands, cried openly, and carried on conversations with imaginary people in empty chairs, talking about feeling lost and frightened. By the time she was whisked in to see the doctor, she had terrified most of the patients in the room, all of whom were glad to see her go.

To the layperson, Sheryl Q was just plain "crazy." But to her physician she posed a special problem of diagnosis, because her symptoms could have been the result of any one of several mental disorders, each requiring different treatment. As an adult child, Sheryl Q's daughter played a key role in helping the medical professional make a diagnosis. That is often the case. In your own caregiving, it is likely that you will be called on to perform the same role. By understanding when your parent needs help for a mental disorder, and by providing critical information, you can prevent needless suffering and improve your aging parent's quality of life.

This chapter is practical. It is not my desire to present theoretical or statistical material on mental illnesses among the elderly. Rather, I want to help you learn when help is in order and how to become an informed consumer of mental health services. Accordingly, the four parts of this chapter answer key questions of importance to any adult child.

Part One addresses two key questions: First, what exactly *is* a mental disorder? You will learn that *mental disorder* refers to two different but closely related sets of conditions. One set consists of *cognitive* disorders. These are disorders characterized primarily by deficits in intellectual functioning, such as dementia. Not all cognitive impairments are progressive and irreversible, as is dementia. The other set of mental disorders consists of disabilities that are, strictly speaking, primarily *emotional* in nature. These disorders, which include anxiety and depression, are problems with mood. An elderly parent who is persistently sad, isolates herself in her room, and refuses to bathe most likely has a mental problem that is emotional (in this case, depression) rather than cognitive. The second question answered in Part One has to do with attitude. As an adult child, what attitude can you take to ensure that your parent receives adequate care for a mental problem? This section shows why the proper attitude is critical. Some shocking data are included on the inadequacy of the mental health care that many seniors receive.

Part Two of the chapter focuses on *why* your elderly parent is prone to mental problems and on which disorders most commonly affect older folks. You will learn about contributing causes of mental illness among the elderly, including physiological changes, life experience, and personal history. Certain disorders are fairly common among the elderly, and you will learn the key characteristics of each and what is known about their incidence and prevalence.

Part Three gives you the information to make a preliminary determination concerning your parent's need for professional help for a mental disorder. A distinction is made between normal cognitive problems and everyday distress on the one hand, and mental problems on the other. The section includes a checklist that will help you recognize the more obvious signs of a mental problem that requires attention. As a family member, you can provide critical data that will help the diagnostician arrive at an accurate picture of what is wrong with your parent. This section includes guidelines on how to help with the process of diagnosis. Finally, Part Three includes up-to-the-minute information on a growing trend in care of the elderly: making what is known as a *functional assessment* of a person's mental state by observing how successfully the person manages activities of daily living.

Part Four of the chapter provides guidance on finding competent help for your parent. Local and long-distance sources of referrals are given, including organizations that can help you locate skilled helpers. You will learn what to expect when you bring in a parent for an assessment—the various tests used to arrive at a diagnosis, and the factors that can adversely influence test outcomes. Suggestions are given for evaluating the quality of help your elderly parent receives. What traits or behaviors should you look for? Which are signals that this particular professional is a person to avoid? Because misuse of medications among the elderly is widespread, there are steps to take whenever a physician prescribes a medication for your parent. Finally, Part Four offers suggestions about what you and your family can do to support your elderly parent while he or she is in treatment. You will read about the common errors families make and how to provide your elderly parent with the correct kind of support.

PART ONE: Two Kinds of Mental Problems

The word *normal* has several distinct meanings when applied to mental illness. Some mental health authorities view *normal* as meaning an ideal state. In this sense, a person is normal when he or she is fully realized and happy, effective, powerful, and fulfilled. To others *normal* means an average, predictable state, not necessarily fully realized or happy. In this sense, the word means the absence of sickness. *Normal* can also refer to a statistical average—what most people experience. For example, mild memory lapses are so typical of people over age 65 that they are considered normal. Or again, following a loss, there is a period of normal bereavement; only if the sadness and distress do not remit after a reasonable time (6 months is the typical yardstick) would the condition warrant attention. A person is considered normal when she can flexibly adapt to changes in her environment and circumstances. Resilience is at the heart of this meaning of the term. Finally, *normal* must always be defined in a cultural context. What is normal within one cultural group is not necessarily normal within another.

Although the word *normal* can have different meanings, keep one key fact in mind: Any marked change in your parent's typical ways of being and behaving can signal a problem and should be a cause for concern. Knowing an individual's personal history is, therefore, important in assessing the presence of an emotional disorder. That is why you, as an adult child, have a key role to play in helping mental health professionals make an accurate diagnosis of your parent's internal state.

Mental disorders are conditions that affect a person's ability to function effectively, to take pleasure and satisfaction in fulfilling everyday responsibilities, and to relate to others in a normal way. When someone has a mental disorder, we see that person as odd, sad, scary, or pathetic—as different from the rest of us. For the person suffering from a mental disorder, the condition causes them to feel frightened, weird, lonely, and out of control. Sometimes the pain and distress are so acute, people choose to end their lives. Statistics clearly indicate that the rate of completed suicides is significantly higher among seniors than among the general population.

There are two broad classes of mental disorders: cognitive or brain disorders and emotional disorders. The distinction between the two classes is somewhat forced, since in reality the two overlap at various points. For example, if your parent has a cognitive problem that affects his ability to make sound judgments or to remember things, he is likely to be depressed as well. Nevertheless, the distinction is helpful because it makes it possible to discuss mental problems in a way that is comprehensible and manageable.

COGNITIVE OR BRAIN DISORDERS

These disorders, the most common of which is dementia, affect conscious mental processes, including memory, judgment, comprehension, reasoning, problem solving, and planning. In its earliest stages, dementia (whether Alzheimer's or another type) triggers minor memory lapses and occasional poor judgment. Later stages are revealed in more serious cognitive impairments that render a person unable to perform simple, everyday tasks like bathing and dressing. Consider these examples:

- Jane, 74, loved to entertain. Over the years she had become expert in giving wonderful dinner parties. In her later years, however, she no longer knew how to plan a party or organize all the tasks required for a successful dinner party. The loss of those skills took away an important part of the way she defined herself. Once an adept and gracious hostess, Jane suffered serious injury to her self-esteem.

- Carlos, 79, had lived in the same neighborhood for over forty years. He knew every street and alley. He had always loved walking, and he would often traverse the familiar streets, chatting with neighbors and making the rounds of familiar shops. In his later years, however, he began becoming disoriented. Once or twice he got lost. To his dismay, he found himself regularly asking strangers for directions.

In both these cases, cognitive impairments resulted in loss of the ability to do things that once were effortless.

Sometimes cognitive impairments have emotional consequences that cause personality changes. These changes include irritability, agitation, depression, frustration, anxiety (the fear of "losing it"), and mood instability. For example, Leon was a kindly man, sociable and gregarious, always ready to lend a helping hand. As his cognitive functioning declined, however, he became antisocial, quick to anger, and suspicious of others. These changes in mood and temperament would not have occurred had the cognitive problem not developed.

Table 4.1 lists the predictable stages in progressive dementia. However, not all cognitive conditions are progressive. Some, like delirium, are reversible. Conditions caused by low blood sugar, vitamin deficiencies, and infections are similarly reversible.

Table 4.1 Stages in Progressive Dementia	
STAGE	**TYPICAL SYMPTOMS OF COGNITIVE DISORDERS**
Early	Problems recalling words; tendency to misplace objects; in demanding social and work situations, the person seems to be functioning below his or her normal level.
Middle	Unable to handle complex tasks (e.g., balancing a checkbook) without help; requires help in choosing appropriate attire.
Later	Unable to bathe or dress without help; limited ability to articulate ideas through speech.
Late	Incontinence; unable to walk, to sit up, even to hold up one's head.

EMOTIONAL DISORDERS

Emotional disorders are illnesses that affect unconscious mental processes and influence the way a person feels, thinks, and behaves. They are clinical entities that often have a predictable course and outcome. They are not simply "problems in living," such as annoyance at a noisy or inconsiderate neighbor. Nor are they the minor variations in mood that all of us experience from time to time.

To qualify as an emotional disorder, a condition must have a persistent adverse impact on the life of the sufferer, regardless of whether the person subjectively experiences the disease as painful or pleasant. For example, an elderly person who suffers from an anxiety disorder may find herself feeling nervous and jumpy when she first wakes up in the morning. A sense of dread may color her days. She may be unable to calm down, enjoy life, or even relax enough to get to sleep at night. The loss of sleep may further exaggerate her jitteriness, put her in a foul mood, and cause her to spend much of her time apart from others. She may even be reluctant to leave the house. On the other hand, an elderly individual who suffers from a personality disorder may not feel anxious or depressed. Yet he may find himself misunderstood by others, perhaps openly disliked for reasons he cannot fathom. His ability to meet his personal goals, to elicit the cooperation of others, and to achieve real satisfaction in life may be compromised.

No one can see an emotional disorder directly. (The same is true of cognitive disorders, of course.) Rather, we infer its presence from external signs and symptoms. Here are some examples of symptoms that may indicate your parent is suffering from an emotional disorder.

- feelings of such depression and hopelessness that he cannot get out of bed and face the day
- a sense of dread, as though something terrible were going to happen
- intense feelings of panic and irrational, inexplicable fear
- exaggerated or extreme worry over trivial or everyday concerns
- belligerence and quarrelsomeness
- lack of emotional control, resulting in inappropriate behavior and the absence of a sense of shame (recall the example of Sheryl Q that opened this chapter)

- Inability to fall asleep because of agitation and feeling that one's mind is racing

- repetitive nightmares or flashbacks of some trauma

- angry outbursts disproportionate to the provocation

- binge eating, vomiting, or self-starvation

- abuse of substances such as alcohol to the point of illness or dependency

THE IMPORTANCE OF ATTITUDE

Table 4.2 contains statistics indicating that mental illness among the elderly often is not treated or is improperly treated. Because of this, a proper attitude on your part is crucial, regardless of whether it is a cognitive or an emotional disorder your parent suffers from.

Table 4.2 Inadequate Care of Mental Problems among the Elderly

Fact: Nearly 75% of elderly people suffering from depression receive no treatment of any kind.

Fact: Throughout the United States, elderly people suffering from a functional mental impairment and living in the community rarely receive treatment. For example, according to one recent study undertaken in North Carolina, only 8% of such people receive help. That means 92% do not.

Fact: 20% of suicides occur in people over age 65.

Fact: Only 5% of the elderly with emotional disorders are referred to psychiatrists for treatment.

Fact: 80% of the elderly who are receiving medications for an emotional problem receive those medications from general medical practitioners rather than specialists in geriatric psychiatry.

To ensure that your parent receives prompt and adequate care, keep the following principles in mind; they are the key components of a proper attitude.

Mental illness is nothing to be ashamed of. The stigma attached to mental problems is a hold-over from a period when ignorance and gross superstition made symptoms an embarrassment. Symptoms that can now be treated and cured by means of talk therapy and medication were once considered signs of demonic possession or attributed to other supernatural causes.

Mental illness does not indicate a weak or morally flawed character. Equating mental illness with weakness is also an antiquated notion, best summed up in statements such as "I should be able to handle this" and "If I were stronger, I'd be able to go on." Seeking help is often a sign of strength, not weakness.

Taking medications is not a "cop-out" or a quick fix. Research has established beyond a doubt that many mental conditions (both cognitive and emotional) are the result of physiological abnormalities in the brain. Depression, for example, once little understood, is now recognized as primarily the consequence of low levels of the neurotransmitter serotonin. Medications such as Prozac and Zoloft that increase the amount of serotonin available in the brain almost always correct the problem. Thus, taking medication for depression is no more shameful and no more of a "cop-out" than taking an antibiotic for a strep infection. Would you deny your parent medication that could alleviate the symptoms of a physical illness, perhaps even cure it?

Mental illness rarely goes away by itself. Like other illnesses, mental illness requires treatment. Properly treated, many mental illnesses can be cured; at the least, the suffering they cause can be alleviated.

Mental illness is best treated by experts in mental health. You would almost certainly take your parent to a specialist for a particular illness or condition. For example, you would see a cardiologist for a heart problem. In the same way, you should take your parent to a mental health specialist if he or she displays signs of a mental illness.

PART TWO: Why Your Parent Is at Risk for a Mental Disorder

Older people are prone to mental illness, both cognitive and emotional. This section of the chapter discusses the factors contributing to the development of mental illness among the elderly and provides an overview of the incidence and prevalence of mental illness among seniors.

CONTRIBUTING FACTORS

There are many reasons your elderly parent is susceptible to mental illness. Some are physical, others are emotional, and still others are of a different nature.

Physical Factors

Of the many physical factors that contribute to the emergence of mental disorders in seniors, three stand out. First, *physiological changes* in the brain that appear to be a normal part of aging affect both cognitive functioning and mood. Whether genetically based or the consequence of living a long life, these changes affect the way our minds function.

Second, *sleep patterns change*. It is estimated that between 30 percent and 50 percent of the elderly have chronic sleep disturbance. This affects their alertness during the day as well as their mood. It may also result in reliance on medication, which creates its own set of problems.

Third, *physical illness*, more common among the elderly, places them at risk. Being ill is in and of itself frightening and depressing. Often, illness carries with it chronic pain and feelings of distress, which can wear down a person. When physical illness is reported to a physician (often among the elderly it is underreported for reasons explained below), the report often results in the prescription of medication, which typically creates side effects. When a person is taking many medications, interactions may occur among them, further complicating the picture and producing new symptoms.

In addition, many physical illnesses and conditions have *emotional components*. Consider something as simple and often easily corrected as hearing loss. It is well documented that undiagnosed hearing loss often results not only in social isolation but in feelings of suspicion and paranoia. Often, hearing loss is incremental—your parent may not realize she is losing the ability to hear, since it occurs so slowly. Because it is difficult to interact with others when you cannot hear them, your parent may withdraw from people without saying why.

Emotional Factors

As seriously as physical factors influence the mental health of older people, it is generally acknowledged that emotional factors are even more important. Following are several of the most obvious emotional factors.

Isolation and loneliness are all too common among the elderly. Living with little sense that one matters to others takes a real toll on a person's emotional health.

The elderly typically experience *multiple losses* of individuals as well as abstract things. Loved ones—family and friends—die. In the course of aging, your parent has probably lost the opportunity to play the useful roles that once were the cornerstones of her life. For example, a once-vibrant educational administrator, long retired, no longer plays an important role in the lives of youngsters in her community. Along with that loss comes a diminution of her status in the community and her sense of worth in her own eyes. She may live out her days with a sense of pointlessness: Her life has lost much of its meaning because she can do little to play a vital role in the affairs of her community.

Another loss your parent is likely to feel is the *loss of autonomy and self-sufficiency.* We all place a high value on being able to chart our own course in life. As that capacity slips away, we feel diminished, and often frustrated and angry as well. Perhaps even more pernicious, an older person may take his cues from those around him. Treated *as though* he is helpless and incapable, an otherwise high-functioning person may begin to feel that he *is* helpless and incapable. He may define himself as less able than he actually is; as a result, his world shrinks.

In a society that values youth and youthfulness, aging means the *loss of one's physical attractiveness and strength*. Pride and self-confidence may suffer as a result.

The *fear of abandonment* and similar worries weigh heavily on many seniors. I cannot tell you how many times older folks have told me they fear becoming a burden to their families. Many fear that if they do become a burden they will be abandoned. Hence, it is no surprise that most of my older clients worry that they will lose the ability to manage their lives by themselves. The dread of institutionalization is behind much underreporting of illnesses or of even simple, easily solved difficulties in managing everyday tasks among the elderly.

There is also a cluster of emotions that come all too often with advancing age: feelings of *disappointment* with one's life along with *disillusionment, regret,* and *sadness* that one's dreams were never realized. Some seniors never healed emotionally from traumas or tragedies in their youth. Others were unfulfilled in their youth, some because they were victims of circumstances and some due to self-sabotage. Such people often become bitter when they reflect back on their lives.

Other Factors

Poverty is a reality for many seniors. They live on inadequate pensions, scrimp on food, and allow their living environments to become run down. In the cold, they save money by lowering the heat. The fear of becoming a burden, mentioned earlier, results in their unwillingness to make demands. "If I manage without imposing on my family," they are likely to say to themselves, "then I won't be a burden."

For some seniors, *neglect and abuse* are part of their everyday experience. Consider the case of one family who was brought to my attention by the department of protective services in my state. Tim Z had been widowed in the early 1990s. For two years he managed on his own, in the small home he and his wife had bought in the 1940s. Late in 1992, however, he was forced by ill health to move in with his only daughter, Sara, and her husband, Hugh. Both wanted him, and both did all they could to make his living arrangements comfortable. However, as Tim's health continued to fail and his cognitive functioning declined, his personality underwent a change. Known as an easy-going and a mild-mannered person, Tim became irascible and sullen, rarely exchanging more than a few words with daughter, son-in-law, and grandchildren. He was demanding and passively aggressive. The next few years were hell for Hugh and Sara.

By 1994 the couple began ignoring Tim's psychological needs. They saw to it that he was fed and clothed and that he visited the doctor when needed. But they rarely did more. They spoke to him little and when they did, their voices had an angry and sarcastic edge to them. Over time, a wall of sullen indifference built up. Hugh knew just how furious Sara was with her father, and he read into her lack of caring a permission to do more than simply neglect her father.

As the situation continued to deteriorate, Hugh and Sara began arguing between themselves. Hugh blamed his father-in-law for the family's unhappiness. Apparently unknown to Sara, he began taunting Tim in her absence. He abused Tim verbally, saying things like "I wish you were dead, you old bastard" and "Things would be a lot nicer around here if some people would just drop dead." Tim pretended not to hear and—out of fear—never told Sara, but in response to the verbal abuse, he began behaving in still more problematic ways, soiling and refusing to cooperate in his care.

Over the months, the verbal abuse escalated to physical neglect, then to physical abuse. Hugh would not feed Tim in Sara's absence. In addition, while providing caretaking services, he would "accidentally" elbow his father-in-law or injure him in other nonobvious ways. Tim suffered these indignities for as long as he could. Not able to talk to Sara and not knowing where to turn, he called his niece one day and told her he wanted to come and live with her. Exploration revealed the reason for his request. The niece called protective services. The complaint was investigated and found to be valid. Arrangements were made to remove Tim from his daughter's home temporarily. I was one of the professionals called in to assist the family.

This was, in many ways. a typical case. The unfortunate truth is that elder abuse appears to be a fairly widespread problem. Because the problem is hidden and rarely publicized, there are no definitive data on its scope. (Elders who are abused or neglected often do not report it. They may be embarrassed. They may fear they will not be believed. They may be reluctant to expose their children. They may fear abandonment and reprisal.)

Despite the difficulties in gathering data, some studies have been done. The best information available indicates that between 4 percent and 5 percent of all seniors are abused; a much higher percentage of seniors suffer from neglect. Moreover, neglect and abuse cut across all socioeconomic levels—they are not confined to the uneducated or the poor. Elder abuse is sufficiently common to be considered a serious public health problem.

COMPOUNDING FACTORS

As I have already suggested, these problems are often compounded because of interactions among them. Physical illnesses may have cognitive and emotional components. Multiple medications may interact with each other and create an array of side effects. Much enlightening research has been done on the incidence and causes of the underreporting of physical and mental illness by the elderly.

- First, symptoms of treatable mental illnesses may be missed by family members and even by physicians. Sometimes they are mistaken for the crankiness and quirkiness so often erroneously associated with old age. Other times the family may simply deny that a problem exists, believing that mental illness is shameful.

- Second, older adults may be unwilling to access care because they cannot afford it or fear they cannot.

- Third, cultural factors may discourage help-seeking. Among the members of some cultural groups, being psychologically strong means not admitting any need for help. Thus, the members of such groups believe that seeking help is a sign of weakness and therefore shameful. In other groups, psychological symptoms are interpreted as religious phenomena and are not seen as a problem.

- Fourth, older people tolerate and accept subjective distress. Once again, out of fear of becoming a burden or of being abandoned, they learn to live with their pain, whether physical or emotional.

MENTAL ILLNESS AMONG THE ELDERLY

Only by being aware of the myriad mental problems to which your parent is vulnerable can you be reasonably attuned to his or her need for help. The following symptoms of mental illness have been identified with some regularity among the elderly (see Table 4.3). Please note that I have grouped these symptoms in one of two categories: cognitive problems and emotional problems. To some degree, however, my groupings are arbitrary, as some symptoms can be attributed to more than one or both conditions.

Table 4.3 Symptoms of Mental Illness among the Elderly

COGNITIVE PROBLEMS AND THEIR CONSEQUENCES

- **Dementia**
  memory deficits
  language and speech difficulties
  lack of orientation in time and space
  poor judgment
  pacing, wandering
  assaultiveness

- **Delirium**
  acute confusion, hallucinations, delusions

EMOTIONAL PROBLEMS AND THEIR CONSEQUENCES

- **Depression**
  sleep and appetite difficulties
  crying spells
  irritability
  feelings of unworthiness or hopelessness
  apathy
  withdrawal
  suicide attempts and gestures
  suspiciousness and paranoia ("people are following me")
  diminished attention span
  inability to concentrate

- **Anxiety and Agitation**
  pervasive sense that something awful is going to happen
  disproportionate worry
  agitation, a feeling that one's mind won't "slow down"
  difficulty falling asleep

The range and scope of these symptoms are impressive. In the next section of the chapter, I will identify specific warning signs and give you the opportunity to complete an inventory that will guide you in determining whether your parent needs help.

PART THREE: Warning Signs—When Your Elderly Parent Needs Help for a Mental Problem

You cannot be expected to know how to diagnose a cognitive or an emotional disorder. Nevertheless, you can learn to recognize the warning signs of mental illness. Having done so, it is essential that you take steps to ensure that a mental health professional makes an accurate diagnosis.

As you evaluate warning signs, keep two principles in mind. First, any change in a person's typical ways of acting should be viewed with concern. If a usually mild-mannered man becomes surly and belligerent, the likelihood is that something is wrong. Similarly, if a feisty and strong-willed woman becomes passive and weepy, something is likely amiss.

Second, any behavior considered to be a typical part of the process of adjusting to a loss or trauma that continues for an unusually extended period of time indicates a likely problem. For example, if your parent is unable to adjust after a reasonable length of time to a predictable life change (say, the death of a friend), then the parent may be experiencing a more serious problem in addition to the matter of adjustment.

To get a very rough gauge of your parent's mental health, complete and score the following questionnaire. It is divided into parts, corresponding to cognitive and emotional problems.

Mental Problem Checklist

Part One: Cognitive Problems

Instructions: Please answer *yes* or *no* to each of the following questions by circling the *y* or the *n* that precedes the question number.

Dementia

y **n**   1. Over a long period of time, has my parent experienced a gradual, progressive decline in a broad range of mental functions, such as memory, judgment, orientation in time and space, planning, language disturbance (for example, the inability to find the right word to convey a meaning), organizing, and the ability to think abstractly?

y **n**   2. If I ask my parent basic questions like the name of the president of the United States, the year, month, and day, or even his name and address, is he unable to answer accurately, even though he makes an effort?

y **n**   3. Has my parent been getting lost going to or from places with which she is familiar?

y **n**   4. Does my parent refer to deceased relatives and friends as though they were alive, or speak as though he were living in another time?

y **n**   5. Are these symptoms quite constant, fluctuating only a little over time?

Delirium

y **n**   1. Has my parent suddenly become confused and out of touch with reality?

y **n**   2. Has my parent suddenly begun to see things that are not there or to hear voices?

y n   3. Has my parent suddenly become agitated?

y n   4. Has my parent suddenly become unable to focus or concentrate?

y n   5. Has my parent suddenly begun to find it more difficult than usual to remember things?

y n   6. Has my parent suddenly begun to exhibit difficulties in interpreting words or using words and language properly?

y n   7. Is my parent experiencing an unusual disturbance in her sleep-wake cycle?

y n   8. Do my parent's symptoms fluctuate during the course of the day, at times growing worse and at times spontaneously improving?

y n   9. Does the emergence of these symptoms coincide with some discrete event, such as starting a new medication, taking a fall, or experiencing some highly stressful event?

PART TWO: EMOTIONAL PROBLEMS

Instructions: Please answer *yes* or *no* to each of the following questions by circling the *y* or the *n* that precedes the question number.

Depression and Bipolar Disorder

y n   1. Does my parent have dramatic mood swings, seeming sometimes very "up" and hyper, and other times rather depressed and hopeless?

y n   2. Is my parent no longer enjoying activities and people that were once a source of pleasure?

y n   3. Is my parent losing or gaining unusual amounts of weight?

y n   4. Does my parent report unusual difficulty sleeping? Does he complain of waking early in the morning and being unable to get back to sleep?

y n 5. Does my parent talk about suicide or about a desire to see life come to an end? Does she seem unusually despondent and hopeless?

y n 6. Is my parent having difficulty concentrating on tasks that were once easy?

y n 7. Is my parent engaging in activities that are atypical for him? For example, is he going on spending sprees or making foolish decisions?

Anxiety Disorders

y n 1. Does my parent seem edgy and frightened for no apparent reason? Does she report feeling that way?

y n 2. Does my parent exhibit behaviors suggesting unusual fear or dread?

y n 3. Does my parent display unusual jitteriness and jumpiness? Does he seem unable to relax?

y n 4. Does my parent experience unusual pain or discomfort that medical tests reveal have no physical cause (for example, shortness of breath, chest pain, sweating, and trembling)?

y n 5. Does my parent report that she cannot get to sleep because her mind keeps racing?

y n 6. Does my parent have sudden and inexplicable attacks of panic? At such times, does he report fearing that he is having a heart attack or that he is unable to breathe?

y n 7. Is my parent unable to let go of certain ideas, fears, or rituals? For example, does she perform a certain act over and over again, even though it does not make logical sense to do so?

y n   8. Is my parent bothered by frightening or ridiculous thoughts that he cannot rid himself of, regardless of how much he wants to?

y n   9. Does my parent report that she cannot stop thinking about some past event that was tragic or deeply upsetting?

y n 10. Does my parent report nightmares or flashbacks of a terrible event in his life?

y n 11. Are my parent's feelings (for example, irritation or anger) in response to an upsetting or annoying event disproportionately intense?

If you answered *yes* to any of these questions, further assessment is strongly recommended. Find a psychiatrist, clinical social worker, or other mental health professional qualified to perform a more thorough diagnostic workup. In the next section of the chapter, you will learn how to do that.

As an adult child, you can help the diagnostician in important ways. Depending on the degree of your parent's disturbance, he or she may be of little help. You, however, have detailed knowledge of your parent's history. You are in a position to answer critical questions that the diagnostician will need to know, and any competent diagnostician will *want* your input. (If the person with whom you're speaking appears defensive or closed to your reports, find another diagnostician.) Here are some guidelines to help you be effective.

Focus on reporting observations, not making interpretations. One of the common mistakes adult children make is to arrive at the physician's office, or that of another professional, with a conclusion already firmly in mind. Not only can this be misleading, it may be upsetting to the diagnostician.

Experienced professionals resist the temptation to jump to conclusions. Instead, they gather data slowly and carefully, often by taking a history, asking for a detailed review of what brings the patient to the office, and speaking with family members or others who know the patient well. Your job is to report what you have been observing, much as people do when they bring their car to a mechanic for repair. Tell the professional what has been going on, for how long, and how consistently; talk about when it started, what you have done to correct the problem, and the results of your efforts; and so on. To help you clarify the distinction between factual reporting and interpretation, compare the examples shown in Table 4.4.

Table 4.4 Factual Reporting vs. Interpretation

FACTUAL REPORTING	INTERPRETATION
My father has been losing his balance.	My father has a brain injury.
My mother has been becoming increasingly uncooperative and angry. This is not like her.	My mother is depressed.
My father has been forgetting where he puts things.	My father has dementia.
My mother is becoming distrustful of others and accuses me of talking behind her back.	My mother is paranoid.

In each of these cases, the facts reported do not justify the interpretation given to them. Professionals are trained to consider all possibilities; and—in fact—there are many possible explanations for each of the conditions observed.

Write down what you have observed and bring your list with you. Your list might include these kinds of entries: "For the past several weeks, I've noticed my mother has lost interest in things. She no longer enjoys talking with people and has begun to stay in bed for much of the day." Or, "Two days ago, my father became very frightened and panicky. He was trembling, sweating, and having a hard time breathing. He said he was having a heart attack. When we took him to the emergency room, they could find nothing wrong with him. They gave him a medication called Xanax, and that helped."

Be specific. Without becoming absurd about it, be as precise as you reasonably can. For example, if your father becomes confused and agitated shortly after beginning a new medication, be sure to write down the name of the medication, the milligram count, how frequently he has been taking the medication, the day he started taking it, the physician who prescribed it, and the reason it was prescribed.

FUNCTIONAL ASSESSMENT

An emerging trend in geriatrics is what is known as a *functional assessment*, which involves determining how effectively an elderly person is able to perform the activities required for daily living.

In Table 4.5 are two lists of activities that each of us needs to perform in the course of everyday life. People's ability to perform these tasks depends on their mental state, as well as any physical limitations within which they must operate. Your careful recording of your parent's ability to perform these functions can help the diagnostician you hire do his or her job.

Table 4.5 Functional Assessment Categories

■ **Instrumental Activities of Daily Living (IADLs)**
Shopping
Cooking
Housekeeping
Doing laundry
Using transportation
Managing money
Managing medication
Using the telephone
Reading
Maintaining a home
Communicating

■ **Activities of Daily Living (ADLs)**
Bathing
Eating
Using the toilet
Grooming
Dressing

In the next chapter, you will see that your parent's ability to perform these activities is a key criterion in determining whether he or she can continue to live independently, and if not, what type and level of assistance your parent may need. For example, suppose an 89-year-old woman is able to perform all Activities of Daily Living (ADLs) and most Instrumental Activities of Daily Living (IADLs), except perhaps shopping and maintaining her home. Then, a nurse's aide or other home-health aide may be all she needs to avoid institutionalization and to continue living in her own home. In the context of this chapter, your observation of how effectively your parent performs these activities will serve as an indirect measure of her mental state.

PART FOUR: Getting Help

In this section you will be given guidance for answering questions such as these: Where do I find help for my parent? What should I expect to happen when I take my parent to a mental health professional? How do I evaluate the quality of the help I locate? How can I support my elderly parent when he or she is in treatment?

WHERE TO FIND HELP

As is the case when securing any medical referrals, it is usually best to begin with your parent's primary care physician. If the physician does not routinely provide the names of local psychiatrists or other mental health experts who work with geriatric patients, ask for names.

Sometimes a referral from a primary care physician is not possible or fails to work out. The physician may not know of anyone. Sometimes the person to whom you are referred has moved away or cannot accept new referrals. In such cases, try these options:

- Your local hospital may have a geriatric health facility or know of a nearby hospital that does. Often, such facilities can point you to competent, local mental health experts. Failing that, your local hospital should have a network of referral sources.

- Local nursing or extended-care facilities undoubtedly have experience with geriatric patients. Try calling their admissions department and see whether they can put you in touch with professionals on their staff or others to whom they regularly refer clients.

- Speak with other medical and health professionals in your community.

- One surprisingly good source of information, rarely called on by members of the community, is your hospital's patient advocate. He or she is in a position to know the physicians in the community who are most responsive and attuned to the needs of elders and their families.

- In every region of the United States, there is an "Area Agency on Aging." Contact that agency for assistance. (The social services section of your phone directory can help you locate the AAA near you, as can the 800-number service called "Infoline.")

- Call the ElderCare Locator service for assistance. This number is 1-800-677-1116.

- Talk with friends who are or have been in situations similar to yours.

- Professional organizations can be a valuable source of referrals. Here are a few; additional resources appear in the Selected Resources appendix.

American Psychiatric Association
1400 K Street NW
Washington, DC 20005
1-202-682-6142

American Psychological Association
1200 17th Street NW
Washington, DC 20036
1-202-336-5500

American Society on Aging
833 Market Street, Suite 511
San Francisco, CA 94103
1-415-974-9600

National Association of Professional Geriatric Care Managers
1604 N. Country Club Road
Tucson, AZ 85716
1-520-881-8008

National Association of Social Workers
750 First Street NE, Suite 700
Washington, DC 20002
1-800-638-8799
1-202-408-8600

WHAT TO EXPECT WHEN YOU TAKE YOUR PARENT FOR AN ASSESSMENT

History Taking

Intake should include a history. This includes a review of your parent's very recent history. What symptoms is your parent experiencing that have resulted in this office visit? When did the symptoms begin? How consistently have they continued? Have they changed over time? If so, how?

The diagnostician should ask for information about your parent's personal and family history. What medical conditions affect your parent? What is his current health? Are there current medical conditions? Past conditions? Any surgeries? Does your parent have a history of emotional or cognitive problems? Has he ever been in treatment (including hospitalization) for a mental problem? Does your parent abuse alcohol or any other substances? Is there a family history of depression or other mental problems? Has anyone in the family ever committed suicide? Is there a family history of drug or alcohol abuse?

Psychosocial Stressors

Intake should also include a review of current psychosocial stressors. What has been going on in your parent's life? Have there been any recent experiences that may have a bearing on your parent's condition? Have there been any accidents or falls, for example? Is he under financial pressure? Did someone die? Have there been any other stressors or losses (relocation, illness, an argument with a friend, the loss of a loved pet)?

You can be a valuable source of information about the recent and remote history of your parent. It is a good idea to bring along a brief family history if there are pertinent facts to remember and report. As mentioned earlier, it can also be helpful to bring a written account of recent experiences that may have a bearing on your parent's condition. This should include notes of changes you have been observing in your parent's mood and behavior and the reasons why you sought the referral.

Medications

The diagnostician should ask about all medications your parent is currently taking. Here, again, you can be an invaluable aid. Bring a medication history, including the names and milligram counts of *all* medications taken by your parent, as well as how frequently and under what circumstances they are taken (time of day, on an empty or full stomach, etc.). Include over-the-counter and so-called "natural" remedies. Make a note of when all medications were begun, how faithfully they are taken, and if prescribed, who prescribed them. As a courtesy, include the name and phone number of your parent's pharmacy. Make copies of your reports and be prepared to leave one with the professional. For an example, see Table 4.6.

Table 4.6 Sample Medication History

Patient Name: Marie Salvos

Prepared By: José Salvos   (Relationship to Patient: son)

Prepared For: Dr. Horn   **Date of Preparation:** 11/12/98

Name of Medication	Prozac
Dosage	20 mg
Frequency	once daily at breakfast
Form	capsule
Prescriber	Dr. Jones
Start Date	2/1/98
End Date	ongoing
Reason Prescribed	depression
Problems, Side Effects	compliance

Pharmacist: Fairwood Pharmacy, New Preston, 333-9999

Physical Examination

A physician or nurse practitioner will conduct a thorough medical examination, the length and complexity of which will be influenced by your parent's current physical and emotional condition. Your parent will be weighed. Blood pressure will be taken. Pulse and other basic functions will be measured. Blood may be drawn for analysis, usually including a complete blood count and thyroid function. A urinalysis may be done. Your parent may be asked to take home a kit to gather fecal smears for analysis.

Family Assessment

In the course of interviewing you and your parent, the professional will also be assessing your parent's family situation and psychosocial functioning. Does your parent have a network of friends? Is she supported emotionally and in other ways? Is she visited and cared for by friends and family? Your parent's ability to perform both the Activities of Daily Living and the Instrumental Activities of Daily Living mentioned above will also be gauged.

Mental Status Exam

Expect that early in the process of assessment, though not necessarily at the first meeting, some measures of cognitive functioning and mood will be taken as part of a geriatric work-up. Certain tests are typically used for this purpose.

By far the most common of these is a mini–mental status exam, sometimes called the Folstein, after one of its creators. A brief, easy-to-administer tool, it consists of a series of questions and instructions for the patient to follow. These questions and tasks test remote and recent memory; orientation (is the senior oriented in person, place, and time?); judgment; attention and concentration (can the senior perform simple calculations?); thought content and process; the ability to assimilate information; and the ability to think abstractly. A score is arrived at by calculating the number of correct responses.

Here are a few of the tasks and questions your parent is likely to be asked to do and to answer. In selecting examples, I have drawn from a variety of mental status exams, not just the Folstein.

- What day of the week is this? What month is this? What year is this? What state are we in? (These questions test your parent's orientation.)

- Repeat the months of the year backward. Who was the president in 1965? (These questions test your parent's memory.)

- Draw a clock with a dial and hands and depict a certain time, such as five after three. (This task measures your parent's ability to think abstractly.)

- Take this sheet of paper, fold it in half, and put it on the floor. (This task measures your parent's ability to follow instructions.)

- Count backwards from 100 by sevens. A variation on this is to ask your parent to spell the word *world* backwards. (Such assignments test attention and calculation.)

- Your parent is shown a card with these words on it: *Close your eyes.* He or she is asked to read what it says and to do it. (This is a test of comprehension.)

It is important to know that the way the mental status examination is administered can affect the score received. Consider these factors:

<u>How such questions are asked</u> can make a great deal of difference in the score likely to be earned. Shooting a series of such questions and tasks at *anyone* without explaining what is being done and why would be unnerving, to say the least.

<u>The setting and psychological context</u> in which the mental status examination is administered can make a difference in the outcome. For example, the room in which the exam is administered should be free of distractions (noise, interruptions), because such distractions

can affect performance. The mood and recent experiences of the test-taker may also affect performance. A frightened person in unfamiliar surroundings is not likely to feel comfortable enough to score as high as a person who is at ease and in familiar surroundings.

Cueing can make a difference in the score. How many times should a question be repeated? How many times should instructions be repeated? What about pointing to items and touching them? Hand gestures, too, can influence the score by "cueing" a patient.

Other tests frequently used are the Beck Depression Inventory and the Zung Self-Rating Depression Scale. These self-administered questionnaires examine mood, self-image, and somatic complaints. Below are a few sample statements. In some cases, your parent will be asked to answer *yes* or *no*. In others, she will record the frequency with which such feelings occur.

- I get tired for no reason.
- I don't enjoy the things I used to do.
- I often feel downhearted and blue.
- I feel I have nothing to look forward to.
- As I look back on my life, all I can see is a lot of failures.

QUALITY OF HELP CHECKLIST

There are several criteria you can use to evaluate the quality of care your parent is receiving. While no single criterion in itself is a definitive measure of quality, several taken in combination provide a reliable measure.

☐ The first and most obvious criterion is the promptness and courtesy with which your initial inquiry is greeted. Are office staff knowledgeable and helpful? Do they seem interested?

☐ The physical location, cleanliness, and orderliness of the facility all signal the level of care you can expect to receive. In addition, look for indications that the facility is tailored to meet the needs of an older clientele. For example, are walkways clear and uncluttered? Are "hand-holds" provided in rest rooms?

☐ Are appointment times respected? With reasonable exceptions, it is a bad sign if you and your parent are kept waiting for long periods of time.

☐ Does the professional appear cordial and concerned, extending simple courtesies? During the initial interview, does he or she display a sensitivity to needs of older patients, pacing the interview appropriately and extending to your parent the respect your parent deserves? Does he or she accommodate for diminished hearing or sight limitations? (For example, many geriatric facilities have amplification devices that make it possible for physicians and staff to communicate with a hearing impaired individual without shouting. When hearing loss is suspected or reported by you, the person speaking with your parent should stand directly in front of him so that it is possible for your parent to supplement what is heard with lip reading as an aid to comprehension.)

☐ What is this person's level of experience in working with geriatric patients? Is he or she certified in geriatrics? What special training or qualifications does the person possess?

☐ When tests such as the mental status examination are administered, is your parent oriented? A skilled professional knows that anxiety and motivation can have a profound affect on performance. Accordingly, the professional will put the senior at ease by introducing the inventory and explaining why it is being administered. He or she will let your parent know that some of the questions may seem obvious and some of the tasks silly; nevertheless, cooperation is needed.

☐ Is the environment relaxing and distraction free?

☐ Before any sort of treatment is begun, are goals clearly specified? Does everyone know what is being sought in treatment and why? Are the criteria for "success" spelled out clearly?

☐ As treatment progresses, look for indications that the professional is consistently reliable and available for questions. Does he or she consult with other experts when doing so would make sense? Are your phone calls returned?

☐ Before arranging for any medications, does the professional insist on knowing all medications your parent is currently taking? Does he or she take the time to discuss the possible side effects of the recommended medication and its possible interactions with other medications?

SUPPORTING YOUR PARENT

Depending on your parent's cognitive or emotional difficulties, treatment may consist of medications, psychotherapy, or some combination of the two. If you find it difficult to know how to behave in order to support your parent, here are a few guidelines.

1. *Stay abreast of your parent's treatment.* Find out what the treatment is intended to achieve. Know with whom your parent meets, how frequently, and in what location(s). Be aware of what your parent is expected to do. For example, if medications are prescribed, do all you can to see that they are taken as prescribed. Report any noncompliance to the prescribing physician or your parent's therapist. If your parent must keep appointments, do what you can to see that he does so. If necessary, you may even provide transportation or accompany him to the therapist's office.

2. *Maintain communication with your parent's helpers.* This does *not* mean making frequent, unnecessary calls; but it *does* mean updating the helpers and alerting them to important developments. A very brief message left with an answering service or on voice mail can be invaluable. I am always grateful when an adult child calls and leaves a message that serves to update me. Two such helpful messages follow:

- "I just wanted to let you know that I've noticed Dad is sleeping a lot better lately. For the past week or so, he's slept through the night. He seems to be in a better mood, too."

- "I'm concerned because since last Tuesday, when Mom began the medication, she has been decidedly more unstable on her feet. She's nearly fallen three or four times."

Such brief, pointed messages alert me to signs of progress or problems; they help me stay abreast of my patient's condition.

3. *Be certain not to undermine the work of your parent's helpers.* Negative comments about treatment—whether about the medications prescribed or about the therapist—can undo any desire on your parent's part to cooperate in treatment and may interfere with her ability to benefit from it. If you have any complaints or objections to the prescribed treatments, take up your concerns with the helpers involved.

4. *Use common sense.* If your parent really seems to dislike her helpers, or if she reports strange behavior in their dealings with her, investigate her complaints. Sometimes personalities do not mix. Other times the treatment given by uncaring or inept professionals harms patients. If, for example, a consistent pattern of discourtesy or aggression develops, find other helpers.

Summary

An aging parent is susceptible to mental disorders that fall into two broad classes, cognitive and emotional. Using the Mental Problem Checklist, you can perform a preliminary assessment of your parent's need for professional help. Another aid is the use of functional assessment, in which your parent's ability to perform both Activities of Daily Living and Instrumental Activities of Daily Living is carefully measured. You have an important role in ensuring that your parent gets the help he or she needs, and you play a crucial part in helping with diagnosis. Finally, there are criteria to keep in mind as you evaluate the quality of the help you locate.

In the next chapter, we will explore the practical and emotional issues that must be considered when determining whether or not a parent can continue to live independently.

CHAPTER 5

Helping Your Parent Stay at Home for as Long as Possible

"My mother was 86 when my father died two years ago," said the middle-aged man who had called my office in some distress the day before. Now he was sitting in my office. "They had retired when my father was quite young—in his early fifties—and they'd lived in the same small ranch house for thirty years. He was ill, so his death was no surprise.

"Now my mother is there alone. So far, she's been managing." He paused. "But, a couple of weeks ago, she fell and injured her shoulder. We're not sure why she fell, but the doctor can't find anything wrong. No evidence of a stroke, no unusual balance or strength problems he could pick up. He suggested she take some medicine for her shoulder and that she be more careful."

The woman was 88. When she fell, she had been carrying a small box of silverware from a cabinet to the dining room table. The box was too heavy for her, and she had stumbled, hitting the corner of the table with her shoulder as she went down.

My consultation with the man was brief and to the point. He, his wife, and his brother had done many things right already, and my client had done his homework even before we met. "I guess it's time to start thinking about getting her more help. I don't even want to think about a nursing home yet. Mom has made it very clear she doesn't want that."

His mother wanted to stay in her own home. In that respect, she is very typical. To that end, she had willingly accepted help. A home-health aide came in three days a week for four hours each day. The aide helped with personal care (now that the mother could not use her right arm, the aide was helping her bathe and dress) and with cooking, laundry, and shopping, as time permitted.

However, the elderly woman's recent accident had brought to light the fact that she probably would not be able to stay at home much longer without more help. We discussed some options, and I impressed on the man the importance of planning for the future. Even though she might not need to be admitted to a nursing home *now*, there was a likelihood she *would* in the future. I recommended that he begin screening some of the local facilities—meeting with the person in charge of admissions (usually a social worker), taking a tour, and completing at least one application—so that his mother could be placed on a waiting list.

The man's experience and his responsibilities are representative of those of many adult children. His next step was to create a *care plan*, a long-term plan that assesses current needs and anticipates future needs, so that there are no breaks in service or lapses in adequate care for a senior as he or she advances in age. Most care plans are based on the premise that the senior will stay at home for as long as possible. The plan includes data on available sources of help and on paying for that help. It also considers alternate living arrangements, including but not limited to nursing homes.

In this chapter you will learn about the care plan you can create for your aging parent or parents. (For convenience, I will speak of one parent, and will assume that parent is female.) You will read about the advantages of keeping a parent in her own home (called *aging in place*) and learn how to increase the length of time she can stay at home by making living and care arrangements that ensure safety, convenience, and optimum quality of life.

Part One gives an overview of the many advantages of keeping a parent at home and the principles that should guide you in formulating a care plan. Part Two offers practical suggestions for making your aging parent's home safe. In Part Three, you will find out about sources of in-home help, learn important distinctions among various kinds of help, and find answers to questions about the qualifications of both the individuals who come to the home and the agencies that usually employ them. Part Four will review alternate living arrangements short of a continuing care community or a nursing home. By the time you have completed this chapter, you will have a reasonable grasp of what you need to do to safely avoid institutionalization for your parent for as long as possible.

PART ONE: Why Home Care Is Desirable

For many reasons, staying at home is often the most desirable option for an aging parent. It often meets the parent's needs as well as those of her adult children. Financial and practical benefits may also result from keeping a parent at home, although there is a point at which it is actu-ally *more* expensive to keep a frail elderly person at home than it is to arrange for nursing home placement.

Before we proceed, there is a principle that warrants mention. It is that of parental self-determination. Put simply, you do not have the right to tell your parent where or how she will live. If she is mentally competent, she retains the final say in just what her living arrangements should be.

Most times this is not a problem, but I do know of cases in which a parent's wishes differed from those of her children. In all such cases, the parent has the right to decide. In one case, the children violently opposed the parent's decision to enter a nursing home. Concerned about her certain impoverishment and its effect on their lifestyles, the adult children did all they could to thwart her desires. In the end, of course, she won. She enjoyed the security the nursing home provided. And although her children were upset with her for a long time, they eventu-ally realized that she had made the right choice for herself.

There are happy stories, as well. Another elderly woman wanted to go to a nursing facility. She was lonely at home—most of her friends and neighbors had moved away. She was a social person, and after visiting a few extended care facilities in her area with her adult children, she elected to enter one. The children, fortunately, were supportive of her decision. To date, she is happy there, leading a busy life. Her social needs are met, and her sharp mind allows her to make a real contribution to the facility.

Let us now look at the more typical cases. Most elderly *want* to stay in their own homes. After all, living independently benefits the individual in several ways. First, one's own home represents safety, security, and familiarity. There is nothing quite like one's favorite chair or the familiar colors and layout of the rooms a person has known intimately for many years.

Second, old people living on their own are given respect by others. They are considered vital, self-sufficient, courageous, and often creative. Pretty heady compliments, I am sure you will agree.

Third, living on one's own enhances self-esteem. A sense of competence is accompanied by pride and self-satisfaction in one's ability to manage on one's own.

Finally, elderly people often enjoy keeping in touch with friends and neighbors. Often, informal care networks develop. People look out for one another. They call to check up on each other's health and see how they are getting through periods of inclement weather. They often share store coupons and ideas about where good shopping values can be found. In times of crisis, they help each other. Thus, not only are socialization needs met, but also the person's need for a sense of meaning and purpose. In the September–October 1997 issue of *Modern Maturity*, the point is made that friendship is important throughout life, but especially as people age, for physical as well as emotional reasons.

Allowing a parent to age in place also has real benefits for adult children. A parent's presence in her own home helps to preserve a sense of stability, security, and normalcy for the children, as well. As one client asked recently, in the course of coming to terms with the fact that her mother was dying, "Where is *home* when Mom dies?"

More than one adult child has confessed that allowing a parent to age in place eliminates the guilt they would otherwise feel at having to institutionalize her. Some adult children feel they are "dumping" a parent when she is sent to a nursing home.

Another benefit to keeping a parent in her own home stems from the fact that most adult children want to feel in control of their parent's care, and they enjoy being responsible for her welfare. To them, this equates with being a "good" child—loyal, devoted, and loving. Allowing a parent to age in place meets the adult children's need to care in a hands-on way.

To a point, there are financial as well as practical advantages to keeping an aging parent at home. Most elderly parents are proud to be able to save the cost of institutionalization and thus preserve their children's inheritance. As a person ages, there is often little she can actively do to help her children. *Not* costing the family money or inconvenience is one of the last things an elderly parent can do for them. In addition to the ease and convenience of visiting a parent in her own home, adult children often feel relieved and pleased that the family inheritance is being preserved.

As I noted earlier, when care needs become intensive, home care may no longer be affordable or feasible. When it becomes too costly to keep a parent at home, practical and financial necessities often dictate that institutionalization is the only viable care option. I well recall one client: I needed many months to convince her that managing two parents in their nineties with dementia was more than any single person should have to do! Only after both were institutionalized was this delightful person able to resume the life of travel and learning that she loved.

We now turn to the prerequisites for successful home care. Like all decisions, the choice to keep a parent at home can only succeed when certain criteria are met. The following five requirements are critical for a parent to age in place successfully.

The parent must want to do it. This is discussed on page 119.

The parent must be able to manage on her own. Later in the chapter, I will introduce you to the concept of *levels of care*, a way of assessing your parent's functional capacities so that a decision about her self-sufficiency can be made systematically and logically. It is one thing to *want* to stay at home. It is quite another to be *capable* of it.

The adult children in the family must be willing to allocate responsibilities fairly, in a way acceptable to all. By this I mean they must be willing to "share" the responsibilities, though not necessarily equally. Services must be provided. Expenses must be met.

There must be a plan for the future. Inevitably, as a parent ages, her needs change. The longer she lives, the more complex and multi-layered her dependency becomes, and the greater the demands on caregivers. A well thought-out care plan can succeed only when it includes provision for growing dependency and demands.

The adult children must be both informed about their parent's rights and fully committed to cooperating for the benefit of the parent. This means consulting with the parent before making *any* decisions that will affect her. It also means talking with *all* family members and achieving consensus before making any important decisions or changes in care arrangements. Here are four examples of decisions that should be made only after consensus is reached.

- the decision to do major repairs or renovations around the parent's house

- the decision to send a parent to adult day care for several hours each day

- the decision to hire a companion or home-health aide
- the decision to have a parent undergo any nonroutine, nonemergency medical or dental procedure

Almost inevitably, failure to consult with siblings in such matters causes rifts. A commitment to consultation and consensus must be part and parcel of adult children's decision to have a parent stay at home for as long as possible.

PART TWO: Safe at Home

By taking certain precautions and making adaptations around the house, you can ensure your parent's safety and security. For your ease of reference, I am providing a detailed checklist rather than discussing all these changes and adaptations. Follow the checklist to ensure you have minimized the likelihood of accidents and maximized the conveniences of living independently.

SAFE AT HOME: A CHECKLIST

Following is a checklist you can use to ensure that you have anticipated most of your parent's safety and convenience needs. In addition to going through the list to be sure that the necessary steps are taken, invite your parent to use it as a basis for a "wish list" of items and conveniences she would most appreciate. Not all of the renovations and changes in this checklist need to be completed at the same time. In keeping with the principle discussed earlier (that as your parent's needs increase, so will your need to make changes), some items can be deferred.

Bathing and Toileting

- ☐ Install a nonskid mat or strips in bathtub or shower stall.
- ☐ Install a shower stall if parent cannot safely step into bathtub.
- ☐ Install handrails by the toilet for aid in sitting and standing.
- ☐ Install a raised toilet seat.
- ☐ If a shower curtain is hung from a rod, be certain the rod is screwed to the wall, not "spring loaded."
- ☐ Be certain the bathroom door has a doorknob lock that can be opened from the outside (without a key) in case of emergency.
- ☐ Install a grab-bar in the shower or tub.
- ☐ Ensure that the hot water tank is set at the "low" setting (120 degrees or lower).
- ☐ Clearly label "hot" and "cold" faucets.
- ☐ Help your parent form the habit of unplugging all small appliances (hair curlers, shavers, hair dryers, etc.) when not using them.
- ☐ Caution your parent not to use hair dryers or other electrical appliances near a sink or bathtub.

In the Bedroom

- ☐ Install a light switch within easy reach of the bed.
- ☐ Provide a step stool and other aids (such as grab-bars or an "over-the-bed trapeze") to help your parent get in and out of bed.
- ☐ Provide clothing, including shoes, with Velcro fasteners, extended zipper pulls, extra-large buttons, and other aids to dressing.
- ☐ If your parent uses an electric blanket, review the proper precautions and be sure she knows how to use the device properly.
- ☐ Replace round doorknobs with lever-type openers for convenience.

Cooking and Meal Preparation

- ☐ To ensure food does not overcook or burn, teach your parent to use a microwave oven if she doesn't already use one.
- ☐ If food is being cooked on the range or in the conventional oven, help your parent develop the habit of using a cooking timer to ensure the food does not overcook or burn.
- ☐ Keep potholders near the stove; caution your parent not to use an apron or a dish towel to pick up hot dishes or utensils.
- ☐ Make certain all spices and cooking utensils are within easy reach.
- ☐ Provide prepared meals that can be reheated simply—perhaps in a microwave or toaster-oven.
- ☐ Ensure that no towels, curtains, or other flammable materials are located next to the cooking area.
- ☐ Make certain the meal-preparation area is well lit.
- ☐ Keep a long-handled sponge mop in a convenient place for spills.
- ☐ Provide an easy-to-use automatic can opener, a jar opener, a food processor, and other devices to make meal preparation simpler.
- ☐ Check the proper functioning of all exhaust fans and ventilating devices; be certain the on-off switches are conveniently located and that your parent knows how to use the devices.
- ☐ Put most frequently used items within easy reach to eliminate any need for climbing.
- ☐ Buy small portions so there is no problem of what to do with leftovers.
- ☐ Replace standard stove dials with large, easy-to-read dials.
- ☐ Discourage the use of clothing with loose sleeves when cooking.
- ☐ Ensure that all wiring is up-to-date and not frayed or dangerous.

□ Install and properly maintain smoke detectors in the kitchen area as well as near the furnace and in other danger spots.

□ Organize pantry and other shelves to eliminate the dangers of climbing and of objects toppling down on your parent's head when she reaches for something.

Hearing

□ Provide a hearing aid.

□ Install extra-loud doorbells and telephone ringers.

□ Ensure that all fire-warning devices emit a signal loud enough to be heard by your parent; make certain your parent knows the prearranged exit plan in the event of a fire.

□ If necessary, supplement devices such as a phone ringer or smoke alarm with flashing lights or devices that make a table lamp light up.

Housekeeping

□ Provide your parent with lightweight, easy-to-use tools for cleaning and home maintenance.

□ Provide non-electric or battery-operated appliances to eliminate the danger of electrical cords. An old-fashioned carpet sweeper can replace a cumbersome vacuum, for example; a self-charging flashlight is always ready.

Keeping Warm

□ Ensure that your parent understands how to use all heating equipment, especially space heaters.

□ Locate all space heaters and other heating devices away from curtains and flammable materials.

□ Instruct your parent never to use a gas range for space heating.

□ See to it that all heating equipment is faithfully maintained, and that the chimney is cleaned annually.

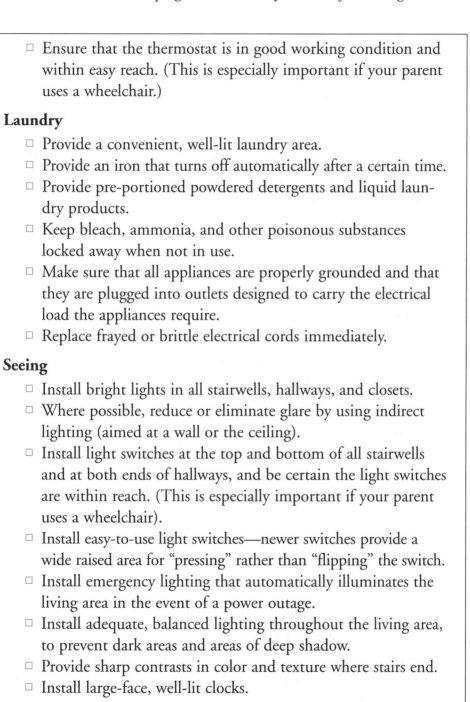

☐ Ensure that the thermostat is in good working condition and within easy reach. (This is especially important if your parent uses a wheelchair.)

Laundry

☐ Provide a convenient, well-lit laundry area.

☐ Provide an iron that turns off automatically after a certain time.

☐ Provide pre-portioned powdered detergents and liquid laundry products.

☐ Keep bleach, ammonia, and other poisonous substances locked away when not in use.

☐ Make sure that all appliances are properly grounded and that they are plugged into outlets designed to carry the electrical load the appliances require.

☐ Replace frayed or brittle electrical cords immediately.

Seeing

☐ Install bright lights in all stairwells, hallways, and closets.

☐ Where possible, reduce or eliminate glare by using indirect lighting (aimed at a wall or the ceiling).

☐ Install light switches at the top and bottom of all stairwells and at both ends of hallways, and be certain the light switches are within reach. (This is especially important if your parent uses a wheelchair).

☐ Install easy-to-use light switches—newer switches provide a wide raised area for "pressing" rather than "flipping" the switch.

☐ Install emergency lighting that automatically illuminates the living area in the event of a power outage.

☐ Install adequate, balanced lighting throughout the living area, to prevent dark areas and areas of deep shadow.

☐ Provide sharp contrasts in color and texture where stairs end.

☐ Install large-face, well-lit clocks.

□ Be certain light bulbs in every lamp and fixture do not exceed the recommended wattage.

□ Be certain switches for bedside lamps are within easy reach, or install adapters that enable your parent to turn on a lamp by merely touching the base.

□ Provide a large, lighted magnifying glass (with its own stand) next to a seating area for reading and close work your parent might enjoy doing.

□ Do not run extension cords or telephone wires under rugs.

□ Provide automatic night lights in all rooms.

Taking Medications

□ Arrange all medications in such a way that the likelihood of confusion is reduced to zero.

□ Use a color-coding system or a "medication minder" (available at your pharmacy) that consists of compartments in which each day's pills can be presorted.

□ Caution your parent against taking any medication in the dark.

Telephoning

□ Provide a telephone with large, well-lit numerals, perhaps even raised numbers.

□ Provide a phone with a memory feature and teach your parent how to use it, so that emergency and frequently called numbers can be dialed with the push of a single button.

□ Provide a speaker phone or a phone with an amplification device.

□ Install a phone beside your parent's bed.

Televiewing and Radio Listening

□ Provide a remote channel changer for the television.

□ Provide a radio/tape/CD player with station presets and a remote control.

Walking and Balance

- ☐ Remove throw rugs and plastic runners.
- ☐ Keep walkways clear by removing all objects on which your parent might trip, such as clutter, electrical cords, protruding furniture, and trash bags or recyclables.
- ☐ Install slip-resistant backing beneath small carpets.
- ☐ Place nonskid stair treads on all steps and mark edges with colored tape. (Vertical "striping" is easier to see.)
- ☐ Install handrails on both sides of all stairways.
- ☐ If your parent uses a walker or cane, rearrange furniture to ensure sufficiently wide passageways.

Outside Maintenance

- ☐ Contract with a landscaping service to provide lawn care and other services.
- ☐ Arrange to have someone shovel snow and put sand on walkways as required.
- ☐ Check outside lights to see that they are all in working order.
- ☐ Install handrails on stairs and walkways.

Please keep in mind that your parent's needs may be more extensive than those reflected in the Safe at Home checklist. Use it as a starting point for identifying the unique changes you may need to make for your elderly parent. In addition, you should consider the following precautions and options.

An emergency personal response system can summon help in case of an emergency. It consists of a pendant, usually worn around the neck, and a small, sender-transmitter console. If your parent falls or if some other emergency arises, she presses the button on the pendant. A 24-hour operator calls immediately, and communication between the operator and your parent establishes what help is needed. The operator, having been supplied with emergency phone numbers (police, fire, ambulance, personal physician, nearest neighbor, friend, or relative), summons help immediately and notifies the closest family member or neighbor. Personal response systems are available through home-health agencies or private vendors. There is a set-up charge and a monthly fee. Some or all of the cost of this system may be paid by your state's Medicaid program.

You can arrange for telephone reassurance for your parent at no cost. Such a program, sometimes known as "telecare," is often available through a community volunteer agency. (Contact the Senior Center in your area, or contact one of the more than 700 Area Agencies on Aging throughout the country for information on availability of these and other services.) Trained volunteers call regularly to see whether everything is all right with your parent, to make referrals as appropriate (if, for example, your parent reports that she needs help taking out the garbage, the volunteer might suggest an appropriate source of help), and to summon help in case of emergency.

You can also arrange for a friendly visitor to drop in at set intervals. Trained volunteers may share a cup of tea with your parent, discuss the news of the day, and help your parent remain in the swim of life.

As noted, some of the services your parent may need and the devices you may need to buy are covered by Medicare. If they are considered medically necessary and are prescribed by a physician as part of a care plan, coverage can be arranged, although the process may be cumbersome.

Whether or not your state provides assistance, some communities provide grants to families who must make these adaptations. In other communities, volunteer help is available. For example, some associations of realtors provide volunteer help in doing minor renovations in order to "elder-proof" homes. Scout organizations may similarly offer help with grounds maintenance or snow shoveling. Again, check with your local Senior Center or Area Agency on Aging for availability and application procedures.

RESPITE CARE

Caregivers' needs must also be considered when the decision is made to allow a parent to age in place. It is unrealistic to think that caregivers can provide quality care and maintain a sense of balance in their lives without taking both physical and emotional breaks from time to time. For this reason, some respite care, utilized on a limited basis, is desirable. Respite care refers to any service that removes some of the caregiving burden from the adult child's shoulders while simultaneously improving the quality of life of the care recipient.

Respite can be provided informally by family members who are not primary caregivers, for example, or by neighbors and friends. Sometimes agreements can be worked out between a family and local, informal care providers, in which services are given in exchange for room and board. In my community, for example, nursing students at a local college often welcome the opportunity to help local seniors in their homes in exchange for free or inexpensive room and board. Provided the contract between the family and the student is clear, the caregiver is trustworthy, and the caregiver's assistance is monitored by the family or others, this is often an excellent arrangement for all concerned.

Respite care can also be provided more formally. Adult day care is one example. So is in-home care, including homemakers, companions, home-health aides, and so on. The subject of home care will be discussed in detail in the next section of this chapter.

Another respite care option is a limited stay in a long-term care facility, a possibility that exists when an adult child goes out of town for several days for a business trip or vacation. Respite care beds must be reserved in advance. Sometimes they are available even when a nursing home does not publicly offer respite care. While there are advantages to such an arrangement (peace of mind for the caregiver being chief among them, along with a chance for the care recipient to see what a nursing home is like), there are also potential problems. Cost, disorientation of the care recipient, and the difficulty of finding a bed are the most frequently reported problems.

Respite care is essential when the needs of your parent are unremitting. Used properly, it can help prevent caregiver burnout and keep your parent at home longer, thereby preventing premature institutionalization. To find out about respite care resources in your community, contact your Area Agency on Aging, your local Senior Center, or a home-health agency, about which you will learn more in Part Three.

PART THREE: At Home with Help

All of the suggestions offered in the previous section of the chapter rest on the premise that your parent is essentially self-sufficient. In this section of the chapter, you will learn about more extensive services that may make it possible for an individual to stay at home when she would otherwise be unable to do so due to some impairment.

When a parent cannot manage to do everything needed to live at home independently, the burden falls on adult children. They must accomplish two key tasks. The first is to determine the kind and level of help needed. Next, they must identify, locate, and arrange for affordable sources of home care.

DETERMINING THE LEVEL OF CARE NEEDED

The phrase *level of care* refers to how much help and what kind of help your parent needs. It implies, as it is meant to do, that care requirements vary from individual to individual and for the same individual over time. Fortunately, there are many tools available for assessing your parent's care needs. The following worksheet, developed exclusively for this book, is based on the work of many gerontologists and professionals in allied fields, accomplished over many years. "Thinking Systematically about Your Parent's Care Requirements" thus represents a melding of ideas derived from countless sources (some are included in the Selected Resources appendix). This worksheet can help you accomplish the key tasks of *assessment, goal setting, planning,* and *problem management.* Whenever possible, you should involve your parent in these processes. In addition, you may want to duplicate this worksheet and redo it from time to time, so that you can make comparative assessments.

WORKSHEET: THINKING SYSTEMATICALLY ABOUT YOUR PARENT'S CARE REQUIREMENTS

ASSESSMENT: GATHERING INFORMATION

What are the relevant facts about my parent's condition?

1. Medical

List any current medical conditions that are affecting your parent's day-to-day life.

Illness or Condition	Effects on Daily Living

(More room is provided on the next two pages.)

Illness or Condition	Effects on Daily Living

Illness or Condition	Effects on Daily Living

2. **Mental**	**Effects on Daily Living**
a. **Cognitive Impairment** (Rank each as *none, mild, moderate,* or *severe.*) memory	
judgment	
wandering	
ability to make self understood	
ability to understand others	
other (specify)	
b. **Emotional Impairment** (Rank each as *none, mild, moderate,* or *severe.*) depression	
anxiety	
paranoia or extreme distrust and suspicion	
other (specify)	

3. Psychosocial Stressors (Briefly identify each.) a. recent loses	**Effects on Daily Living**
b. changes in living arrangements	
c. isolation	
d. financial difficulties	
e. problems with access to health-care system	
f. other (specify)	

My parent's strengths and weaknesses: In what areas is my parent able to manage with little or no difficulty? In what areas is she unable to manage? (Rank each as *self-sufficient, needs some help,* or *cannot do.*)

1. Activities of Daily Living	**Effects on Daily Living**
a. bathing	
b. dressing	
c. toileting	
d. transfer	
e. continence	
f. feeding	

2. Incidental Activities of Daily Living	**Effects on Daily Living**
a. using the telephone	
b. getting to places beyond walking distance	
c. shopping	
d. bill paying and money management	
e. housework	
f. minor "handyman" household tasks such as changing a light bulb	
g. laundry	
h. taking medications faithfully	

Obviously, if your parent cannot manage most activities of daily living, rather extensive in-home help is required. If she can perform all activities of daily living independently but is less able to manage incidental activities, less extensive help is required.

GOAL SETTING

In arranging for care for my parent, what do I want to achieve—

1. for my parent?

2. for myself?

How will I evaluate progress and measure "success"?

What specific, measurable criteria will I apply to evaluate my parent's progress?

Goal and Criteria for "Success"

Example: With the help of a home-health aide, my mother will be able to get up in the morning, bathe, dress, eat a nutritious breakfast, and take required medications at least five days per week.

PLANNING

Have I/we formulated a "care plan" that will meet my parent's needs?

What will be done? Why? How?

Have responsibilities been clearly allocated?

Need to Be Met	Name of Individual	Responsibilities

PROBLEM MANAGEMENT

Have I/we formulated a course of action that will solve (or at least manage) the problems my parent is currently experiencing?

If so, specify:

Are back-up plans in place in case the original plan fails to meet the objectives? This is especially important, since home-care agencies are not ultimately responsible for implementing care plans. Moreover, sometimes an aide may not show up when scheduled or may not be able to be scheduled by an agency. Review back-up plans here:

What problems may arise in the future, as a result of either current plans, further deterioration in my parent's physical or mental condition, or psychosocial stressors? List each possible future problem and likelihood of occurrence (for example, 90%):

Do I/we have a plan to prevent each problem that is preventable?
Describe the plan(s):

Do I/we have a plan to manage each problem that cannot be prevented? Describe the plan(s):

While a checklist may seem a mechanical way of assessing your parent's needs, it does afford a systematic way of tackling an otherwise complex and easily bungled process. However, as noted, you must be prepared to complete this worksheet more than once. You may choose to do so at regular intervals, such as every six months. More likely, you will repeat the process when a need arises.

Below are several signs that a need for a change in level of care has arisen and that care requirements are changing and need to be reassessed. (I am assuming that requirements are increasing, although under some circumstances—say, after a person recovers from surgery—

they decrease.) Changes in your parent's behavior or experiences that signal the need to review care level requirements include these:

- She becomes more forgetful; she may forget to turn off burners on the stove or how to make a favorite dish.
- She stops eating when alone, although she eats when others visit.
- She falls or has a "close call."
- She forgets to take important medications.
- She becomes incontinent.
- She leaves the house on a routine errand and becomes disoriented.
- She undergoes a personality change, perhaps becoming very passive or, at the other extreme, very aggressive.
- She cuts off social contacts and isolates herself.

Changes in your own experiences and behavior may signal the need to review care requirements. Here are several indicators:

- You miss work or you are often late for work.
- You lose sleep regularly.
- You spend less and less time with your spouse and children because of caregiving responsibilities.
- You fail to pursue social activities and leisure activities because of caregiving responsibilities.
- You become resentful of the care you must provide.
- You feel overwhelmed by your caregiving responsibilities.
- You become physically or emotionally ill due to excess stress.

Any of these indicators should be viewed as warnings that something has to change. Levels of care may have increased slowly but relentlessly, to such a degree that you need to rethink altogether the care plan you have been following.

LOCATING AND ACCESSING HELP

Once you have some sense of your parent's care requirements, your task is to arrange for people who can confirm your assessment and provide that help. This task can be broken down into four phases.

1. Levels of Home Care

Your first task is to inform yourself about the levels of home care available through public and private-pay agencies. This includes finding out about payment arrangements and benefits available through Medicare, Medicaid, and other programs. This is not as daunting a task as it may seem, although you need to stay abreast of the laws and regulations governing benefits, as they are changing even as this book goes to print.

Up until now, I have deliberately been using the term *home care* broadly, to refer to a wide range of services provided in the home. There are, however, many kinds of home care. Different people provide these services, and providers' training and credentials vary. Furthermore, for reimbursement purposes, the government distinguishes between *nonmedical home care* and *medically oriented services* (also known as *home-health services*). Whereas the former are not covered by Medicare, the latter are, but for a limited time and with additional caveats.

Who are the people who provide both *nonmedical home-care services* and *home-health services?* Table 5.1 outlines the various types of caregivers. As you can see, there is a correlation among the skill level of the providers, their credentials, the costs of the services, and the likelihood that the services will be paid for by Medicare. Note that unskilled care is the least expensive, requires the least training, and is the least likely to be reimbursable. Skilled care is the most costly, the providers are better trained and credentialed, and their services are more likely to be covered.

2. Sources of Help

Next, you need to find out about sources of in-home help in your area, including publicly funded, private pay, and nonprofit agencies.

Table 5.1 Home-Care Providers

SKILL LEVEL Unskilled	Modestly Skilled	Skilled
TYPE OF CAREGIVER *Companions* Provide socialization, accompaniment on walks and errands, etc. *Homemakers* All that companions do, plus housekeeping tasks, laundry, grocery shopping, meal preparations.	*Home-Health Aides* Perform all previous duties plus personal care (bathing, dressing, help with medications, bandage changes, management of incontinence, etc.).	*Nurses* Provide professional medical care (wound care, injections, intravenous feeding, assessment, teaching, etc.).
CERTIFICATION, LICENSING, AND TRAINING Not certified or licensed; no training is required, although most have taken classes through a home-care agency.	These providers are trained to deliver personal care. They are certified through exams. Most work under the supervision of a registered nurse (RN). They are usually employees of a home-care agency.	Licensed and certified, these skilled workers undergo extensive and ongoing training. In addition to state licenses, many are certified by their professional associations.
COST (1998 Dollars) Least costly ($5–10/hr, with a minimum number of hours per week)	More costly ($12–20/hr, with a minimum number of hours per day)	Most expensive ($60/hr, with minimums)
INSURANCE COVERAGE Not covered by Medicare; may be covered by Medicaid (varies by state).	Some home-health services are covered by Medicare if prescribed by an MD as part of a care plan. Strict eligibility requirements pertain.	Most services are covered by Medicare if prescribed by an MD as part of a care plan. Strict eligibility requirements pertain.

Fortunately, there is a great deal of information (which is also changing as of this writing) available on services covered by the Medicare and Medicaid programs as well as many helpful agencies and individuals who can provide this information. In addition to appreciating the dif-

Table 5.2 Sources of In-Home Help

TYPE OF AGENCY

Publicly Funded		Private-Pay (for profit) (some, state regulated)	Nonprofit (volunteer, hospital affiliated, Visiting Nurse Associations)
Medicare (eligible for Medicare reimbursement)	**Medicaid** (funded by state and federal governments, but administered by states)		

COST/COVERAGE

Medicare	*Medicaid*	*Expensive* (per hour fees, plus minimum number of hours)	*Competitive rates* (few or no minimum number of hours—varies by agency). Some offer flat fees for specific services; most offer sliding fee scale.

TYPE OF CARE PROVIDED

Skilled care only (nursing, rehabilitation)	Unskilled care (personal care, cooking, shopping; help with chronic, unchanging conditions)	Many levels of care; wide range of services.	Services vary widely. (Some VNAs, for example, offer an extremely wide range of services. Other nonprofits offer very limited services.)

ELIGIBILITY

No means test; strict eligibility requirements; MD approval required; time-limited.	Means tested (income and assets); strict eligibility requirements; limited services and hours.	Clients pay out of pocket or with long-term care insurance.	Medicare pays for services for clients over age 65; some self-pay; some pay with long-term care insurance

ferences in training, fees, and reimbursability of the different providers, it is useful to understand differences among the various sources of in-home help. Table 5.2 provides an overview of the most important characteristics of each of these sources.

3. Screening and Selection

Your third task as an adult child attempting to provide in-home care for your parent is to develop a systematic set of procedures to follow when contacting an agency to inquire about in-home help and when choosing among the agencies and providers with whom you will contract. These procedures are necessary, whether the services provided by the agency you contact are funded by the federal government, the state government, or some combination of the two, and whether the agency is for-profit or not-for-profit. Without adequate procedures and meticulous record-keeping, you will be quickly overburdened by facts and left more confused about what to do than when you began.

The following set of procedures represents the fruit of many years of experience. I have learned from my own mistakes and from those of my clients, and I have attempted to provide adequate guidelines for you to follow. It is unlikely that you will be able to avoid or ignore any of these guidelines. At the same time, your unique situation may make it necessary to change or add to the procedures outlined here. If so, feel free to come up with your own procedures, of course.

STEPS TO FOLLOW WHEN CONTACTING AN AGENCY: A CHECKLIST

WHAT TO ASK

Certification, Licensure, and Accreditation

- ☐ Is the home-health agency Medicare-certified? This makes a huge difference, for only Medicare-certified agencies are eligible for reimbursement.
- ☐ Is the agency licensed by the state? Although not all states require licensure, many do. In my home state of Connecticut,

all home-health agencies must meet state licensing requirements.
- ☐ Is the agency accredited by a health-care accreditation organization such as the Joint Commission on Accreditation of Health Care Organizations?

Experience and Business Practices
- ☐ How long has the agency been in business?
- ☐ Is the agency available after business hours, on holidays, and in emergencies? The better agencies provide 24-hour, 7-day-per-week coverage in the event of an emergency. Such coverage must be provided in states that require licensure.
- ☐ Is it the policy of the agency to arrange a home visit before taking on a client? The best agencies do this, not only to assess the client's needs but also to gauge the sort of caregiver with whom the care recipient might best get along.
- ☐ Is it the policy of the agency to schedule occasional visits after care has begun, to see whether things are going well? The best agencies do this.
- ☐ Is it the policy of the agency to provide continuity of care? Will the same caregiver be providing help continuously, or will providers change?
- ☐ If the caregiver is unable to come to work due to illness or an emergency, will the agency provide coverage? What procedures are followed in such a case?
- ☐ Is the family consulted and involved in creating and implementing the care plan? This is often a good idea.

Services
- ☐ What services are available through the agency? What are the costs? Note that services vary widely within and among all categories of agencies. For example, some nonprofit agencies

provide only homemaker services, while others have staff people who can provide personal care. A Visiting Nurse Association, while technically a nonprofit agency, may provide skilled nursing care.

□ What are the eligibility requirements for care recipients?

□ What documentation does the agency need in order to verify eligibility for services?

□ Is physician approval required to arrange for service? Are any other approvals needed?

□ How long is the waiting period between the time services are requested and the time services begin?

□ Based on the information provided by you, the caller, precisely what services will the agency likely provide? Are there alternate ways of meeting your parent's needs?

□ What is the name of the contact person for the desired services?

Policies Regarding Payment and Expiration of Medicare Benefits

□ If services are funded by Medicare, for how long are they available? What are the renewal criteria, if any? Be aware of the fact that Medicare's policy is to *gradually reduce* the services your parent receives and the number of hours of service per day. For example, your parent might receive services for four hours per day initially, but unless her needs are extreme, those four hours will be reduced to two or three hours before very long.

□ What arrangements can be made to see that the agency continues to provide service even after Medicare benefits expire?

□ Does the agency accept *assignment* (insurance reimbursement as payment in full)?

□ Does the client pay the care provider directly, or does the client pay the agency?

- How are fees calculated? Are there any "up-front" costs?

Hiring Practices

- How are applicants selected for positions at the agency?
- Do applicants complete a written application?
- Does the agency conduct personal interviews?
- Are applicants' references checked? By whom?
- Is a criminal background check done on applicants?
- Are police and motor vehicle records checked?
- Will the caller or other members of the family have the opportunity to conduct a personal interview with the caregiver recommended by the agency?

Information about the Caregiver Who Will Provide Services

- What is the caregiver's license or certification, if any? Who accredits him or her? What criteria must be met for accreditation to be issued?
- Does the agency have the results of the caregiver's current screening for communicable diseases?
- Is the caregiver insured and bonded? The better agencies provide malpractice and liability insurance for their hires, and bond them as well.
- For whom has the caregiver worked in the past? How long did he or she stay on the last job? Why did the caregiver leave?
- Does the care provider drive a car that appears to be in good repair and reliable? Is his or her driver's license valid?
- If the care provider will be using his or her own car to provide transportation for the care recipient, is there proof of adequate insurance coverage? Many agencies expressly forbid the caregiver to provide transportation services. You will need to know the agency's policy.

WHAT TO BE PREPARED TO TELL

- ☐ name of care recipient, address, social security number, contact information
- ☐ whether the recipient is homebound and in need of skilled nursing and/or rehabilitation services
- ☐ care recipient's current medical problems and home-care needs (Be precise and specific—for example, if your parent is incontinent, say so; if she is obstreperous, that needs to be said, as well.)
- ☐ care recipient's medications, both prescribed and over-the-counter (names, start dates, dosages, frequency, prescribers, and any medications recently discontinued)
- ☐ name, address, contact numbers (voice, fax) of care recipient's primary physician
- ☐ your wants and expectations (The "contract" you negotiate should be clear and specific—for example, if the care provider must not smoke, say so.)

WHAT TO KEEP TRACK OF

- ☐ name, address, contact numbers (voice, fax), and e-mail address of agency contacted
- ☐ date of call
- ☐ name of person with whom you spoke
- ☐ answers to all pertinent questions (Make careful notes on information that will spare you the need to repeat data gathering.)

Needless to say, it is best to organize this information so that retrieving it is easy. You may want to use a spiral-bound notebook divided into sections, or you may prefer large index cards organized into a mini-filing system. If you are computer-literate and spreadsheet-minded, you may wish to organize the data in a spreadsheet. The method is less important than the outcome: accuracy, convenience, and speed when retrieving data.

4. Monitoring and Supervising Delivery

Once you have selected an agency and your parent begins receiving in-home care, you should develop and implement a specific plan for monitoring and supervising the delivery of services. This requires two sets of skills. The first skill is communication. The second skill is anticipation, or forethought. Let us look at each set of skills in turn.

Communication Skills From the outset, you must be clear about the care recipient's needs and problems. What, exactly, will be expected of the home-care provider? For example, if vision is a problem and the caregiver will be expected to read to the client, that must be specified early in the discussion.

Daily routines must be spelled out. Remember that *personal* care must constitute the bulk of services provided by skilled and semi-skilled, Medicare-reimbursed personnel. Routines might include items such as the following:

- Morning routine: Mom likes a shower first thing in the morning. She also needs to take medications with her breakfast. If possible, breakfast should be finished by 9:30 or so. Please load dishwasher in preparation for your running it before leaving in the afternoon.

- Privacy requirements: 9:30–11 A.M., private time. Mom enjoys television watching and reading alone in the family room. Please read or pass the time in another room.

- Unless agency or other rules prohibit this, take Mom to and from the grocery store on Tuesday and Thursday at noon, back by 1:30. On Mondays, Wednesdays, and Fridays, this hour and a half can be spent playing cards, shopping for personal items at the mall, or running errands (picking up medications, etc.). Ask Mom how she would like to spend the time.

Not only must you be able to make your wants and expectations clear to the agency and the care provider, you must also be skillful in giving feedback to the agency. Whether communicating satisfaction or dissatisfaction, you must develop the habit of letting your voice be heard promptly and clearly.

Anticipation There is no substitute for forethought. If home care is to be successful, you must anticipate problems and be prepared to tackle them as they arise. The following are good practices any adult child should follow when arranging for home care for an elderly parent. These practices grow out of typical problems that seem to crop up over and over again unless the adult child anticipates them and makes his or her expectations clear.

- Post all emergency phone numbers by the telephone. This includes fire, ambulance, police, the local hospital, and the patient's personal physician. A neat, framed listing, easy to read and not likely to get mislaid, is best.

- Provide written instructions for using the washer and dryer, VCR, television, microwave, and other appliances and utensils.

- If the caregiver is providing meals, be clear about food to be served and avoided, preferred meal times, and cleanup after meals. For example, will all items be placed in the dishwasher? Are there fragile items that must be washed by hand? Will the caregiver be expected to run the dishwasher every time it is full, or at the end of each day? If the care recipient is a vegetarian, keeps a kosher kitchen, or has other dietary requirements, specify the procedures that should be followed.

- If the caregiver does the shopping, are there particular markets or brands to favor? Are there any that should be avoided?

EVALUATING SERVICES

Like all solutions to a problem, home-care arrangements need to be evaluated for effectiveness. Thorough and ongoing monitoring of the services provided for your parent is as important as careful screening of the agency and health-care personnel. Below is a form you may find useful in judging the quality of care your parent is receiving from a home-health agency and its personnel. While the specifics of your parent's situation will be unique, you should carefully evaluate each of the items listed in the chart.

INVENTORY: EVALUATING THE QUALITY OF CARE YOUR PARENT RECEIVES

In order to determine whether your parent's needs are being met, answer the following questions. Make notes if ideas come to you.

Assessment: Has all information relevant to your parent's needs been gathered and systematically recorded for planning purposes?

Problem Definition: Have all the problems faced by your parent been completely and carefully defined? (This includes medical, psychosocial, cognitive, financial, and other problems.)

Goals: Has the purpose of care been spelled out so that it is possible to evaluate progress and to measure "success" by applying specific, measurable criteria?

Planning: Has a "care plan" been formulated to meet your parent's needs, with responsibilities clearly allocated?

Problem Management: Has a course of treatment been spelled out that will solve (or at least manage) the problems your parent is currently experiencing? Are back-up treatments in place in case the original course of treatment fails to meet the objectives?

Anticipated Problems: Have care providers thought about problems that may arise in the future, as a result of either current treatments, further deterioration in your parent's physical or mental condition, or psychosocial stressors? Is a plan in place to prevent problems that are preventable and to manage problems that cannot be controlled?

Planning for the Future: Has consideration been given to the circumstances under which your parent will be discharged from care when treatment goals are met? What arrangements for follow-up care have been provided?

HANDLING RESISTANCE TO IN-HOME CARE

It is important to recognize that your parent may not be receptive to in-home care for a variety of reasons. She may cherish her independence and her privacy and resent sacrificing any of either. She may be unaware of just how dependent she is. Other reasons could be at work as well.

If your parent resists, it is understandable that you may become frustrated and annoyed. She may seem foolish or obstinate, uncooperative and unaware of how hard you must work to provide the care she needs. Given your own annoyance and urgency, it is predictable that your unthinking tendency will be to silence the opposition in order to force the care upon her. That is a very bad idea.

Your goal must be not so much to argue away your parent's opposition as to understand its origins and to provide the appropriate remedies or reassurances. By looking beyond her opposition, you can overcome your negative feelings and simultaneously become more accepting and compassionate. Table 5.3 can guide you through the process. It provides common indicators of resistance to accepting in-home care, along with possible factors motivating that resistance, and suggestions concerning how you might respond.

Table 5.3 Recognizing and Overcoming Resistance to In-Home Care

EXTERNAL SIGN OF RESISTANCE	HIDDEN MEANING OR MOTIVATION	POSSIBLE REMEDY
"I don't need help."	(1) Your parent may truly be unaware of how dependent she is. (2) Your parent may fear conceding that she can no longer manage on her own.	State that the family's intent is to allow her to stay at home for as long as possible. Use examples to show how dependent she is.
"I don't want to spend my savings." "I want to leave something to my children."	Your parent may fear admitting that there is no future to save for because the final stage of life has arrived.	Demonstrate that she *can* afford help. Address her distress by acknowledging that her life is ending.
"Nobody knows how I want things done." "Nobody cleans like me."	Your parent may fear being unable to supervise and direct an in-home worker.	Involve your parent in creating a "to do" list. Teach her to supervise and monitor her worker's performance.
"I don't want to be alone with someone I don't know."	Your parent may fear being robbed, victimized, exploited.	Arrange for a family member to stay with your parent the first few times. Make random visits to monitor the worker.
"I don't want any of *those* people in my home." Your parent exhibits condescension or suspiciousness and has petty complaints about the worker's performance.	Your parent may have racist attitudes.	Address the issue of racism. Encourage her to give the worker a try.

PART FOUR: Home Away from Home

The word *home* can mean many things. In this section you will learn about housing options that fall between living more or less completely on one's own and entering institutionalization. Some of these living arrangements will be familiar to you. Others will be new. Your task as you read is to avoid ruling out any housing option without seriously considering it, because each option offers real advantages over institutionalization. Throughout the discussion, I will try to be as candid and as succinct as possible.

OPTION ONE: LIVING WITH AN ADULT CHILD

For many people, as care requirements grow and expenses build up, arranging for a parent to live with an adult child's family seems like the most logical and affordable option. By having the parent live in, the adult child becomes capable of providing many of her care requirements, albeit at some personal sacrifice. I refer here to having the parent share a home or apartment, not settle in an attached or "in-law" apartment. (That option will be covered shortly.)

Just because this option seems so seductively simple, it warrants scrutiny. After all, if the choice were so obvious, why would home-health agencies, adult day care centers, and nursing homes exist? The fact is, having a parent move in, while not without its advantages, has some potentially serious drawbacks. Rather than listing advantages and disadvantages, I will summarize the points worth considering in an inventory you can use as a starting point to evaluate whether you, your immediate family (spouse, children), and your parent are candidates for a shared living arrangement.

As the questionnaire shows, the decision to have a parent actually move in with an adult child is not one that should be made lightly. Only by weighing the many considerations hinted at in the questionnaire can you be reasonably assured of the success of such an arrangement.

Inventory: Can You Make a Go of Sharing a House or Apartment with an Elderly Parent?

Instructions: This questionnaire should be completed by each person involved in the decision about whether or not to have an elderly parent move in. (Make copies as necessary.) Answer each question fully and honestly. There are no "right" answers. However, each question addresses an issue that warrants scrutiny. As appropriate, discuss your answers with all parties involved, including children. It may be advisable to consult with a family therapist so that he or she can play the role of facilitator and mediator as you weigh this important matter.

Questions about You

1. If your parent moves in, what will be the effect on your family? On your career? On your personal life and leisure time?

2. Have you the stamina and willingness to learn the skills required to become a hands-on caregiver?

3. What are your personal motivations in allowing your parent to move in? Beyond the obvious ones ("to help her, to fulfill my responsibilities to her, to save money"), do you have a hidden agenda? Do you, for example, want to "show up" a less-involved sibling?

Questions about You and Your Immediate Family

1. Are you and your partner in agreement on whether or not to have your parent move in?

2. What sacrifices will have to be made by your partner in order to accommodate your parent? How is he or she likely to react?

3. What sacrifices will have to be made by your offspring in order to accommodate your parent? Will someone have to give up the privacy of his or her own room, for example? How willing is the

youngster to do that? What arrangements will have to be made to provide for sleeping space, etc.?

4. How will your parent's moving in change the family's routines—whether TV viewing, entertaining friends, holding rock band rehearsals, etc.?

Questions about Your Parent

1. Does your parent welcome the chance to enter your family?

2. In temperament, is your parent flexible and willing to make accommodations to your needs and those of your family?

3. Knowing yourself, your parent, and your family, will it be possible to set down clear rules governing what people may and may not do at home? For example, if you argue with one of your children, will your parent respect your wishes to avoid becoming involved or taking sides? (Put another way, will your parent, your spouse, and your children respect rules you set down to ensure there are clear boundaries at home?)

Questions about Space

1. Assuming your parent will be able to have her own bedroom, is there a bathroom nearby? Will it be shared, and is that likely to cause a problem?

2. Will wheelchair ramps or other adaptations have to be made so your parent can get around safely and comfortably? What other changes will be necessary? (See the checklist on pages 123–129.)

Other Considerations

1. If you have siblings, what arrangements will be made with them to provide respite care or to share the costs of such care? What, exactly, will you expect of them (and they of you) if your parent moves in?

2. What mechanisms are in place, or which ones can be put in place, to prevent the buildup of resentments, hurts, and anger among all people involved in this care arrangement, whether directly (your parent and you, for example) or indirectly (your siblings and your parent's siblings, for example)?

OPTION TWO: ACCESSORY, "IN-LAW," OR "GRANDPARENT" APARTMENTS

This is the familiar arrangement in which an adult child or other relative either remodels a garage or basement or adds a wing to their home and prepares it for Mother. This option is so similar to the previous one that the same checklist should be used to evaluate it. While this often preserves the privacy of both senior and adult child to some degree, it is technically often difficult to finance and pull off. However, creative arrangements are often made within families. For example, an elderly member might release some of her child's rightful inheritance early in order to make it affordable for the adult child to complete the renovations. The will may have to be changed if there are other siblings, and all family members should be involved in making a decision as important as this one.

Alternately, the adult child might look into sources of financial assistance for the renovation by contacting the local housing department, Area Agency on Aging, or other sources of help. He or she would also be wise to check with the local zoning board to see whether such changes are allowed as a matter of course or whether an appeal must be made to the board. (Under such circumstances, the zoning board may be willing to grant a zoning variance, otherwise known as a "special use permit.")

In fact, however, accessory apartments can also take other forms. First, the senior in question might arrange for the remodeling of her *own* home. She could then live in the newly created apartment while renting out the larger space she no longer needs. Of course, all of the problems that come with tenants must be anticipated and planned for before any such option is chosen. Tax implications must also be considered. In addition, bear in mind that any rental income your parent receives will affect her eligibility for Medicaid services.

There is yet another option within the "accessory apartment" category. An apartment in the home of a person unrelated to the senior can be rented by her or on her behalf by her children. This often enables a senior to enjoy the privacy of her own dwelling, in her own neighborhood and surroundings, without "imposing" on her children, without appearing to play favorites among her offspring, and without assuming more of a burden than that of paying the monthly rent. (Sometimes, the "surrogate child's" family will even take on caregiving responsibilities, either out of kindness or for a small fee—providing laundry or transportation services, for example.)

Provided an elderly parent can be cared for in such a setting, and provided the arrangement doesn't cause more problems than it solves, the accessory apartment option is worth considering.

OPTION THREE: FOSTER HOUSING

Another option worth considering is foster care for seniors. A relatively new concept, some states' social service departments have adapted the foster family idea from the model of foster care for troubled, neglected, or abused youngsters. Simply put, a foster family agrees to allow a senior to "live in," often in his or her own apartment or at least in a room designated for the senior. The family is paid an allowance by the state. In return, they provide services such as laundry, transportation, and meals. The senior may often agree to help out in areas where she can. For example, some seniors baby-sit for youngsters who would otherwise be "latch-key kids."

The foster family idea works for many people. But, like all the options discussed in this section, it has its own inherent drawbacks. How is the quality of care provided by the foster family measured? What about the place of the adult children of the senior? Can they visit? How often? Some people worry that the foster family might take advantage of the senior. Another consideration is the guilty feelings such an arrangement evokes in some adult children, who feel someone else is doing what the children themselves should be doing.

OPTION FOUR: SHARED HOUSING

The roommate situation is more frequently associated with young people just starting out in life. Many of the same advantages and disadvantages apply when considering this option for an elderly parent. She can take in a roommate to live with her, perhaps arranging for a rental payment or for living space in exchange for services. The possibilities are many, but so are the potential problems. An obvious one is the lack of privacy; for some, this is compensated for by companionship. Another problem is posed by the lack of a clear contract—expectations, rights, and responsibilities must be clear and explicit or disagreements are bound to arise. What about visitors? Will there be a no-smoking policy? To whom will it apply? Who will do laundry? What if the parties' sleep habits differ widely? How about meal preparation and cleanup (what does cleanup *mean*)? Who does the grocery shopping?

Successful shared housing is possible, but it requires a great deal of thought. All potential problems between roommates must be either anticipated or addressed as soon as they occur. It is also important to respect the fact that neighbors might object. Two or three people sharing a home or apartment might not cause problems, but more than that are almost certain to cause neighbors to begin raising questions. Neighbors may wonder, "Is this condominium apartment or 'single-family home' now a 'multi-family apartment'?" Legitimate concerns about parking spaces, privacy, and other matters are almost certain to arise.

OPTION FIVE: *ECHO* HOUSING

The acronym *ECHO* stands for *Elder Cottage Housing Opportunity. ECHO* housing refers to temporary, modular housing—whether a camper-trailer, mobile home, or small, factory-built, garage-like structure—that is erected on the property of an adult child, adjacent to his or her home. These structures are all built with seniors in mind. They are wheelchair accessible, single-level, and stand-alone dwelling units.

In addition to being unsuited for many but the most rural residential areas, ECHO housing can pose special problems associated with zoning laws and utilities. It is imperative that an adult child or senior exploring this option check carefully to determine whether local authorities look kindly on the construction of such a temporary structure.

OPTION SIX: SENIOR HOUSING OR SENIOR APARTMENTS

Senior housing is designed with elders in mind. It is built from scratch (or remodeled) with ramps and wide pathways for wheelchairs, elevators, tight security, and excellent lighting in common areas. Often located near public transportation and within walking distance to stores, senior housing affords each resident the privacy of his or her own apartment but ample opportunity to socialize with and help peers. Senior housing is usually in the form of apartment buildings varying in size from a few apartments to many hundreds. Most senior housing provides on-site emergency medical assistance, including "call" buttons in each room. Some even have a medical staff and a social work staff.

Despite these similarities, several alternatives exist within this category. Some of this housing is subsidized by federal, state, and local authorities, or some combination of all three. Subsidized apartments are inexpensive and usually in high demand, with waiting lists for apartments. Furthermore, because their care is dependent on municipal employees with little incentive to keep the property in top condition, many subsidized apartments are poorly kept. Nonsubsidized senior housing is more costly but usually (not always!) cleaner, more attractive, and kept with more care.

Policies vary from one senior housing complex to another with respect to your aged parent's ability to care for herself. Some routinely welcome tenants so long as they are self-sufficient, but evict them if they are no longer able to manage for themselves, even when help is available from family or hired caregivers. Caution and a clear understanding of the contract you are entering into are essential if the senior housing option is going to work for you and your parent.

SUMMARY

This chapter was devoted to helping you formulate an adequate care plan for your aging parent. Throughout, the unspoken assumption was that the best time to plan for care is *before* a crisis arises, since anticipating the future and planning for it are the two keys to successful aging and successful caregiving. Emphasis was placed on keeping a parent in her own home and on ways you can help her stay there safely and conveniently.

For the caregiver, anticipating a parent's needs means not only understanding what is likely to happen as a parent ages but also identifying and learning to access sources of appropriate adaptations and assistance. To that end, this chapter offered suggestions about how to "elder proof" a home. In addition, the chapter provided information on various sources of in-home help and on ways of accessing them, using them, and evaluating them. The last section of the chapter described alternate living arrangements short of a nursing home or a community with a nursing facility at its heart.

In the next chapter, you will learn about assisted-living facilities and similar alternatives that have nursing care at their core, even though not all options to be discussed are limited to "extended-care facilities" or "skilled-care facilities" in the conventional sense of the terms. The situation with respect to elder care is changing almost daily. As the elder population grows, and as opportunities for profit and service grow, many individuals, corporations, and institutions are getting into the act of providing living arrangements. This carries with it both opportunity and risk for adult children and their parents.

CHAPTER 6

*W*hen a Parent Must Leave Home

Eldercare is big business. Consider the following facts, based on "A Profile of Older Americans: 1997," published by the American Association of Retired Persons with the assistance of the Administration on Aging, Department of Health and Human Services:

- Since 1900, the percentage of the American population above age 65 has more than tripled—from 4.1 percent in 1900 to 12.8 percent in 1996. The number of Americans above age 65 has swelled from 3.1 million in 1900 to 33.9 million in 1996. That number is expected to grow to 39.4 million by the year 2010.

- Four percent of United States citizens above age 65 (1.4 million people) lived in nursing homes in 1995. Not surprisingly, the percent increased with age: 1 percent of people between 65 and 74 lived in nursing homes, 5 percent of people between 75 and 85 lived there, and 15 percent of people aged 85 or older lived there.

According to research undertaken at the Mayo Clinic, there is a marked trend toward an increase in nursing home residents.

- Currently, almost 2 million Americans live in nearly 20,000 nursing homes, at an annual cost of $53 billion.

- By 2030, 5 million Americans are expected to require nursing home care, at a cost of $700 billion or more each year.

These numbers explain why the nursing home industry has grown rapidly during the last twenty years. This growth is both a blessing and a curse. It is a blessing because, as the population ages and entrepreneurs see the advantages of offering a variety of services, an increasing number of options has become available to the elderly and their families. Furthermore, competition has resulted in an overall improvement in care and cost management, both of which benefit the elderly. It is a curse because it requires that the elderly and their families inform themselves about the growing number of options available to them and learn how to evaluate and compare the various long-term care options.

In Part One of this chapter, you will learn the most common reasons why elderly people are institutionalized. A questionnaire will help you determine whether it is time to consider institutional care for *your* parent. You will learn about the importance of (1) keeping all interested parties, *especially your parent*, informed about and involved in discussions of care arrangements, and (2) planning ahead in order to avoid having to make decisions without adequate investigation and in an emotionally charged atmosphere.

In Part Two, you will explore the institutional care options, from continuing-care retirement communities to more traditional nursing facilities. You will find suggestions for early planning and strategies to ease the transition to institutional care. You will discover the benefits of viewing the nursing home as an extension of home care and viewing the staff and administration as members of your eldercare team rather than as usurpers who have wrested responsibility from you.

In the course of learning how to choose an institution, you will discover that funding of nursing facilities goes hand-in-hand with the level of quality assurance at the facilities. By asking a few simple questions, you will be able to gather key data about an institution's ratings in such areas as safety, cleanliness, programming, and staffing. You will also be given pointers on how to evaluate an institution's suitability for your parent.

Institutionalization is traumatic, not only for the elderly parent but for every member of the family as well as other involved parties. In the last part of this chapter, you will learn how to ease adjustment problems by anticipating and managing them. By the time you have finished reading this chapter, you will be in a position to reduce the trauma of institutionalization and to do your best to make it a positive experience for your elderly parent, yourself, and other family members.

PART ONE: Three Pathways to Institutionalization

There are three basic pathways to institutionalization. The first involves voluntary long-range planning on the part of elderly individuals or couples. When a couple decides to take up residence in a continuing-care retirement community, they are jointly approaching institutionalization.

The second pathway is incremental but involuntary—the health of an elderly individual who is being cared for by family or others, perhaps with some home-health and other assistance, deteriorates over time. As the person's condition worsens, and as caregiver burdens increase concomitantly, institutionalization eventually becomes necessary.

The third pathway is unfortunately the most common and the most traumatic. An intervening event, such as a fall, a stroke, or a sudden worsening of a person's physical condition, suddenly makes institutionalization necessary. Typically, under circumstances like these, admission to a nursing facility immediately follows a period of hospitalization.

In this section of the chapter, you will learn more about each of these pathways to institutionalization as well as three key principles to guide you in making the decision to institutionalize your aging parent.

TAKING UP RESIDENCE IN A CONTINUING-CARE RETIREMENT COMMUNITY

Over the past several years, a new kind of living arrangement has begun to evolve. Known alternately as *continuing-care retirement communities* and *continuing/life-care centers*, these facilities offer a range of living options for aging individuals, most of whom, upon admission, are capable of living independently.

The decision to take up residence in a continuing-care retirement community is almost always made by aging individuals themselves and under conditions that are entirely free and voluntary. Typically, the people who choose to live in a continuing-care retirement community have these characteristics:

- They foresee that their health situation will not be stable forever. They are long-range planners and prefer to be in charge of their own lives.

- They want to avoid becoming a burden to their family.

- They can afford the luxury of this kind of living (see below for a comment on the affordability of these communities).

Most of these self-contained communities offer "apartment-home" style living, sometimes even small, private homes. A full-time staff provides housekeeping, groundskeeping, apartment maintenance, and basic laundry services. Residents decorate and furnish their living space independently, with whatever personal items they wish. Each living unit is linked by an emergency-response system to an on-campus health-care facility where services are available 24 hours a day.

Most of these communities are a bit like destination resorts, offering the basic necessities of a full life: shopping, banking, beautician and barber services, dining (one meal per day is usually included in the monthly fee), travel and transportation facilities, structured social activities, even educational opportunities. No one is forced to participate in any activities or to dine in the facility's restaurants. However, all activities and all facilities are open to all residents.

What distinguishes these communities from typical retirement communities is that on the same continuing-care campus, graduated levels of medical and home health-care services are available. As a person ages and his needs increase, he moves to the next level of care—say, from totally independent living to assisted living. For example, in the beginning, a companion may come in a few days a week to help with cooking, shopping, and cleaning. Later, a home-health aide may also come for a few hours per day to provide personal care. The facility responds to the individual's needs, providing more services as needed. Every continuing-care retirement community has a nursing facility on premises as well as a full range of medical and nursing services—described as "intermediate care services" and "skilled nursing services." (These terms are defined in detail later in the chapter.)

Living in a continuing-care community has many advantages. The obvious one is that seniors are able to remain independent and as active as they desire, while enjoying opportunities to socialize with peers. Many choices are open to the elderly individual. Life is lived on one's own terms. In addition, residents have the security of knowing that once they have moved into the community, they will not have to move again. Continuity of relationships, not only with friends and acquaintances but with medical staff, is also reassuring.

Unfortunately, the cost of living in these communities excludes most seniors. They charge a hefty admission fee and monthly fees, both of which are tied to the size and luxury of the home or apartment-home selected. In 1998, entrance fees at a typical continuing-care retirement community in the Northeast section of the country ranged from $88,000 to as high as $289,000, and monthly fees ranged from $1,600 to $3,000.

INCREMENTAL FACTORS

For many people, the nursing home decision is made after a long period during which the senior has been cared for in her own home or that of a child. (Typical care arrangements were discussed in Chapter Five.) As the parent's physical and cognitive capacities decline and her needs increase, institutionalization becomes unavoidable. For example, a parent with Alzheimer's may be manageable when the disease is in its early stages. As time passes, however, and as cognitive and physical declines become more dramatic, it becomes increasingly difficult to provide adequate care. Even the most informed and conscientious caregivers find the burdens unbearable.

On other occasions, the decision to institutionalize a parent is made because the caregiver is unable to maintain a life of his or her own while providing adequate care. If you are a caregiver, the following questionnaire can provide you with guidance in judging whether the burdens of caregiving are exacting too high a toll on you.

INVENTORY: IS IT TIME TO CONSIDER A NURSING HOME PLACEMENT?

Instructions: Please answer *yes* or *no* to each of the following questions by circling the *y* or *n* that precedes the question number.

y n 1. Is your parent experiencing any health problem that cannot be managed successfully at home and that therefore jeopardizes his safety and comfort? (Examples include recurring infections, bedsores that do not heal, incontinence, etc.)

y n 2. Despite training that you or other caregivers have sought out and been provided, are there certain physical tasks you can no longer manage and which are likely to cause, or have already caused, personal injury? (For example, have you injured your back while lifting your parent from a bed or otherwise helping him get around?)

y n 3. Are you consistently sleep-deprived or ill as a result of caregiving responsibilities?

y n 4. Do you ignore your own injuries or illnesses in an attempt to provide uninterrupted care?

5. Are you experiencing any of the following problems or stresses with some consistency, regardless of whether or not they are the direct result of your caregiving responsibilities?

y n work difficulties (lateness, absence, unsatisfactory performance reviews)

y n marital problems, including strife, infidelity on the part of either or both partners, looming separation or divorce

y n difficulties with your children or stepchildren

y n serious illness or injury of family members other than your care recipient

y n financial problems

If you answered *yes* to more than one of these questions, it is certainly time to begin considering a nursing facility.

A third incremental pathway to institutionalization involves the gradual realization that a person can no longer be cared for adequately at home. The reason may be that home care can no longer meet the needs of the care recipient, due either to equipment demands or other factors. It may also be that home care *could* meet your aging parent's needs, but the cost has become prohibitive.

INTERVENING EVENTS

The primary intervening events that lead to institutionalization are accidents, health crises, or injuries that require hospitalization. A broken hip is an example; a stroke is another. Typically, the elderly person is admitted to the hospital, stabilized, and discharged to a nursing facility.

In one case, an elderly gentleman had been cared for at home by his wife. As his dementia progressed, however, he became increasingly unmanageable. He was admitted to the hospital after a fall at home. It was apparent to the physicians and discharge planner that he could not be sent home in the care of his spouse. She was physically and emotionally exhausted, and ill-prepared for the demands that would be placed upon her. The decision was made to discharge him to a nursing facility. Other cases are certainly familiar to you. Here are just a few:

- A woman falls and breaks a hip and can no longer care for herself. Her home is not adapted to her needs.
- A man has a stroke and is paralyzed on one side of his body. He can understand what is said to him but cannot speak.
- A woman is injured in a devastating fire in her home and simply has nowhere else to go after she recovers from her injuries.

As these examples illustrate, whether the intervening event is a true crisis in itself or an event that triggers a "caregiving crisis," the final result is that the person is discharged to a nursing facility.

GUIDING PRINCIPLES

I am convinced on the basis of my experience that one of the reasons so many nursing home placements are made with little or no planning, usually on discharge from hospitals, is that families do not want to consider institutionalization until it is absolutely necessary that they do so. Such resistance, while understandable, is unfortunate. Three principles can guide you as you weigh the decision to institutionalize an aging parent.

Principle One: Keep all interested parties, especially your parent, involved in all planning for institutionalization.

Plans for a nursing home placement should *never* be made without the active involvement of your aging parent, assuming she is conscious and mentally competent. As I have mentioned elsewhere in this book, client self-determination is a fundamental principle in all helping, and it is applicable throughout the caregiving process.

Discussions should certainly be held regarding any plans to institutionalize an elderly person. Whether these are limited to family members and other interested parties or facilitated by a professional therapist or counselor (often a very good idea), such discussions provide an opportunity to accomplish many objectives, such as these:

Explore alternatives and review the rationale for admission to an institution. Discuss: Why is it necessary? What purposes would it serve? What problems would it solve? What are the advantages and disadvantages of institutionalization? How would it serve the best interests of the senior? How would it help other family members?

Validate the feelings of your elderly parent. For the vast majority of seniors, placement in a home is a depressing prospect. The pain and sadness of the senior are hard to witness, let alone validate; yet that is precisely what is required. You must *hear* these feelings as well as others your parent is experiencing, acknowledge them as valid, and avoid the impulse to manage your own distress by saying useless, unhelpful, and guilt-inducing things such as, "It's not going to be so bad," "You shouldn't feel that way," or "You should be grateful we care enough to look after you by arranging this admission."

Ferret out the basis for your elderly parent's reluctance to accept an admission. For example, he may fear being abandoned by the family, simply "dumped" and left to rot. While it is important to acknowledge and respond to such fears, it is equally important to resist the temptation to make false promises. "We'll visit every day" may be an admirable expression of your good intentions, but it may be an unrealistic promise.

Principle Two: The nursing facility can be seen as an extension of the same care you would provide at home.

A common misunderstanding is that once a person is admitted to a nursing home, that facility and its staff take over care—or, more precisely, *take away from the family the right to care for the senior*. Thus, admission is seen as a surrender, a handing over of care responsibilities to strangers. The family sees itself as pushed aside, reduced to a role of visiting the senior and complying with the rules of the institution to which their parent has been admitted.

While this attitude may be fostered by some inferior long-term care facilities, it is most certainly *not* fostered by the best institutions. Quality care facilities and their staffs view themselves as entering into a partnership with the family when a senior is admitted. In effect, they are picking up the slack, providing care that is beyond the capacities of family members.

The professionals in a nursing home have the training, judgment, experience, supervision, and equipment to provide appropriate care for the senior. This not only results in improved care and—for many seniors—improved quality of life, it actually frees up family members so that visits can be focused on pleasant things. On the one hand, the senior is no longer hamstrung by feelings of guilt at being a burden. On the other hand, family members, no longer buried by responsibilities, can better enjoy the company of the senior.

Principle Three: Plan ahead.

Earlier I observed that the vast majority of nursing home placements are made upon discharge from a hospital. Such a time is almost invariably the worst possible time to make such a decision.

First of all, the atmosphere is almost always emotionally charged. Individuals are trying to manage a range of strong emotions, including guilt, shame, feelings of failure, and relief. Such situations are especially difficult when siblings are involved and conflicts exist. At a time when such strong emotions abound, these conflicts are likely to erupt in unpredictable and often very destructive ways. I recall an instance in which one adult child physically assaulted a sibling, raging as he did so, "If you were more of a daughter, if you'd done *anything* to help Mom out over the past six months, we wouldn't be talking about this right now!"

Second, there is limited time for rational thought and calm deliberation. Most often, under such circumstances, family members are given a photocopied list of local facilities (often out of date) that contains limited information and is often difficult to read and interpret. Armed with this information, and having access to little other data about additional care options, families are asked to make one of the most important decisions in their lives and in the life of their parent.

Third, there is little time for learning about area nursing facilities by visiting, talking with staff, or arranging a trial stay for your parent. There are many reasons why visits are useful. They afford an opportunity to assess the professionalism and caring style of the staff, to talk with residents and family members, and to learn whether the institution is a good "match" for your elderly parent.

Fourth, when a parent is acutely ill, family members are often faced with many pressing issues simultaneously. Thus, a decision about a placement may have to be made at the same time as decisions about health care, allocation of family responsibilities, and end-of-life care. It would take an extraordinary individual or family to handle adequately so many pressing and crucial decisions at the same time.

To help you plan ahead, Part Two will explain the kinds of information you need to gather well before making the decision to institutionalize.

PART TWO: Long-Range Planning

Long-range planning for institutionalization makes the entire process—from selecting a home to adjusting to admission and settling in—less traumatic and more systematic for all family members. In this section of the chapter, you will find guidance on educating yourself and your elderly parent about (1) the kinds of institutions that exist, the differences among them, and the care standards that (at least on paper) they all must meet; (2) matching an individual and an institution; (3) payment issues and options; (4) and narrowing the search to a final choice.

KINDS OF INSTITUTIONS AND STANDARDS OF CARE

By understanding how nursing homes are categorized and funded, you will be better able to understand the differences among institutions, appreciate the standards of care all homes must meet, and lay the groundwork for choosing the most appropriate home for your parent.

Kinds of Institutions

Nursing facilities are described differently by different people. For two reasons, I will review the two most common classification systems—first, so that you will know the terminology, and second, so that you will be able to determine the kind of institution that will best serve your parent's needs.

The most common method of classification describes three categories of institutions based on the kinds of care an institution provides. (To muddy the waters a bit, sometimes a single institution will provide more than one—perhaps all three—levels of care. Sometimes different floors or different wings of a single floor will be earmarked for each varying level of care. At such institutions, a certain number of beds may be devoted to each kind of care. Thus, there may be a longer waiting list for "skilled-nursing-care beds" than for other types. The term "bed availability" is one with which you will become familiar as soon as you begin your search for an adequate facility for your parent.)

1. *Custodial-care institutions provide help with activities of daily living such as bathing, dressing, and so on.* The care is nonmedical and is administered by aides rather than medical personnel. Such institutions are typically for people who are in sound health but are too infirm to care for themselves. These are not really "medical" institutions, and they do not provide treatment.

2. *Intermediate-care institutions provide rehabilitative services such as occupational therapy, physical therapy, and speech therapy.* Care is provided by licensed therapists (such as occupational therapists) as well as registered nurses and licensed practical nurses. A person who has had a stroke but is otherwise in sound health will almost always be cared for in an intermediate-care facility. Most residents in intermediate-care facilities are discharged after a time. Such institutions are not meant to be more than places providing relatively short-term care leading to discharge. There are roughly 5500 Medicare-approved intermediate-care institutions in the United States.

3. *Skilled-nursing care institutions provide extensive help with all aspects of living.* Referred to in the past as "acute-care facilities," they are designed to meet the needs of bedridden and seriously incapacitated people. Many of the residents are post-operative and chronically ill. Care is delivered by licensed medical personnel who work under the orders of an attending physician. The care provided includes intravenous (IV) therapy, wound care, and rehabilitative services. There are about 9000 Medicare-approved skilled-nursing facilities in the United States.

Very recently, this system of categorization has changed, so that "intermediate-care institutions" and "skilled-nursing care institutions" are currently grouped together under the heading "nursing institutions." Thus, they can be categorized as follows:

Table 6.1 Kinds of Institutions
▪ **Custodial-care institutions**
▪ **Nursing institutions** intermediate-care institutions skilled-nursing care institutions

Another, somewhat less common system categorizes institutions into these three classes:

1. *Homes for the aged* are equivalent to the custodial-care institutions, described above. Personnel provide help with activities of daily living. Residents are usually in sound health but are too infirm to manage for themselves.

2. *Rest homes with nursing supervision* have facilities and personnel to provide personal care (assistance with activities of daily living), as in a home for the aged. In addition, they provide nursing supervision under medical direction 24 hours per day. This does not mean that a physician is on duty 24 hours per day, only on call. However, an RN (registered nurse) is on duty around the clock, by law.

3. *Chronic and convalescent nursing homes* are equivalent to the skilled-nursing care institutions described previously. They are long-term care facilities. In addition to providing nursing supervision under medical direction 24 hours per day, they are also able to provide simple nonsurgical treatment and dietary procedures for those who are chronically or acutely ill. Services include intravenous therapy, wound care, respiratory therapy, and rehabilitative services.

Regardless of the type of institution, all nursing facilities share certain characteristics in common:

- Their overriding goal is to promote as much independence as possible on the part of residents.

- They develop a care plan for each resident, with goals and means of attaining these goals spelled out.

- They encourage active family involvement in the life of the family resident. (In this respect, they differ from hospitals, which view family members as visitors with severely limited rights and little voice in the care of patients.) Although care must be managed by the professionals, the staffs of all three kinds of nursing institutions encourage family members to play an active role in the life of the institution and in the care of residents.

Funding and Standards of Care

Most people do not know that *every* nursing facility must make available to prospective families on request an assessment document that provides information on the quality of patient care as well as on institutional safety. This document, updated annually as a result of a mandatory on-site inspection, is evidence of the fact that funding of nursing facilities is inherently tied up with standards of care.

The reason for the connection between funding and standards of care is that the federal government pays the majority of all nursing home bills directly or indirectly through Medicare, a federal insurance program, or through Medicaid, a state-administered welfare program. Because of many past cases of inadequate care, abuse, neglect, maltreatment, and unnecessary deaths, the government has taken on the task of ensuring that care providers meet certain criteria in order to qualify for reimbursement. This is an example of the "power of the purse string"— the one who pays has a say in what is paid for.

To participate in the Medicare or Medicaid programs, a facility must be certified by the federal government as complying with federal participation requirements. (At last count, more than 4000 nursing facilities were *not* Medicare approved.) Compliance with federal standards is determined by means of on-site surveys performed on a regular schedule. Trained personnel conduct these surveys over several days, using standardized forms and procedures, including interviews with residents. The purpose is to compile information about such factors as the following:

- adequacy of care plans for residents
- cleanliness
- provisions for privacy and protection of personal property

- meal quality
- timeliness of food service
- fire safety (fire alarms, sprinkler systems, emergency exits, etc.)

Areas of strength and weakness, as well as any outright violations of standards (known as a health deficiency or a life-safety code deficiency), are noted in the survey results. The institution is given an opportunity to correct deficiencies.

The results of these surveys are available on request. Therefore, as an informed consumer, you may ask to see them. Include them in making a decision about whether a facility is appropriate for your parent.

A Word of Caution

The vast majority of institutions provide clean, safe places for residents to live, while offering sensitive care, well-planned services, wholesome meals, and appropriate treatment. Procedures are in place to ensure that *all* institutions meet at least minimal standards in all these areas. Nevertheless, a word of caution is in order.

Even the most caring and well-intentioned administration and staff are subject to burnout and cynicism. Moreover, where there is money to be made, the unscrupulous often find their way. As a result, sometimes horror stories *do* unfold.

Recently, in my own state of Connecticut, a nursing home owner, 77 years old herself, was accused of assaulting an 84-year-old resident suffering from dementia. The resident had resisted efforts to restrain her when she attempted to leave the facility. In response, the owner is alleged to have kicked the resident. As this book goes to press, the owner is facing trial.

Or take the case of an adult child whose story is briefly summarized in the November–December 1997 issue of the AARP publication *Modern Maturity*. Early in 1995, she testified before the Texas state legislature about the substandard care her mother had received while residing in a number of state-licensed nursing facilities. In her testimony, she spoke of bedsheets that reeked of urine, cockroaches that swarmed when she accidentally disturbed a nest, and worse. Perhaps most disturbing, she voiced well-founded suspicions that administration and staff were routinely forewarned of "surprise" inspections by state survey teams.

The movement for nursing home reform was born in response to such abuses. Led by the National Citizens' Coalition for Nursing Home Reform, the movement's mission is to expose and ultimately prevent abuses such as those mentioned here. It is supported by residents and their families, by local, state, and federal officials, and also by the most conscientious administration and staff of long-term care facilities. (For address information, see the Selected Resources appendix.)

As an adult child, not only should you be very vigilant in selecting an institution for your parent, you should be quick to notify nursing home staff and administration of any abuses or problems of which you become aware at any point in your dealings with a facility. If there is no response, notify your local officials. The most appropriate resource is your state's long-term care ombudsman. Established in every state in 1978, when the Older Americans Act (originally passed in 1965) was amended, the Long-Term Care Ombudsman Program is intended to serve as an overseer of all long-term care institutions in your state. When a complaint is made, volunteers from the ombudsman's office investigate; they have the legal authority to intervene aggressively, and they sometimes arrange for legal assistance to protect the health, safety, and rights of residents in long-term care institutions. Your state's long-term care ombudsman can be reached through a variety of sources, including your Area Agency on Aging, your state's Office of the Aging, and your town's Municipal Agent on Aging.

The elderly and the infirm are among the most vulnerable members of our society. They deserve nothing less than the active, aggressive support of those of us in a position to make a difference. Vigilance is the least we owe them.

MATCHING AN INDIVIDUAL AND AN INSTITUTION

In educating yourself, you must go beyond simply learning about the kinds of institutions that are available and factors such as accreditation and licensing, cleanliness, and safety. You must also have a sense of the distinguishing characteristics of the institution. Ask yourself whether *this* institution, with *these* characteristics, would most likely suit your parent. Here are some guiding questions and procedures you can use to match an institution to your parent's needs.

> ***Does the facility provide the level of care my parent needs?*** By taking an inventory of what your parent can do for herself (always a good starting point in any decision about the level of care an elderly parent might need), you will find that it is easy to rule out some facilities simply because they do not provide the appropriate level of care required.

> ***Does the facility provide the nonrequired services we want?*** After narrowing your choices to several facilities that meet your first three criteria, move on to preferences. Look into opportunities for socialization, entertainment, and the observance of religious practices. Find out the cost of extras such as laundry service and a private television.

> ***Are staff well qualified and attentive?*** In evaluating each facility, consider such factors as staff credentials, caring, and attentiveness. Find out about night coverage and about the presence of a pharmacist on staff to make it easier to monitor medications.

Ask yourself whether the facility provides the kind of atmosphere that is likely to feel like home to your parent. Having toured many facilities, I can report with first-hand knowledge that the "feel" of an institution is a major factor in creating a climate of welcome and homeyness or sterility. Some have a dreadful institutional quality to them. Others are warm. Rather than institutional furniture, for example, warm institutions often have normal residential furnishings, even occasional antiques. Sometimes they have older furniture that has the wear and tear of home about it. I recall one dining room that was furnished not lavishly, but with furniture from the 1930s and '40s. Dinner was being served as I walked by. Animated conversation filled the air, and one had the impression that residents looked forward to their meals and were enjoying this one, not only for the food but for the socialization that was encouraged and fostered by the staff.

While we are on the topic of the "feel" of an institution, let me call your attention to a movement begun several years ago in New York State. Known as the "Eden Alternative," this movement calls on nursing home administrators and staff to revamp the way they think about and provide care for residents.

Most nursing homes follow the model of a hospital. Nursing stations, tight scheduling, and orderliness are characteristic of the hospital environment. Residents are most often seen as "patients," and days are structured around treating patients and providing services. Residents are, to a great degree, objects to be acted upon. The Eden Alternative calls on directors to think of nursing homes as *habitats*—places where people live. "Edenists" advocate creating a living environment that is modeled on nature rather than on hospitals. Variety and diversity become the norms. "Edenized" nursing homes foster, among residents, active involvement in life as well as *mutual* caregiving. Such homes may:

- replace lawns (or at least some portion of the lawn area) with flower and vegetable gardens, and at mealtime serve foods raised on the grounds by residents or with their advice and counsel;
- bring into the home many plants of various kinds, with a diversity of color, texture, and so on;
- bring animals (dogs, cats, birds) into the facility and encourage residents to provide care and companionship;

- bring children into the home, sometimes providing after-school care and summer day camps for youngsters.

An Edenized nursing home is clearly very different from a traditional one. In such facilities, residents require less medication, complain less of pain, and display a better attitude. While an Edenized nursing home may not be for everyone, it certainly represents a clear alternative and may be worth looking into for your adult parent. (See *Life Worth Living* by Dr. William Thomas, listed in the Selected Resources appendix.)

PAYMENT ISSUES AND OPTIONS

For most families, the cost of an institution is a major factor in the choice they make. Nursing home costs alone, exclusive of doctors' bills, medications, physical therapy, x-rays, lab tests, and other expenses, average $50,000 per year in many sections of the country as of this writing. In addition, many homes charge extra for television, transportation, and other near-necessities. When speaking with an admissions director, it is essential that you ask about charges. It is wise to imagine or "walk through" a typical week in your elderly parent's life. Picture him doing the things he does at home—calling relatives, watching TV, going into town to have lunch with a friend—and ask whether associated expenses are included in the monthly nursing home charges.

Overall, consider not only what you should expect to pay but also what arrangements can be made for payment and the quality of help you will get in making those arrangements. Most facilities will help you with Medicare and Medicaid paperwork, although not all have the trained staff to provide knowledgeable assistance.

It is beyond the scope of this book to provide detailed information on the financing of nursing home care. However, the following paragraphs will alert you to some of the crucial information you must have on hand when considering the affordability of a home and its expenses.

For information specific to your region of the country, contact your state's Department of Social Services and Office of the Aging or your regional Area Agency on Aging. For planning advice tied to your family's financial circumstances, consult a financial advisor or an elderlaw attorney in your area.

As of this writing, the following data are accurate, although the picture is likely to change in the near future. Unfortunately, any changes will certainly be in the direction of decreased benefits.

- About half of the country's long-term care bill (that includes both institutional care and home-care services) is paid for by care recipients and their families.

- Most nursing home residents enter as private-pay patients because their assets make them ineligible for state assistance (Medicaid). Many eventually use up their assets and become impoverished and therefore eligible for Medicaid assistance.

- Medicare, the federal health insurance program for disabled people and those over age 65, was *never intended* to pay the bill for long-term care. The same is true of "Medigap" policies, which are designed to supplement Medicare payments so that Medicare recipients will not be liable for out-of-pocket medical expenses incurred (a) when they visit a physician or other health-care provider, or (b) when they enter a hospital or skilled nursing facility for short periods, or (c) when they receive home care for short periods.

As a result, at the present time Medicare pays less than 10 percent of the nation's long-term care bill. Specific Medicare benefits and limitations are in flux. For up-to-date information, you are best advised to contact your local Area Agency on Aging.

Long-Term Care Insurance

Long-term care insurance provides coverage for assistance you need over a long period of time to manage (not cure) a chronic condition or to fulfill the tasks of daily living (ADLs). Most, but not all, long-term care insurance pays not only for institutional care but for home care as well.

In most states, long-term insurance policies enable policyholders to protect their assets. That is, policyholders do not have to become impoverished (and therefore Medicaid eligible) in order to have their care needs paid for. This is a major advantage, but as you will soon see, it also makes long-term coverage an expensive frill for those who do not have assets to protect.

This kind of insurance has become a necessity for more and more people, as the cost of care rises and the pool of state and federal funds shrinks. According to one estimate, almost half of Americans who reach age 65 will eventually need some form of long-term care insurance to pay for either home care or institutional care. Recent federal laws require that long-term care policies meet certain requirements. Here are several:

- A policy must be noncancellable, except for failure to pay premiums, and guaranteed renewable should a policyholder fail to pay premiums in a timely manner. A policy must also allow the purchaser to name someone other than the care recipient as the person who must be notified in the event that the policy is about to lapse due to failure to pay premiums.

- A policy cannot require that a care recipient enter a nursing home before benefits are paid.

- A policy cannot exclude coverage for Alzheimer's once a policy has been issued.

These and other minimum criteria must be met by all long-term care policies. However, there are many variations among policies and many qualitative differences. Thus, one basic question remains: How do you evaluate a long-term care policy? Following are several factors to keep in mind.

When does a policyholder become eligible for benefits? Usually, policies specify that to become eligible for benefits, the policyholder must be unable to perform at least two of the Activities of Daily Living (see page 104) and that he or she would be unlikely to be able to do so for another 90 days. However, eligibility criteria differ from one policy to the next. Obviously, very strict eligibility criteria reduce the usefulness of the policy while saving the insurance company money. Check into the various eligibility criteria specified in several policies before choosing any of them.

What terms are used in the policy, and how are they defined? How, for example, does the insurance company define terms such as "severe impairment." Does "care" include home care as well as institutional care? Policies differ widely and need to be investigated thoroughly.

In addition to institutional care, does the policy enable the purchaser to arrange for coverage of a wide array of home-based and community-based benefits? These would include skilled nursing care, adult day care, services of a home-health aide, and speech/occupational/physical therapy.

What minimum benefits will the policy pay for services? In 1998 dollars, $107 daily is considered a minimum for nursing home care; $53.50 is the minimum for home- and community-based care.

Does the plan provide for inflation? Health-care costs continue to rise; therefore, it is essential that a long-term care plan take that factor into account. The usual minimum rate of inflation is 5 percent.

Despite what some people in the insurance industry would have you believe, long-term care insurance is not appropriate for everyone. Premiums are quite high, and they become higher with the age of the purchaser. Someone without many assets may simply be throwing money away by purchasing long-term care coverage. If you do not have many assets to protect—few savings or investments and perhaps only the home you live in—then long-term care insurance is *not* your preferred option. There are at least two other options worth weighing.

The Reverse Mortgage

This enables homeowners to tap into the equity of their homes to pay current bills. For example, suppose your elderly mother owns her home free and clear, after having paid off the mortgage over many years. The home is worth $150,000. A bank offering a reverse mortgage will advance her most of that $150,000. Banks use various formulas to calculate the amount they will advance. That advance can be paid out either in the form of a lump sum or in monthly payments. The money she receives is tax-free, but the bank charges interest on the money advanced. In some cases, the loan is not repaid until your mother either dies or sells her home, at which time a portion of the proceeds of the sale equal to the amount advanced by the bank (plus interest charges and applicable fees) is paid to the bank. Alternately, in some cases the reverse mortgage loan has a time limit (say, 5 or 10 years). At the end of that period, you must repay the loan. Your state's Department of Social Services or Office of the Aging can provide details.

Viatical Settlements

Relatively recently companies have sprung up, offering to purchase a senior's life insurance policy for a percentage of its face value. Essentially, your parent agrees to accept a cash settlement now—perhaps 80 percent of the face value of her life insurance policy—in return for making the company providing the cash the beneficiary for her life insurance policy when she dies. It is a quick way to raise needed cash, but the cost of the convenience is high. On a $100,000 policy, for example, your parent may receive $80,000; and of course, when she dies, the company is the insurance beneficiary and is entitled to the face value of the policy ($100,000).

ADDITIONAL CAUTIONS ON ADMITTING A PARENT TO A NURSING HOME

A few other cautions are in order. First, be aware that nursing home admissions agreements are contracts. When you admit your parent to a nursing facility, you sign a legal document that guarantees rights and imposes responsibilities—the conditions under which your parent is admitted.

Always ask to be allowed to take the contract home. Take the time to read the contract carefully. Make sure you understand the terms. It is a good idea to have the contract reviewed by an elderlaw attorney *before* you sign. If certain terms of the contract are not acceptable, ask to have them changed. If the nursing home refuses to make reasonable changes that your attorney feels are important, go elsewhere.

Second, understand that Medicare eligibility is a major issue. If you are told by the nursing home administrators that your parent does not qualify for Medicare, you have the right to ask that they send Medicare a "no payment" claim. This is a report that says, in effect, "We have told the family that it is our best judgment that Medicare will not pay for this service. However, the family wants us to bill Medicare anyway." Once Medicare receives this, they will review the matter and, in all likelihood, issue a written denial of benefits. This ruling (the denial of benefits) can be appealed; and in a small number of cases Medicare's decision is reversed on appeal.

NARROWING THE SEARCH

As noted earlier, your local Area Agency on Aging has on staff a long-term care ombudsman. One of his or her jobs is to provide you with not only a list of institutions in your area but also objective and frank information on the quality of each institution. Find the number of the Area Agency on Aging in your phone book or by calling the National Association of Area Agencies on Aging at (202) 296-8130, your state's

Department of Social Services or Office of the Aging, your local Senior Center, or Municipal Agent on Aging. A call to the ombudsman is invariably a helpful experience.

To narrow your search to a few institutions in your immediate area, contact the institutions about which you are particularly interested. Request literature. In addition, consider factors such as the personal recommendations of friends and associates who have placed their own relative in a home. Consider, too, the reputation of a particular facility among local professionals such as hospital discharge planners, home-care workers, and social workers. Always supplement these strategies with personal visits, during which you review survey results, talk with residents and families, and so on.

Bed availability is a major concern in scouting out an institution. For all but those people admitted on an emergency basis, the normal procedure is to place your parent on a waiting list. You will be called when a bed becomes available. If placement is not required at the time you are called, your parent goes to the top of the list unless you make other arrangements, and you are called again when another bed becomes available. This procedure is repeated until the right time arrives.

Finally, weigh factors such as transportation and access. Since you and others will be traveling to the institution to visit your aging parent, it is important to be realistic about these: Is the facility easily accessible by car? By mass transit? Is it in a safe area?

Meet with the intake worker or admissions counselor, usually a social worker or a nurse, and arrange for a tour of the institution. Bring your parent. Talk with residents and families. If possible, arrange for a trial stay of a few days or even, if possible, a few weeks. The following checklist provides some guiding questions you can use as you tour and then evaluate a facility.

Questions to Ask When Evaluating a Facility: A Checklist

☐ What personal belongings may be brought into the facility? (You will see later that this is an important consideration in facilitating an adjustment to nursing home life.)

☐ Are residents' rights posted and respected by nursing home staff? Because of past abuses, a Bill of Rights for nursing home residents has been created and adopted by virtually all institutions. In a well-run home, the Bill of Rights is prominently displayed. More important, it is taken seriously.

☐ What arrangements exist for the management of residents' personal finances?

☐ Are private rooms available? In a shared room, how are roommates paired? What provisions exist for making changes, if required?

☐ What arrangements exist for telephone access? For televiewing? For radio?

☐ Are activities and current and upcoming events clearly posted in places residents will find easy to access?

☐ Do the institution's administration and staff encourage family involvement? Is there a family council that has the power (at the very least) to disseminate information and recommend changes in institutional policies and practices?

PART THREE: Adjusting to the Nursing Home

No decision to enter a nursing home is easy. Institutionalization affects both the senior and the family, as well as other interested parties. By anticipating adjustment problems, preventing those that are preventable, and being prepared to cope with those that are not, you can ease your parent's adjustment as well as that of others. This section provides tips on the management of adjustment issues, not only for your parent but for yourself, your siblings, and other concerned parties.

YOUR PARENT'S ADJUSTMENT PROBLEMS

The first thing you need to bear in mind is that adjustment problems are normal. We are territorial creatures, and our environment is our territory. It provides privacy, a safe haven, a place we can feel entirely at ease. Often our roles are bound up with the places we call our own. One's home is the place where a mother raised her children or where a man ran a small business. One's home or living space symbolizes autonomy, self-sufficiency, and worth. In our homes we can do exactly as we please: eat when we want, go to bed when we want, dress as we like. When this territory is invaded, or when we lose it, we feel edgy, angry, or worse. Little wonder that older adults are so often reluctant to give up their personal space.

When the move to a nursing home is made in haste, without the thoughtful consent of the older person, or when it is made under emergency conditions, perhaps as a result of sudden dependency or illness, the admission is even more traumatic. Lack of time to prepare oneself emotionally may result in depression, rage, and a host of other negative emotions.

Moreover, one's personal space usually contains prized possessions. Though not necessarily of great monetary value, the things that surround us are often charged with personal meaning. For example, the favorite painting your mother bought on a vacation trip with your dad many years ago may carry emotional weight far beyond its market value. The furnishings and knickknacks are almost literally pieces of a life once lived with passion, meaning, and purpose. To surrender these is to relinquish one's hold on the only life she's known. To leave them behind, even in the care of one's children or others, is extraordinarily painful.

I recall one elderly woman who had moved from her home in a distant state to a small apartment in my town. Despite her daughter's distress, the woman insisted on having many furnishings moved with her. To her, their presence in her apartment made the move more bearable. It took many months before the daughter came to realize just how significant these possessions were to her mother. When a nursing home admission became necessary, the daughter was much more aware of how important it would be for her mother to be able to take certain of her prized possessions with her. Wisely, the daughter spoke about this issue at length with nursing home personnel. As a result, her mother was able to furnish her own room with at least some of the possessions that meant so much to her.

DEALING WITH YOUR PARENT'S ADJUSTMENT PROBLEMS

When adjustment problems cannot be anticipated or avoided, they must be managed. Here are several typical indicators of adjustment difficulties along with some thoughts on how to handle them.

Complaints about Staff and Other Residents "These people aren't nice," or "These people are too old for me."

Possible responses: Encourage your parent to avoid snap decisions. Accompany him to activities in the home. Introduce him to people close to him in age and with whom he is likely to get along. Alert the staff to the fact that he is having difficulties adjusting.

Complaints about Food "The meals are awful here—cold, tasteless," etc. Some complaints are about the fact that dietary restrictions are not respected. "They serve me pork even though they know I don't eat it."

Possible responses: Visit at mealtime and see for yourself. If the complaints are valid, advocate on your parent's behalf. Bring food.

With the permission of staff, arrange for food to be delivered.

Global Complaints "I want to go home."

Possible responses: Encourage your parent to give it time. Try to determine the specific disappointments that are at the heart of her distress. Perhaps there is something you can do to make her living arrangements more homey. A few personal touches in your parent's room can make it feel much more like her space. Perhaps an avoidable annoyance (too much light from the hallway) can be eliminated.

Isolation Your parent may elect to isolate herself. She may not leave her room, may decline to participate in activities, and so on.

Possible responses: Become involved in the life of the institution. Take your parent along to ease the transition.

Depression Your parent may say things like, "I'm here to die," or "This is the end for me. I'd rather be dead than live out my days here."

Possible responses: Allow your parent to vent these feelings, then encourage him to make the most of his circumstances. If you can do so without lying, avoid speaking of placement in the home as permanent; instead, hold out the realistic hope that he may be discharged one day. Maintain regular contact. Often, relief that he is not being abandoned in the home will make it easier for your parent to overcome his depression. If depression does not remit after a reasonable period of time, and if it affects his appetite or other activities, alert staff. A psychiatric consultation may be in order.

STAGES IN THE ADJUSTMENT PROCESS

Research suggests that there are four phases in the adjustment process. While these stages are a useful way of understanding what happens as a person comes to terms with the fact that she is now living in an institution, they need to be taken loosely as they provide only rough guidelines of what is likely to occur in most typical cases.

The first phase is called *acute distress*. Emotional reactions during this phase include feelings of loss, anxiety, depression, abandonment, and anger. Overt manifestations include lack of self-care (a person who is usually meticulous about herself may not bother to bathe or wash her hair), silence and surliness, teariness, and refusal to eat. Her behavior may lack purpose. She may have no sense of what she is doing or why.

The second phase is *initial acceptance*. Emotionally, the person may begin to experience the feelings less acutely. For short periods of time, he may actually accept some aspect of living in the home, perhaps even take pleasure in some experience or person. Behaviorally, as he gets to know the routine of the institution, he may join in certain activities, perhaps even anticipate them with a certain satisfaction. An outgoing person might help himself by assisting "newcomers" as they learn the ropes.

Tentative friendship often follows the period of initial acceptance. Emotionally, a person might begin to experience feelings of relief and security as he makes the acquaintance of like-minded people. He may meet a friend who enjoys cards or who becomes an ally in some effort to improve the quality of life in the home. People who have shared experiences—as parents, or tourists, or professional working people—can often commiserate with each other and recall pleasant experiences. Behaviorally, the senior may take pleasure in introducing his new friends to family members when they visit. Grandchildren, for example, may often be "shown off" when they visit.

Finally, *final acceptance* occurs. The raw emotions experienced on admission subside, and the person lives a more or less normal life within the parameters set by the institution. She takes part in activities, perhaps volunteers to help out in the library or media center, and otherwise contributes her knowledge and expertise in improving life within the institution.

The movement from one phase to the next is gradual, and "loops" are not unusual. For example, a person might regress during the tentative friendship phase to the acute distress phase. Ordinarily, however, such setbacks are temporary, and over time they become less frequent. Nevertheless, adjustment is not a one-way street; regressions are not at all unusual. They need to be taken in stride by the family.

YOUR OWN ADJUSTMENT PROBLEMS

The senior is not the only one who experiences adjustment problems; so do the family and other interested parties. It is difficult on many levels for an adult child to come to terms with a parent's admission. The sights, sounds, and smells of a home may be distressing and upsetting. Staff may not be sensitive to the many new experiences facing a family whose member has entered the home. (Some homes provide excellent support for new families. This may be a criterion you consider when selecting one home over another.)

As noted previously, trial periods of residence prior to institutionalization often ease adjustment problems for all parties. Among the many feelings adult children have discussed with me, several stand out:

- Guilt, shame, and self-reproach: "I should be able to take care of Mother. Her being here is a measure of my lack of caring and my ineptitude as a caregiver."

- Anger: "If other members of my family were more cooperative and compassionate, we might have avoided this."

- Pity: "It's so hard to see my mother as a *patient*, and as a dying one at that. She was always so full of life."

- Guilty relief: "Having Mother in a home is such a relief for me. I feel awful admitting it, but I'm secretly very happy she's off my hands."

These and other emotions are perfectly normal and appropriate, though it is often difficult without professional help to accept them and move on. Let me share an experience. Some years ago, a woman was referred to me by a neurologist who had been treating her for intractable headaches. When, after the usual treatments failed, the neurologist inquired about what was going on in her life, he learned that she had two elderly parents whom she had cared for virtually alone for many years. A distant sibling had washed her hands of the responsibility. When my patient complained to her sister about how difficult it was to manage both parents alone, the sister's reply was a glib, "Put them in a home." Her suggestion was less a serious attempt at a solution to the problem than it was an expression of her disinterest and disinclination to help.

As my client's parents' health declined, it became obvious that both were facing admission to a home. She had thought about the possibility but was extremely reluctant to arrange it. Her headaches were in part the result of the physical and emotional stress she was under, and in part they were a somatization of the guilt she felt at the prospect of arranging the admission.

Through counseling, she was able to come to terms with the need to take action. After her parents were admitted, she slowly worked through her feelings. Not long afterward, she retired from her job as a bank mortgage officer and began to pursue interests she had put off for a long time. She maintained a schedule of regular visits to the home, and eventually she was able to acknowledge that she had made the right decision.

Her parents died some years later, and she was able to accept that. She was also satisfied that they had received the best possible care in the home. "I could never have done for them what was done by the staff," she observed one day. Not long after their deaths, she was able to enjoy travel and self-improvement classes. When I last saw her, she reported that she felt she had been given a new lease on life. Counseling had helped her make an excellent adjustment to her situation.

EASING THE PERIOD OF ADJUSTMENT

For your parent's sake and your own, you can do several things to make the period of adjustment more smooth. The first is to visit regularly and productively. If your family is a large one, and if members are cooperative, share the responsibility of visiting. Work out a schedule that meets everyone's needs.

For many people, visits can become burdensome. "What do I do?" adult children often ask me. "We're running out of things to say." It may seem surprising, but often conscious thought must be put into making visits productive and pleasant. On a recent visit to a local nursing facility, I was given a list called "101 Things to Do When Visiting Your Elderly Adult." Here are some of those suggestions:

- Bring things to do and talk about that are related to the season or to an upcoming holiday.

- Read letters or listen to audiotaped messages from family and friends.

- Have grandchildren bring or send artwork or school papers.

- Work on a project or hobby you both enjoy doing. For example, begin collecting stamps or unusual items. Build a bird feeder to hang outside your parent's window, or a terrarium to place in her room.

- Learn a new word each time you visit together. A dictionary of word origins can be both entertaining and instructive.

- Have your parent create a "wish list" of items she would like in her room—a particular plant, for example, or a goldfish—and fulfill the realistic wishes.

- Read a book together. The joy of being read to is one that we all experience throughout life. If possible, take turns reading chapters to one another.

Second, become involved in the life of the home. Get to know staff and form alliances to ease your own and your parent's discomfort. Attend activities, lectures, and workshops. Volunteer your time, if you can, to help staff make life in the home more varied and fun.

Third, listen. No matter what your parent is presenting, and so long as he is not manipulative or abusive, it is important to provide as open an ear as possible. At the same time, convey by your words and actions your expectation that your parent will have the resources to enter into the life of the institution and make a satisfactory adjustment.

Fourth, find creative ways to maintain your parent's involvement in the family and the outside world. The more a person focuses on himself, the more likely he is to be aware of pains, aches, and other sensations that might otherwise be appropriately ignored. The result of such self-scrutiny is often the prescription of medication, which, of course, causes side effects that become problems in themselves. In turn, additional medications are prescribed. (The fancy word for this is *polypharmacy*.) This entire, unfortunate process can be avoided by encouraging your parent's healthy involvement in the world.

While none of these steps is a definitive answer to the problem of adjustment, all collectively can make a difference and facilitate the process by which your parent experiences the highest possible quality of life during his stay in the home.

SUMMARY

The three ways in which elderly people most often arrive in nursing facilities are (1) after voluntary long-range planning, or (2) along an incremental and involuntary path, or (3) on sudden placement after a traumatic event. There are ways to gauge whether your elderly parent is a candidate for institutional care. The many institutional care options currently available include continuing-care retirement communities and several types of more traditional nursing facilities. The chapter emphasized the importance of keeping all interested parties, especially your parent, informed and involved in the decision to institutionalize; planning ahead in order to avoid making last-minute decisions without adequate thought and in an emotionally charged atmosphere; and viewing the nursing home as an extension of home care and viewing the staff and administration of any institution as members of your eldercare team.

There is a correlation between the funding of nursing facilities and quality assurance, and there are ways to evaluate an institution, both in general and in terms of its suitability for your parent. Finally, one can ease adjustment problems by anticipating, planning for, and managing the problems.

In the next chapter, you will read about decisions associated with planning for the end of life, including advance directives and other topics.

CHAPTER 7

Making End-of-Life Decisions

Allowing your parent to stay in control of her final days and hours of life is the very last gift you can give her. Too often in my work, I hear of people whose deaths became events over which they lost all control. A physician, a hospital administration, or some other entity became the decision maker, leaving both the family and—more important—the dying person feeling like passive spectators or victims in a situation in which they had every right to be in control.

Complicating the act of dying in today's world is a basic fact. We are heirs to sophisticated technology that makes it possible to prolong physical existence by artificial means almost indefinitely. Ventilators, feeding tubes, pacemakers, IV's that provide artificial hydration, and other life-sustaining devices have all been touted as "advances" in medical science.

It is a curious but indisputable fact that technology of all kinds tends to spawn more technology; the result is run-away "progress" that sometimes defies common sense. President Eisenhower coined the expression "military-industrial complex"; I would identify the "medical-technological complex" as a sometimes unholy alliance between medicine and technology. The result is a self-perpetuating machine that keeps grinding out new "life"-sustaining medical devices without regard to their effects on the *quality* of human life and human dying.

Technological developments have made many new things possible— from the duplication of human beings to the harvesting of human body parts. The question is: Is it always wise (that is, moral and desirable from an ethical point of view) to do what it is possible to do? Practical concerns about care of the dying cannot be separated from the same fundamental question spawned by cloning, genetic engineering, and other new technologies. We *can* keep people "alive" by artificial means, but should we? Consider the following players in the death scenario, each of whom has his or her own agenda:

> **The _hospital administration_ is concerned about lawsuits and wants to ensure that every step is taken to prolong existence, lest a suit be initiated.** Some charge that hospitals seek profit, as well, and *that* motivates them to keep patients alive. However, prolonging life often reduces profits, since life support can be extremely costly. Thus, this criticism is not entirely fair.

> **The _doctor_ is trained to prolong life.** Taught that "losing" a patient to death is a personal "defeat" (the metaphor of war is no accident), the physician is dedicated—mindlessly so at times—to prolonging "life" at any cost. In the United States, physicians receive little or no training in what is known as palliative medicine. Our physicians are not prepared to accept the fact that a person is dying and then ease pain, relieve symptoms, and otherwise comfort the individual. (In other countries, palliative medicine is a specialty, just like family medicine and endocrinology are in the United States.)

In addition, for some doctors, especially those who are strangers to the dying person and the family, concern about lawsuits is as strong as for hospital administrators. In a series of interviews conducted in 1997 on National Public Radio, one expert used the phrase "stranger medicine" to refer to the fact that dying people and their families are often placed in the care of physicians with whom they have no prior relationship. The absence of a connection puts the physician in a precarious position and may cost the dying person dearly. For example, near death, Mrs. O may be transferred to the hospital from an extended-care facility. The chances of her personal physician being available in the hospital at the time of her admission are very small. More typically, the physician who receives her does not know Mrs. O, so he instructs the staff to do everything possible to keep Mrs. O alive. Unless she has made it absolutely clear ahead of time that she does not wish to be kept alive, every conceivable step will be taken to prolong her life, regardless of the wishes of Mrs. O and her family.

One of the many roles of <u>nurses</u> is to implement the physician's instructions. If nurses do not do so, even when they disagree violently with the physician's thinking, they risk losing their job and worse. Many nurses are well trained for and well attuned to the human side of patient care, as well as the technological side. They appreciate the negative aspects of sustaining life by artificial means. Regardless of how strongly they feel, however, their hands are often tied by the rules and requirements under which they work and by their status within the medical hierarchy.

Pressure is on the <u>patient</u> and his <u>family</u> to comply with the medical establishment's directives. Compliance with the wishes and needs of an institution makes life easier for the institution and its professionals. Research conducted decades ago demonstrated that hospital staff members prefer "good" patients over "bad" ones. "Good" patients comply, do not ask too many questions or insist on their rights, and fit into the routine. They do not demand special accommodations. By contrast, "bad" patients make life difficult for physicians and staff. They ask questions and demand explanations. They know their rights and insist that they be respected. They are aware of their own needs and preferences, and they reject the institutional routine when it fails to serve them. (Interestingly, researchers further documented that—contrary to what might be predicted—"bad" patients get better more quickly and do better overall than "good" ones!)

As players in the death scenario, patients and their families all too often allow themselves to be pushed along in directions they do not want to go. Needlessly ashamed of their ignorance of medical terminology, they may feign understanding when they do not grasp what is said. Guilty and uncertain about how to proceed, lacking knowledge, unsure of their rights, they allow themselves to be cajoled into choices that run counter to common sense and their personal values. Sometimes those choices are based on incomplete information, as when a physician urges a course of treatment without providing accurate and complete information on the long-term effects of making the choice. Anxious and upset, family members might hear a recommendation but fail to consider its implications. "What would you do, Doctor?" they are likely to ask. Or they might go even further: "Do what you think is best, Doctor." There is no replacement for a good relationship with a physician who knows the patient and the family and feels comfortable enough with them to level with them, and then respect their wishes.

The pressure to prolong life is so great that institutional personnel will make decisions to maintain life support *unless aggressive actions are taken both to make the dying person's wishes to the contrary known and to see that those wishes are respected.*

In this chapter, you will learn what you and your parent can do to stay in control of the last days and hours of life. My job will be to familiarize you with the tools at your disposal, such as living wills, but also with strategies you can use to see that your parent's wishes are not disregarded. (It is an alarming fact that in the majority of cases a person's expressed wishes are simply not taken into consideration by medical decision makers at the time of death! I will have more to say about this later in the chapter.) On the way to those goals, you will read about the difficulties most people experience talking about death and find suggestions on how to overcome these difficulties. While I have no magic formulas to offer, I will suggest lines of thought and communication techniques that can facilitate necessary discussion. By the time you finish reading the chapter, you will know what must be done to ensure that your parent leaves this world gracefully and with dignity, and you will also know how to go about doing it.

There are specific topics that this chapter will not address. You will *not* learn about estate planning, probate, or other legal topics. My best advice is to contact an attorney for advice on those matters.

PART ONE: A "Good Death" Is Not an Oxymoron

An oxymoron is a word or phrase that is self-contradictory. "Square circle" is an example. So is "sad happiness." For many people combining *death* with *good* also seems to give rise to a self-contradictory term. Not so. Anyone who has overseen the death of a loved one or otherwise been a party to the death of another knows that just as the quality of life is variable, so, too, is the quality of death. Few would use the phrase "good death" to refer to the act of dying alone in a sterile hospital room, connected to machines, wires, and tubes, unable to make any but the tiniest movement. By contrast, dying in a warm, familiar setting, surrounded by loved ones, able to say good-bye and offer reassurance to those about to be left behind—this death can be considered a "good" one.

BENEFITS OF STAYING IN CONTROL

The hospice movement was born of the recognition that death can be good. Originating in Britain and brought to this country in 1974, the modern hospice movement is dedicated to the concept that dying patients have the right to a dignified passing in the company of their families. Further, loved ones have the right to be a part of the dying process, not shunted aside as they so often are by the professionals in a health-care setting. Physical, psychological, and spiritual needs are all attended to in hospice. The only word not likely to come up in a hospice setting is "cure," because no illusion is maintained that the dying person can somehow be snatched from the jaws of death.

From the perspective of this chapter, hospice can be seen as advocating staying in control of the dying process. Just as it is desirable to talk about a nursing home admission before a crisis arises (see Chapter Five), it is desirable to make end-of-life decisions before your parent reaches death's door. Being in control provides benefits to your parent, to you, and to the professionals who are your partners in the process.

Benefits to Your Parent

We are inclined to reduce the element of chance in our lives. Most of us wear seat belts when we drive, in case of an accident. We plan our trips to ensure we do not get lost on the way to where we are going. Similarly, we see a physician when we notice an unusual, lingering pain or when a sore throat does not clear up after a week or so. Business people forecast sales and anticipate inventory needs. As a society, we set schedules for our public transportation and take comfort in knowing that the morning flight to Chicago will leave the airport at 7:15 A.M. Even youngsters rely on predictability. They are flustered when their teacher is out sick, and they like knowing what will happen from day to day in their school and family environments.

The situation is no different when it comes to your elderly parent's dying. There is something reassuring about knowing one's wishes are clear and that they will be carried out. Such knowledge places the dying person in control of what will happen to him. Rather than feeling subject to the values and needs of others, he has the satisfaction of being the choice maker. It also gives your parent the peace of mind associated with relieving loved ones of the burden of making decisions he himself should make. As you will see later in the chapter, mechanisms exist for creating an *advance directive* to make your parent's wishes known, as well as for appointing someone to act as a stand-in if and when he becomes incapable of expressing them himself.

Benefits to the Adult Child

Knowing what your parent wants and does not want during the last days and hours of his life helps you because it defines and simplifies your role. In its essence, your task is to see that your parent's wishes are carried out. You are relieved of having the responsibility of making decisions for him without having any clear sense of what he would want. (Even when, as a health-care agent, an adult child must weigh facts or treatment alternatives of which a parent might not have been aware when he expressed his wishes, the agent is still basing a decision on a set of values implied in wishes previously expressed. More information on health-care agents is provided later in this chapter.)

When a parent makes his preferences known, the family benefits by working together. Cooperation ensures that his wishes are fulfilled, not those of some physician unknown to him or to you, or worse yet, some impersonal medical establishment more concerned with avoiding a lawsuit or making efficient use of institutional resources than with accommodating your parent's needs. Just as important, cooperation brings about a sense of family unity—crucial at such an emotional and stressful time.

Benefits to Health-Care Providers

A clear and specific statement of your parent's wishes provides important reassurance for the physicians and other professionals involved in his care. It is a relief for them, too, to know what your parent wants and does not want. Not only does this knowledge eliminate their need to make decisions more properly made by the dying person, it also eliminates the personal burdens of weighing often conflicting values. Such a set of conflicting values comes into play when it is necessary to choose between allowing a dignified death or sustaining life by mechanical, sometimes inhumane means. Knowing the patient's wishes and being reassured that the family supports them also relieves the physician of the potential burden of legal proceedings arising from misunderstandings or from the failure to do what the patient *might* have wanted had he been able to state a preference.

There is an important caveat, however. One's wishes *must* be stated in *very specific* terms. Later in the chapter, you will learn about *medical directives,* which allow you to become as specific as necessary to ensure that your parent's health-care providers receive the guidance they need.

Financial Considerations

Research on the cost savings associated with advance directives is inconclusive. It is well known that the majority of an elderly person's medical expenses are incurred during the last weeks of life. Consequently, some argue, with research findings to back their claims, that advance directives save money by eliminating expensive and point-less procedures. However, a number of recent studies have indicated that there are no significant cost savings associated with advance direc-tives. Thus, the matter remains unresolved. In the end, however, finan-cial considerations should *not* be the determining factor in making decisions about the end of life. Instead, considerations such as personal values, dignity, and mutual understanding among those involved in car-ing for the dying person should be paramount.

For all these reasons, end-of-life decisions are best made as early as possible—long before a crisis arises and circumstances make it impossi-ble for cool heads to weigh logically the options available and the costs and benefits of each.

PART TWO: The Right to Die Movement

The movement leading to the widespread acceptance of advance direc-tives can be compared to a river fed by many tributaries as it makes its way to the sea. A variety of factors converged in the 1970s, resulting in a powerful push that culminated in the Right to Die movement with which most people are familiar today.

TRIBUTARIES THAT LED TO ADVANCE DIRECTIVES

The Technological Tributary

The United States has long led the way in medical technology. Beginning before World War II and accelerating rapidly as a result of developments born of necessity during the war, technological advances made their way into the field of medicine. As a result, during the 1950s, 1960s, and 1970s, the face of medicine was transformed and the care of the dying underwent marked changes. As it became possible to keep bodies alive after the people they contained had long since died, ethical concerns often clashed with technological advances. Yet, few "front line" medical technologists asked the question, "Should we be sustaining life in this way?"

The Underground Tributary: Little-Publicized Horror Stories

For many families, extreme psychological trauma and financial disaster resulted from the use of the new technologies. Hundreds and thousands of ordinary people suffered tremendously. Dying became a sterile and high-tech process, control of which was taken over by medical professionals trained to preserve life at any cost. Among families and friends, stories were told of tragic endings, financial ruin, and protracted agony—all in the name of "good medicine."

Thousands of these stories never received a word of media publicity, because the media were less pervasive than they are today and because the people whose lives were affected were neither famous nor wealthy. However, having grown up during the early fifties, I can assure you that the stories were circulated among friends and family, and the anger conveyed during the telling of these stories was often quite intense.

The Legal Tributary

From both ends of the spectrum, the medical community became embroiled in lawsuits around the issues of death and dying. Some families, angered at the foolish and agonizing prolongation of life, sued because they felt the patient's right and their own had been infringed upon. But the opposite also occurred. Because in our culture death has always been the great enemy, fighting death has been the primary mission of the medical profession. Therefore, unfortunately, the physician's failure to take all possible means to preserve life, at times, resulted in lawsuits. Hospitals, too, were sued, sometimes successfully. (Even today, lawsuits are initiated far more frequently because of the "failure to treat" than because of unwanted treatment. It thus makes perfect sense for hospitals and physicians to err on the side of caution—which means providing unwanted treatment.)

Like the family horror stories mentioned above, tales of these lawsuits circulated among the medical community rapidly and with alarm. Physicians began to practice "defensive medicine," taking every possible step and using every possible test and technological tool to preserve life. Professionals and the institutions for which they worked sometimes became more concerned with preventing lawsuits than with treating the patient compassionately and sensibly.

During this period, the very meaning of *death* itself became a legal issue that continues to be debated today. In a simpler time, death was considered to have occurred when the heart stopped beating and could not be started again. But now that life can be sustained even after the heart stops, the word *death* has been redefined by ethicists, attorneys, and medical professionals to mean *brain death*—the irreversible loss of brain function, with the resultant inability of the brain to sustain basic life functions such as respiration and circulation. *Brain death* has, in turn, been refined. It can mean, first, the death of the upper portion of the brain, referred to as *neocortical death*, also known as *cerebral death*. (People in this state are not always considered "dead," because a portion of their brain continues to function. They exist in a sort of limbo technically referred to as a persistent vegetative state or coma.) *Brain death* can also mean death of the brain stem, the most elemental and primitive brain component.

As you can see, legalities and technicalities have long been debated and will likely continue to be. As the debate continues, patients and their families suffer. The Right to Die movement emerged as an attempt to add another voice to the scientific, legal, and ethical debate. It is the voice of common sense, urging an awareness that physicians treat *people*, and that while it might be very stimulating for professionals to engage in learned discussions of what it means to be dead, people view the subject of death quite differently! They need to be in a position to decide what will happen to them during their final days and hours of life.

The Media Tributary and *Causes Célèbres*

During the late 1960s and 1970s, as a result of all that had occurred during the previous quarter century, thoughtful people began writing and speaking intelligently about a new concept, that of *patients' rights*. The phrase carries many connotations, including the right to refuse unwanted treatment, specifically unwanted life-sustaining treatment. It also means the right to stay in control of what happens to one after admission to a hospital.

My own experience as a college professor who began his career in 1968 is typical. In the early 1970s, a colleague and I designed a course in interpersonal communication, which I still teach. Early in the evolution of the course, I created a segment called "Knowing and Enforcing Your Rights as a Consumer of Medical Services." That unit was the product of my own growing awareness of the importance of patients' rights. There are a large number of nursing majors at the college where I teach. One day in 1975, one of my students, a nursing major, showed me a handout about patients' rights that she had received in one of her nursing courses. Among the twenty questions on the handout were items having to do with the right to refuse unwanted treatment, but also the right to refuse to be examined by medical students, the right to be informed about the seriousness of one's condition, and the right to sue a doctor for withholding information or for imposing unwanted treatment. The quiz was an eye-opener for me at the time, and I now use it in updated form in my classes, where it continues to be revealing for many students. The very concept of *patients' rights* remains a novel idea for many people, even today. My experiences are typical of many people whose knowledge and sensitivity to these issues have grown dramatically over the last thirty years.

The growth and development of the Right to Die movement was fueled by a few dramatic and well-publicized cases that caught the attention of the media. The case of Karen Ann Quinlan is the best known. In 1976, this young woman suffered a respiratory arrest that left her comatose for many months. She was kept alive by an artificial respirator and a feeding tube. When it became clear there was no hope of recovery, her parents requested that she be disconnected from life support. To their shock and dismay, the physicians and hospital servicing Karen Ann refused to comply. It soon became clear to the Quinlans that control of their daughter's death had been wrested from them by the medical establishment. When they sued for the right to disconnect their daughter from life support, the case gained national publicity. (Although the Quinlans won the case, their daughter continued to live for another nine years, dying in 1985. The feeding tube that kept her alive during those years had not been the subject of the court case.)

The case of Karen Ann Quinlan placed a spotlight on the issue of the right to die. Other cases and related media events also caught the attention of the public.

- In 1967, the Euthanasia Society of America (known later by the name The Society for the Right to Die and currently by the name Choice in Dying) devised the original living will. Today, Choice in Dying, a national, nonprofit group, provides education, counseling services, an electronic registry system, and forms for advance directives tailored to the specific legal requirements of each of the fifty states. It has become a responsible and articulate voice in support of patients' rights.

- In 1978 English writer Derek Humphry published *Jean's Way*, an account of how he had helped his wife end her life when her spreading cancer made living unbearable. His subsequent publication of other books on the same topic, most notably *Final Exit* (1991), a highly successful publication, highlighted the issue of the right to die.

- Other organizations have been born. Derek Humphry's creation of the Hemlock Society in 1980 placed him in the position of the foremost authority on assisted suicide.

- In 1985, a then well-known media personality, Betty Rollin, wrote *Last Wish*, a book in which she detailed her actions in helping her aged and ailing mother end her own life.

- In 1990 the Supreme Court heard the case of Nancy Curzon, whose parents fought for four years to get their daughter disconnected from life support, including a ventilator and artificial hydration and nutrition. The Court's decision recognized that the right to refuse medical treatment is protected by the U.S. Constitution.

- In the late 1990s, Dr. Jack Kevorkian's invention of a "suicide machine" and his participation in scores of suicides earned him the label "Dr. Death." As of this writing, advocates of patients' rights and even of assisted suicide consider Kevorkian a loose cannon because of his maverick nature and his refusal to await changes in the law. Nevertheless, his controversial actions have certainly highlighted the fact that the terminally ill have options.

Other Tributaries

It would be possible to identify many other tributaries in this stream fueling the Right to Die movement. For our purposes, however, it is enough to recognize that the movement was the culmination of many individual cases, legal battles, and personal tragedies. The net result was the passage in 1991 of the Patient Self-Determination Act, a federal law that changed the face of care of the dying. As a result of the passage of this law, advance directives became the prime means by which the will of the patient can be stated and implemented.

PART THREE: The Patient Self-Determination Act and Advance Directives

Profound societal changes are often signaled by the occurrence of two concurrent events: the passage of legislation that articulates a change in values, and the emergence of mechanisms by which those changed values are implemented. The Patient Self-Determination Act, passed by Congress in 1991, reflects a major change in the way we think about health care and in the values that govern decisions about the care of the dying person.

The mechanisms collectively known as advance directives existed before the passage of the Patient Self-Determination Act. However, they are incorporated into the act, signaling widespread societal acceptance of the thinking upon which those mechanisms are based, and providing each individual with the means by which to stay in control of the medical procedures to be employed at the time of death.

THE PATIENT SELF-DETERMINATION ACT (1991)

The first federal law requiring that patients be informed of their right to express their wishes about how they choose to be cared for when dying was passed in 1991. The agencies that must inform patients of those rights are those agencies receiving federal funds—that means virtually every hospital in the United States, along with home-health agencies, skilled-nursing facilities, and other health related organizations. The law requires that patients be informed of their right to accept or refuse certain medical treatments in advance—that is, while competent—so that their wishes can be carried out even if they become incompetent due to illness or injury. Institutions must also provide information on their policies in regard to advance directives and any relevant state laws.

Further, upon routine admission to a hospital or any other health facility, every new patient must be asked whether he or she has prepared a living will and a durable power of attorney for health care. The patient's response must be included in her permanent medical record; the documents, if prepared, must also be placed in the patient's file. It is further stipulated that the patient's care is not to be altered by virtue of her having completed advance directives. This is to prevent discrimination for or against anyone, regardless whether or not the individual has executed advance directives.

Unfortunately, these mandates are not always followed. In the case of an emergency admission, for example, there is usually insufficient time—and too much anxiety—to ask about advance directives, and the questions never get asked. Practical advice from health-care professionals is simply this: Families should *not* wait to be asked whether the patient has prepared an advance directive. You should tell the nurse or physician upon arrival at the hospital. If you do not make a point of informing them, you risk having others assume decision-making power.

The law requires that all institutional personnel be given ongoing training about advance directives. Institutions must provide educational programs not only for employees but for the community at large so that all parties may become aware of patients' rights and relevant laws in their particular state.

ADVANCE DIRECTIVES

As noted, advance directives are at the heart of the Patient Self-Determination Act. Yet as this book goes to press, there is a growing recognition that serious problems exist with these supposedly airtight expressions of preferences. Let us look first at a more thorough definition of advance directives, and second at why they remain problematic.

Throughout the discussion you will find suggestions on how to make certain your parent's advance directives stick.

What are advance directives and how many kinds are there? The term *advance directive*, like all words in a living language, has evolved over time. Once roughly equivalent to the term *living will*, a document intended only to make clear an individual's wishes about end-of-life care, *advance directive* has come to mean any expression of preference about medical treatment. Formally defined, an advance directive is a legal document, signed and witnessed, spelling out preferences regarding medical care and appointing another person to make choices in accord with those preferences when the signer is no longer able to do so.

There are three kinds of advance directives that you will learn about here. In order to keep the functions of each kind clear and to draw distinctions between them, I will divide my discussion of each into three parts: *What It Does, Requirements*, and *Additional Facts*. Please note that I am not a legal authority on the subject of advance directives. While the discussion that follows is accurate and complete to the best of my knowledge, as of the date of this book, the law is always in flux and by the time you are reading this it may have changed. Furthermore, the specific requirements and contingencies for advance directives differ slightly from state to state. If there is any doubt whatever in your mind about the correct preparation of a living will or any other advance directive, consult your local hospital administration, county medical society, or Area Agency on Aging. National organizations can also provide up-to-date requirements. One is Choice in Dying, mentioned previously (contact them at 1-800-989-WILL). Perhaps best of all, speak with an attorney who specializes in elderlaw.

The Living Will (or Advance Health-Care Declaration)

What It Does In a living will, an individual makes known his or her preferences regarding the use of extraordinary measures to prolong life in the event the individual becomes unable to make or to communicate decisions due to permanent unconsciousness. For example, does he wish to be placed on a respirator in the event he can no longer breathe independently? Does he wish to be resuscitated if his heart stops and he would not return to life without resuscitation? If he were to go into a coma, would he want artificial hydration and nutrition?

Requirements To be binding, a living will must meet two criteria. First, the person must sign willingly—that is, freely, without coercion, intimidation, or interference of any kind in her decision-making. She must also be mentally competent at the time of preparation of the document—free of any condition, psychological or physical, that might affect her ability to understand the full implications of what she is doing and to choose freely. Put more precisely, a person completing a living will must act with *informed consent*—that is, with an understanding of the meaning of her decisions. *Informed consent* is a legal term whose meaning includes, but goes beyond, freedom of action and mental competence. To act with informed consent, the patient must have a good grasp of all the medical options open to her, including the benefits and risks of each, as well as any other matters relevant to an intelligent decision. Given the difficulty of understanding some medical concepts and the complexity of choosing among treatment alternatives, it is hardly surprising that some living wills are thrown out on the basis that the preparer did not act with a full understanding of the options open to her and of the potential risks and benefits of each.

Second, the document must be signed, dated, and witnessed (states vary in the number of witnesses required) by people who are not blood relatives, family members, or beneficiaries of property. In some states (a *very* small number), the living will must be notarized.

Additional Facts Before a living will is signed, the document and its meaning should be thoroughly discussed with *all* people involved in caring for the senior. This includes the family (the term is used loosely here to include spouse or domestic partner, offspring, siblings, and all other interested parties), health-care providers, and the senior's attorney.

Doing this reduces the likelihood of family conflicts over what should be done for the dying person. As noted previously, if a health-care provider becomes aware of family disagreement, it is extremely likely he or she will choose to err on the side of caution and to keep a patient alive, even against her will, in order to ward off litigation. (The odds of this happening are nearly 100 percent, because even one surviving family member can initiate a suit, regardless of the number of family members who agreed with the decision to withhold treatment.)

Once the document is signed, multiple copies should be made. The person signing the document should ensure that everyone involved in his care receives a copy of the document and that it be placed in his medical records. That includes the senior's primary care physician (if there is one) and any other physicians treating him. All such directives should be placed in the patient's file. In the unlikely event that an advance directive is mislaid or lost from the patient's file, it is a good idea to have extra copies on hand so that one may be supplied, if requested. (Note that copies of advance directives are adequate; it is not necessary to provide physicians or others with the original.)

A copy of the living will should always be placed in a prominent (or at least strategic) place at home, in the event of an in-home emergency requiring a call to the Emergency Medical Service. By law, EMS personnel *must* make every effort to save the life of an individual for whom they are called. Only clear and unmistakable directions to the contrary can justify their taking no action to preserve life. Even then, the wishes of the dying person *may* be disregarded.

Steps are being taken in individual states to clarify the ambiguous position in which EMS personnel find themselves. In Connecticut, for example, EMS personnel *must* resuscitate a patient unless he or she is wearing a special orange bracelet (called a DNR bracelet, for "Do Not Resuscitate"). In nursing homes and hospitals, and (rarely) in homes, a properly completed DNR form may suffice. Such forms are issued by physicians.

While it may seem extreme, some people recommend that elderly persons carry a copy of their living wills with them at all times. I know of one case in which an elderly woman was kept alive for several months by techniques that she had clearly stated in her living will she did not want used. The problem was that she had had a stroke while visiting friends in a nearby state, and no one knew her wishes. She was resuscitated, attached to machines, and lingered for almost half a year before dying.

A living will should be reviewed and updated from time to time—some say yearly. I recommend that the document be reviewed and updated *at least* yearly, depending on a number of variables, including your parent's age and state of health, but that the precise interval should be flexible and determined by significant events. For example, the document should be updated whenever your parent changes his address and when new medical or technological developments occur that may affect the medical care he receives. Changes in your parent's wishes regarding life support measures should also trigger updating the living will, as should changes in his condition.

What should be done when changes are needed in a living will or other advance directive? According to the legal experts I consulted, only a change of address is regarded as a nonsubstantive change. When an address change is made, simply strike out the old address and write the new one in its place. Photocopy the document and send copies (again) to all interested parties, with a cover letter noting the reason for the revision and asking that the old living will be removed from the patient's file and replaced by the new one.

All other changes are substantive. When substantive changes are made, the entire document must be redone, and the same procedures followed as when it was drawn up originally. That is, the document must be signed, witnessed, copied, distributed, placed in your parent's medical records, and kept on hand at home. Extra copies should be made.

It is always possible to revoke a living will. A person who has signed one always has the option of changing her mind, assuming, of course, that she is conscious and able to do so.

The Health-Care Agent (or Health-Care Proxy)

What It Does A health-care agent is often appointed at the same time that the living will is signed. In some states, the two documents are "bundled" so that both are completed essentially simultaneously. By appointing a health-care agent, the elderly person agrees that that agent will serve as a stand-in for him, exclusively for the purpose of conveying the senior's wishes regarding life support only. The health-care agent does not make any other treatment decisions or become involved in any other health-care decision making. He or she is an *agent* whose function it is to convey the wishes of the senior on one topic and one topic alone: life support. The health-care agent document authorizes the agent to act to ensure that the senior's wishes are fulfilled. That may mean advocating with physicians and others, and even going to court or taking other extraordinary measures.

Requirements These are the same as for a living will. The power to act as a health-care agent must be given freely by a person who is competent at the time the agent is named. The senior must act with informed consent.

Additional Facts Fulfilling the role of a health-care agent is sometimes quite difficult. It requires not only a full understanding of the wishes of the senior, but the ability to keep clearly in mind the distinctions between the senior's wishes and the agent's. Once again, the agent's role is to act as a stand-in for the senior. It is the elderly person's wishes and values, *not those of the agent*, that must be the determining factors in decision making. If the agent is too emotionally involved with the dying person, he or she may not be able to make decisions based on the patient's wishes and needs. Careful selection of the agent is, therefore, very important.

Furthermore, a health-care agent may well become involved in making difficult choices about fairly technical matters. The agent must be able to understand medical terminology and procedures. The agent must be willing to question a physician, to request (perhaps even demand) clarification of procedures that have been explained inadequately, and once armed with a full understanding of the options, to argue a case in support of the senior's desires. For that reason, very careful thought should be given to whom a senior chooses as an agent, otherwise an uncaring medical professional or establishment may easily find justification for disregarding the wishes of the dying person. I know of health-care agents who have encountered uncooperative and unresponsive hospital physicians, and who have had to go to the hospital's chief of medicine, risk manager, attorney, and administration to see that a patient's will has been respected. Clearly this is not a job for the faint-hearted or the inarticulate. (Once again, there is no substitute for sound, open communication among all those involved in the dying person's care.)

On occasion, the competency (the legal "ability" of a person to make decisions or to execute any legal document, including an advance directive—be it a living will, the appointment of a health-care agent, or any other directive) is questioned. For example, suppose a person's capacity to understand complex matters or to make sound judgments is impaired due to age or illness, or as a result of a stroke or an accident. Under such circumstances, the individual's competence would necessarily be called into question. If that individual has not appointed someone as a stand-in to handle financial or personal matters prior to becoming incompetent, the court (usually a probate court) will appoint an individual to serve as a conservator to perform the tasks of caring for the person's financial affairs and/or personal needs. By appointing a conservator of any kind, the court is acting as a stand-in for the incompetent person.

Conservators are voluntary when they are chosen by the senior or appointed with her consent. They are involuntary when appointed over the objections of the senior. For example, if a person does not believe he is incompetent, but he is, the court will appoint a conservator provided it has been given adequate evidence of the individual's incompetence.

There are different types of conservators. A *conservator of the estate* has authority over property only. For example, if a house must be sold or other assets liquidated (to pay for medical care or for other reasons), the conservator of the estate will do that. A *conservator of the person* has authority over personal matters only, such as questions of residency (does the impaired person require long-term care?) and medical decisions.

Once again, I recommend you contact an attorney experienced in elderlaw if matters of competency, guardianship, or conservatorship arise. Most laypeople (I include myself among them) lack the expertise to behave knowledgeably in such matters.

Durable Power of Attorney for Health Care

What It Does There is a difference, often misunderstood, between giving someone general power of attorney and giving them power of attorney for health care. The former means giving them the power to act as one's stand-in (one's "attorney-in-fact") in all legal matters. For example, if a person is not able to attend a real-estate closing (perhaps due to illness) at which a piece of property will be sold, that person may appoint someone to act in his or her stead at the proceeding. The stand-in is authorized to do all necessary things to successfully complete the sale. A person with general power of attorney can do many other things as well, including paying bills, opening or closing bank accounts, and selling stocks.

A person given power of attorney for health care has more limited powers. This designation refers to a person who is appointed by another to serve as a stand-in for the elderly person to make general health-care decisions about all aspects of medical care *except life support.* In other words, if a senior is not dying but is nonetheless incapable of making decisions about medical procedures such as those designed to maintain her comfort (for example, a surgical procedure), the person with the power of attorney for health care does this.

The word *durable* in this context means only that the appointment of the other party survives the incompetence of the person giving the power. In other words, if your parent gives you power of attorney for health care and later becomes incompetent, that designation survives her incompetence.

Requirements To give someone power of attorney, the grantor must be competent at the time the power of attorney is given and must act with informed consent. Unlike other advance directives, the durable power of attorney for health care must be notarized in order to be legal and binding.

Additional Facts The same person may be appointed as the health-care agent and be given the durable power of attorney for health care. As with all important documents, it is advisable that this document be prepared with the help of an attorney.

Medical Directives

Recently, as a result of a number of court cases initiated when a dying person's wishes were disregarded, a new and highly desirable practice has arisen. The practice has grown out of the fact that living wills are often too general to provide adequate guidance for the physician and others charged with the patient's care (including the health-care agent). For example, one living will form I have seen provides only a general statement of preference that "my attending physician withhold or withdraw treatment that merely prolongs my dying." Another lists only three life-support measures to be avoided: CPR (cardiopulmonary resuscitation), artificial respiration, and artificial means of providing nutrition and hydration. According to the experts, the problem with these forms is that they lack specifics. A carefully prepared living will should list any and all possible life-support means that might be employed, as well as any variations on the basic tools available. Some living will forms allow for the preparer to write in specific techniques and then to specify whether or not she wants them provided. These statements are called *medical directives*.

It is my personal recommendation that a living will also include a statement in which the senior addresses means of life support of which he is unaware or which have not been developed at the time the document is executed but which he rejects nonetheless. Such a statement might read as follows:

> I am aware that additional life-support measures may exist of which I am unaware at the present time, or may not exist on the date of the signing of this document but may exist when I am dying. Nevertheless, my intent is to avoid all life-support mechanisms of any kind that merely prolong my dying, whether they exist now or come into existence in the future. I hereby direct that no techniques of any sort whatsoever be used to prolong my dying by any means.

Such a statement can hardly be mistaken as not capturing the will of the preparer to avoid any and all measures that merely prolong dying.

THE PROBLEMS WITH ADVANCE DIRECTIVES

Despite the apparent effectiveness of advance directives, they are not the foolproof and readily implemented tools they appear to be. It is possible to identify three basic problems with them.

First, too small a percentage of seniors have advance directives. According to one team of researchers who published their findings in a professional journal in 1996, only 31.8 percent of people sampled reported having a living will, and only 40.3 percent reported having appointed a durable power of attorney for health care.

Second, a large percentage of those who do have advance directives have made errors in preparation, including the following:

- insufficiently specific information (see above section on medical directives);

- incorrect witnesses (recall that a living will cannot be witnessed by a family member or anyone else with a stake in the estate of the senior);

- failure to establish informed consent—that is, to reveal that the senior has a grasp of the various options open to him and the risks and benefits of each, and that a reasonable amount of time was spent in making the decisions stated in the living will;

- appointment of a health-care agent who lacks the ability to fulfill the requirements of the role (some experts also recommend the appointment of a back-up agent, equally qualified, in case the senior's first choice is unavailable at the time of death); and

- failure to prepare documents in compliance with your state's laws.

Third, many seniors do not follow adequate notification procedures. As noted, a living will should not be a family secret! Unless all parties involved in the senior's care are notified, including the local hospital and other offices and agencies, it is likely your parent's wishes will *not* be followed.

As a result of these or other potential flaws, your parent's advance directives may well be ignored by his physicians. It is up to you to see that they are not.

PART FOUR: Communicating about Death and End-of-life Decisions

Despite the many obvious advantages of talking about end-of-life decisions, and despite the need for clear and unmistakable statements of preferences, many families avoid discussions of end-of-life matters. There are reasons for this, and they are neither beyond understanding nor beyond overcoming. In this section of the chapter, you will find suggestions for recognizing, understanding, and overcoming resistance to talking about death and dying.

RECOGNIZING RESISTANCE

How can you recognize resistance—either your own or that of your elderly parent—to talking about end-of-life decisions? There are several signs. The first is *postponing*. Comments such as, "This is not the time" and "We'll talk about it later" are hallmarks.

I know of families in which planned discussions took many months to schedule and complete because of repeated postponements. In these cases, at one time or another, almost everyone involved objected to the timing of the discussions that had been planned:

- The elderly parent objected, saying she was "too upset right now to talk about it."

- A son objected because it was "too close to the holidays."

- A daughter objected because her own child had just gotten engaged and she did not want to get upset during that happy time.

- Another adult child's busy work schedule made meeting "impossible for now."

An even more obvious sign of resistance is *avoiding* the subject outright. This occurs when someone, not necessarily the elderly parent, changes the subject or steers the conversation in a different direction every time the topic comes up. Avoidance can also take the form of saying all the right things, but just not getting around to doing what needs to be done. For reasons that are never quite clear, no actual discussion ever takes place and the issues are never resolved.

In one case known to me personally, when the family pressed a senior to discuss advance directives, she resorted to manipulation, thereby effectively enforcing her desire that no discussion take place. The manipulation took the form of guilt induction. She said her family wished her dead, or else they would not insist in bringing up the topic. When that failed to work, she resorted to intimidation: If they insisted on talking about it, she said, she would have no more to do with them.

In all such cases, the senior is avoiding the topic. But there are other, less obvious ways to resist talking about advance directives. One is by *forgetting*. Sometimes a family meeting is planned and one of more key persons "forgets" to attend. Other times, important documents such as living will forms are misplaced.

Regardless of the form of resistance, you may be certain that when a subject is resisted, there are reasons.

UNDERSTANDING RESISTANCE

Resistance to talking about end-of-life decisions is a bit like resistance to talking about life insurance. None of us wants to face the fact that we will die and that the people we love will die. Death is the great unknown. We may fear death itself or the uncertainty of what comes after death. To avoid having to confront our fears, it is convenient to pretend that death will not visit us. Both elderly parents and their adult children are equally as likely to resist talking about death for this reason.

Sometimes, the resistance originates with the senior. Elderly parents may not want to face the fact that they will die before long. Or, they may be reluctant to burden their children with the weighty issues and serious decisions that need to be made in advance of their death. Rather than addressing the issues and relieving their own minds (as well as those of their adult children), seniors may hesitate to bring up the subject or may resist talking about it altogether.

Children may hesitate to bring up the matter not only because they do not want to face the fact that their parent is going to die, but because they fear their motives might be misinterpreted. They fear being seen as uncaring or as wanting to be rid of the elderly family member. They worry that they may be seen as greedily looking forward to their inheritance if there is one.

Latent sibling conflicts due to unexpressed anger over uneven distribution of caregiving responsibilities, past family favoritism, or other matters may inhibit discussion. Adult children may fear that barely contained disagreements might erupt. There may be status conflicts over who should have the biggest "say" in what will and will not occur. In such cases, a cold distance may be maintained in which no real discussion can take place.

There may also be *practical* reasons why a discussion of end-of-life decisions is avoided. The medical issues are daunting and complex. Many people can speak in general terms but lack the knowledge to speak in specifics. Involving a medical doctor, although desirable, poses its own problems. First of all, a connection is necessary with a caring and humane physician with a genuine interest in the senior and her family. Yet even if that exists, a discussion may be difficult due to constraints on the doctor's time and his or her own discomfort with the topic of death (physicians may be just as uncomfortable talking about it as the rest of us).

OVERCOMING RESISTANCE

Whatever form the resistance takes, everyone involved can benefit from overcoming it. Here are several ways to do that.

First, accept and validate the discomfort—yours, your parent's, or anyone else's.

This involves avoiding the tendency to judge yourself or others by saying things such as "I (or you, or we) *should not* be feeling this way!" and "We're all adults now, and these things need to be talked about—we have just got to stop acting like babies." Such remarks, while seeming to provide an impetus to overcoming resistance, may actually deepen it. The reason is that people feel one way or another (in this case, they may be reluctant to talk about the death of a loved one) whether they *want* to or not, whether they *should* or not. Feelings simply are.

While it is true that critical remarks such as the one just presented may sometimes overcome the resistance, they typically do so at the expense of inducing guilt, shame, and other undesirable feelings. The need to defend one's reactions, or at the least to save face, may make surrendering or overcoming the feelings all the more difficult.

It is far better to acknowledge the feelings of resistance and validate them. For example, remarks such as the following can be very constructive: "We all feel awful talking about this—I know I do—but there's no avoiding it. We have got to do it!" Such a comment is reassuring and nonjudgmental. It gives everyone "permission" to feel as they do and indicates that their feelings are valid and understandable. There is no stifling of feelings, no shaming or blaming. It is a simple acknowledgment of the fact that everyone involved is entitled to their feelings, but that at the same time, action is necessary.

In the course of acknowledging and validating resistance, pose basic questions or make a case in favor of taking action.

By posing a question or making a case in favor of taking action, you carry the discussion forward. Here are a few approaches you might take:

Ask your parent, "Are you afraid of death or of dying?" If he fears death itself, explore his fear. It may be desirable to contact a member of the clergy to provide the reassurance he needs. If it is the process of dying he fears, find out what about it frightens him. Is it prolonged suffering? Being a burden? Spending the resources and savings he has accumulated? The humiliation of being "hooked up" to wires and machines? Alone or with the help of a health-care professional, answer whatever questions you can. Use information as well as the power of logic to try to dispel the fears.

Explain the desirability of making decisions early. Talk about advance directives. Explain their purpose and how they work. Show your parent the actual documents and explain what would be involved in completing them. Discuss the advantages of being in control of the dying process. You may find your parent needs time to accept the idea. Allow that time! Use these quiet moments together to ascertain her real wishes. Avoid rushing because of your own discomfort. Face the moment with as much equanimity and love as you can muster.

For these strategies to be successful and reassuring, careful planning and thorough preparation are essential. If you need to educate yourself, read books and articles. Attend hospital workshops. Contact organizations such as Choice in Dying. Find a compassionate pastor, physician, nurse, or hospital social worker who will take the time to educate you and answer your questions.

The following additional suggestions can help family members overcome their resistance to talking about end-of-life decisions.

Remind family members that taking action is in your parent's best interest. Few people are comfortable with the prospect of losing a parent. Love and gratitude for all our parents have done, as well as many other emotions—not always positive—course through us when we think about losing them forever. Yet these very emotions can be an impetus to taking action. After all, it is out of love and respect for your parent that you want to see her maintain control of her passing. As I noted earlier, allowing your parent to stay in control of the final days and hours of her life is the very last gift you can give her.

Absolve them of guilty feelings. Planning for a parent's death does not suggest coldness or indifference. Nor does it grow out of a desire to be rid of the parent. On the contrary, it suggests thoughtful and compassionate concern. If we cannot be rational, deliberate, and humane when we most need to be, then how can we take pride in our humanity?

Even if it is not essential, it may be desirable to see a professional—medical or nonmedical—just to get the discussion off the ground.

Mental health professionals with an interest in eldercare and issues such as death and dying can facilitate discussion, provide reassurance, and educate family members. Their services are well worth the expense.

Consider that a formal discussion may be less desirable than a series of brief, informal, but pointed ones.

My own mother, who is 89 years old as I write these words, has made her wishes known to me in a series of brief, seemingly "off the cuff" discussions we have had during outings and conversations about friends and neighbors. "Not me!" she will say after discussing a friend who had been put on life support. "I'm 89," she will say, "and I'm not going to live forever, you know! I don't want to be a vegetable."

Summary

Technology has made it possible to keep people "alive" for almost indefinite periods through the use of machines designed to provide respiration, hydration, and nutrition. Given the existence of that technology and of compelling professional and practical reasons why physicians want to preserve life (or some vestige of it) at all costs, it is easy to lose control of one's parent's dying. Nevertheless, being in control is important—not only to the dying person but to the family.

This chapter traced the origins of the Right to Die movement, a now powerful societal force that, like a river, has been fed by many tributaries as it has grown. The passage of the Patient Self-Determination Act in 1991 was a major milestone in the journey toward an enlightened attitude about dying. At its heart are advance directives: the living will, the health-care agent, and the durable power of attorney for health care. Each of these serves a vital purpose, yet none is flawless. Too often, advance directives are ignored. By discussing them with all interested parties, preparing each one according to the letter of the law, and notifying all appropriate individuals and agencies of their existence, you can make advance directives stick. Finally, the topic of resistance to talking about death and advance directives was addressed.

In the next chapter we will turn to what to expect and what to do after a parent dies.

CHAPTER 8

When a Parent Is Gone

The responsibilities of caring for an elderly parent may end when he or she dies, but the process of saying good-bye has only begun. This chapter is devoted to helping you understand what happens after a loss, both to an individual and to the family as a whole. In the first part of the chapter, you will learn about the nature of grief and about the four critically important functions it serves. You will learn about normal and abnormal grieving and how to distinguish between the two. You will also become familiar with the warning signs that suggest grieving is not accomplishing its goals. Throughout the chapter, you will read about the variables that affect grieving and you will learn to recognize the need for help. You will see how a therapist can assist both individuals and families with the grieving process.

In the second part of the chapter, the focus is on you as an individual. You will learn what you are likely to experience after a death. Most people feel sadness, of course, but you may also experience confusion, disbelief, anger, relief, guilt, and a host of other feelings. You may have flashbacks; you may even forget your parent is dead. You will find suggestions on how to manage all these grief reactions.

Death affects both the individual and the family, and the impact on each must be attended to. In the third part of the chapter, you will read about the family issues that need to be addressed after the death of a parent. You will find answers to questions such as these: How does a family change after a parent's death? What variables affect a family's response to a death? How can you know whether a family is having trouble handling a loss? What can go wrong, even among future generations of a family, when grieving is not successful?

PART ONE: Grieving, Mourning, and Bereavement

Throughout the chapter, I use the terms *bereavement, grieving,* and *mourning* interchangeably to mean "the normal process by which human beings come to terms with the loss of a loved one." Let us look at the key elements in this brief definition.

A NORMAL EXPERIENCE

Mourning is universal. In all cultures and at all times, humans have mourned the loss of loved ones. Rituals may vary and the manner of expressing grief may vary, but there are always rituals, and grief is always expressed.

While mourning is normal, it is also an unfamiliar experience. Fortunately, for most people, significant losses (such as the death of a parent) occur infrequently, and mourning is outside the ordinary course of events. As a result, for many people, grief is a frightening and almost overwhelming experience, especially at first and especially when the person who dies is a parent. Not only is mourning frightening to experience, it can also be frightening to witness.

Mr. J, 31 years old, came to me some weeks after his mother's death. Hers was the first significant death to touch him. He was a sophisticated and successful young man who was nonetheless having a very difficult time coming to terms with his loss. Despite his best efforts and the encouragement of family and friends, he was still crying almost every morning as the reality of the loss hit with the dawning of consciousness. He was experiencing nightmares, panic attacks, and a host of bodily symptoms, from diarrhea to chest pains, for which every physician consulted said there was no organic basis. "Am I going nuts?" he asked me. "Will I lose it? I feel like I'm going to break!"

Mr. J's experience *was* extreme. However, it was clearly not outside the normal order of things. Because he had been spared significant losses before his mother's death, mourning was a totally novel and terrifying experience for him. The symptoms of grieving triggered intense anxiety, and the anxiety compounded the symptoms. A vicious cycle developed, and Mr. J was almost out of his mind with worry. Reassurance that his symptoms were normal and would eventually remit of their own accord was met with skepticism at first. In time, though, and with the help of supportive therapy and a brief course of medication, that is exactly what occurred. What Mr. J needed most was information and reassurance.

Mourning is normal for children as well as for adults. Mrs. S brought Jeffrey, her 11-year-old son, to see me because at his grandfather's wake a few days earlier, Jeffrey had become angry with Mrs. S and with other relatives who were crying. He was disruptive and finally ran out of the funeral parlor and onto the street. Jeffrey's father pursued him, and the two struggled. Jeffrey eventually had to be taken home and given a mild sedative to calm him down.

Jeffrey's anger, as well as his running away, were his ways of coping with the terror he felt when he saw those he loved breaking down. Most of us—adults and children alike—can see a child's tears and accept them without too much personal distress because it is not unusual to see a child cry. However, seeing an adult cry or lose emotional control is far more unsettling. Therefore, children, especially, are very likely to feel uncomfortable in the presence of adults who are grieving. Jeffrey's carrying on was his attempt to silence the tears and to escape an extremely painful situation. In therapy, he was able to express some of this; as a result, he was visibly relieved.

THE PROCESS OF MOURNING

Mourning is a process that unfolds over time. It might even be called a *predictable* process, although I mean no disrespect by that term. (The process of childbirth is predictable, too, but hardly run-of-the-mill or without significance.) While there are many theories about mourning, the most well-accepted view is that successful grieving enables us to go on with life after a loss by allowing us to accomplish four crucial tasks, each of which can be considered a stage in the mourning process. By the time grieving is over, a mourner has passed through each of these stages. While it is usually true that the tasks of mourning are completed more or less in sequence, grieving is not a neat, orderly process. Mourning has no correct timetable, no schedule to keep or mileposts that must be reached by a certain time. Moreover, all four stages may overlap each other; we sometimes loop back and return to an earlier stage.

Another important point: because mourning is a process that comes to an end, it is possible for us to know when it is over. In healthy and normal mourning, there is resolution, a feeling of closure. Mourning has been compared to the healing of a psychic wound. When we fall and scrape a knee, the resulting wound requires healing. When properly attended to, a scab forms and we know the wound has begun to heal. In time, the healing is complete. As with physical wounds, there may be long-term scarring. Although we may never be quite the same, we can go on. Later in the chapter, you will learn about the signs that mourning has not been successful, that no resolution has occurred. In such cases, it is highly desirable to seek professional help.

The process of mourning serves four main functions. It allows us to accept the reality of the loss, to work through the pain and grief, to adjust to an environment from which the deceased is missing, and to relocate the deceased person emotionally and move on with life. These functions are explained more fully below.

To Accept the Reality of the Loss

This is the most basic task of all mourning. Whatever we may believe about an afterlife, death is final. Once dead, a parent is lost to us forever. As one person told me not long ago, "My father had an infectious laugh. *No one* I know can bring a smile to my lips the way he did." A long, melancholy silence followed as the finality of this loss embedded itself in the psyche of my client.

To Work through the Pain and the Grief

Talking about your deceased parent with others—sharing stories, memories, and feelings—is a way of working through your pain. Similarly, the public display of grief has a beneficial effect, because shared grief somehow facilitates healing. Stoically holding the tears inside robs the mourner of the support of others and the knowledge that others have experienced and validated the mourner's grief.

Funerals and memorial services certainly help us, both to accept the reality of our loss and to work through the pain and loss. Public, shared, or social grief is common at a funeral or memorial service. Such communal grieving affords everyone a chance to turn to, lean on, and garner support from others at a time of intense sorrow and vulnerability.

To Adjust to an Environment from Which the Deceased Is Missing

When someone dies, many things change. It takes time to adjust to these changes. Many surviving spouses have told me about the silence in their homes. They miss the footsteps, the familiar voice. Others have told me they miss seeing the deceased person in his usual places in the home—in his chair, at his desk. In addition, survivors may have to take on new roles. One woman had relied on her husband for handling the family finances. She missed him as a companion, she told me, but—she was almost embarrassed as she said what followed—she was also saddened by the fact that she must now take on the dreaded task of managing finances.

To Relocate the Deceased Person Emotionally and Move on with Life

In the end, the ultimate task of mourning is to make it possible for survivors to disengage from the person. Of course, you will remain aware of your parent's impact on your life and the lives of those around you. In a sense, you must affirm the fact of her existence while accepting her death. One client whose father had died several months earlier put it very well: "Loving my boyfriend doesn't mean I love my father any less. I have to go on. But Dad will always be a part of me."

AN INDIVIDUAL PROCESS

While there is a certain predictability to mourning, everyone grieves at their own pace and in their own way. There is no timetable—people cannot be rushed through the grieving process. Each person's way of grieving is unique, and many variables can impact the manner in which one grieves.

The experience of the W family illustrates how people grieve differently. The W family consisted of middle-aged parents and two daughters who were single. Mrs. W had a stormy relationship with her mother, who was a selfish, manipulative, and at times even cruel woman. Her feelings for her mother were very mixed. Mr. W had never been close to his mother-in-law, and he resented her when she upset his wife. The children hardly knew their grandmother, since she was anything but a warm and affectionate figure.

After the death of Mrs. W's mother, the family came to see me for several reasons, of which two were predominant. First, because she had been unable to acknowledge her negative feelings toward her mother, Mrs. W was having a hard time coming to terms with her mother's death. Second, Mrs. W was upset with her husband and children for not caring very much about her mother's passing. "They're so cold about it," she cried. "It's like they don't care at all."

Husband and children felt bad about Mrs. W's pain and did their best to offer her support, but they were being quite honest in saying that her mother's death had little effect on them. "My mother-in-law managed to reduce my wife to tears and rage more times than I can count," said Mr. W. He paused a moment, clearly struggling with mixed feelings. "I'm sorry, but I can't feel too bad that she's gone. Frankly, it's a relief to know she won't be around to screw things up any more."

The children were equally candid. "I lived on the opposite coast for four years," said one daughter. "Not once in those years did I get a call or a card from my grandmother. And now I'm supposed to be sad?" Her pained face set, she added, "If anything, I'm *angry* with her, not sad!" The younger child's comments were similar in tone. "Sure, I'll miss knowing she's there, I guess," she observed. "But I can't say she made much of a difference in my life. Most of what I remember is Mom being upset whenever she spoke with Grandma."

Each of these four people had a different relationship with Mrs. W's mother. It would be unrealistic to expect that they would all grieve the same way, to the same degree, and for the same length of time. In treatment, it became clear that Mrs. W's ambivalence caused her to wish for more feeling from her family. If they were sadder, she reasoned (without being aware of it), perhaps her attempts to idealize her mother would have been successful. In fact, their honesty was more useful to her. As our work progressed, she began to acknowledge her own negative feelings. In the end, she left treatment with an acceptance of her family's reactions to her mother's death. Just as important, her own grieving came to a satisfactory end as she arrived at a realistic picture of her mother as a troubled woman—"She was neither saint nor sinner," she said, "but she was a lot less than I wish she had been."

As the W family's experience indicates, many variables have an impact on how we grieve, among them the nature of the relationship between the deceased and the survivor, the degree of closeness between them, and the degree of interdependence between the parent and the survivor. You will read more about these and other variables later.

IMPORTANT AND FUNCTIONAL

Like most other important activities that are the focus of rituals in human communities around the globe, mourning serves many valuable purposes. Viewed positively, mourning enables us to go forward with our lives after we have sustained a blow. It is healing, as noted earlier. It is purging, allowing us to rid ourselves of the physical and emotional afterbirth that lingers after a deep attachment has been rent. Bereavement provides a sense of closure, a "good-bye" that—painful as it is—brings a note of finality to something that simply is over and will never be known or experienced again in quite the same way.

But grieving can also be looked at from the perspective of what happens when we do *not* grieve. The failure to grieve affects not only us but others in our lives. It can also affect future generations.

Individual Consequences of the Failure to Grieve

The failure to grieve almost always results in problems of one kind or another. While these problems may vary widely, depending on the age and life circumstances of the person involved, they can nevertheless be traced back to the same cause. In extreme cases, these problems can lead to psychiatric symptoms.

For example, Mr. M was told by more than one person that he had never really gotten over the death of his father, which had occurred two years prior to my meeting him. This was confusing, he told me, because he did not *feel* depressed (nor did he appear to be). However, when I took a detailed history and spoke with family members, I learned that his personality had changed. A once pleasant and caring person, Mr. M had become cynical, cold, and argumentative. These changes were symptoms of masked depression. As a consequence of these personality changes, Mr. M began to experience serious job problems that almost resulted in his being fired. In treatment, the underlying depression emerged and became so serious that it was life threatening. After a period of hospitalization and intense therapy, Mr. M realized that he had not grieved his father's death. He then began the long process of coming to terms with his loss. In the end, Mr. M was profoundly grateful for the experience. "My life had become a quiet kind of hell," he reported. "Now I feel like I've found myself again."

In another instance, Johnny G was an earnest and hard-working 27-year-old whose life changed dramatically when his father succumbed to cancer after a long illness. This usually stable fellow began drinking. Within months he began to experience job problems. After a weekend of his drinking, punctuated by a one-night stand with a former girl-friend, his wife threatened to leave. His entire life was unraveling. By the time he came for help, he had run from his grief as far and as fast as he could. It took many months of both individual and joint therapy for Johnny G to put his life back together.

Among teens, delinquency, sexual promiscuity, truancy, and poor school performance are frequent warning signs of the failure to grieve. Take the case of Meryl H, a well-behaved and conscientious high school student from an upper middle class family. Her teachers loved her. Her family could not have been more proud or supportive. Everyone agreed she had with a bright future. However, when her mother died unexpectedly, Meryl was traumatized. Although she appeared to handle the loss in stride, she soon began to spiral downward. She became swept up in the wrong circle of friends. Within several months she was arrested for shop-lifting. During court-mandated treatment, Meryl began to experience the full impact of her loss. A long and painful healing process began.

Each of these individuals suffered the consequences of the failure to grieve. Only when they accepted that fact and began working through their losses were they able to recognize their behavior as aberrant.

Effects on Others

As each of the preceding examples shows, the failure to grieve affects not only oneself but others as well. Relationships suffer as a result of misdirected anger and resentment, emotional withdrawal from the family, remoteness, and the lack of sex in intimate relationships. All these are usually quite obvious signs of the failure to grieve. Sometimes, however, the effects are less apparent although no less harmful.

For example, Mr. Y was the happily married father of a bright 18-year-old girl. His hitherto normal attachment to his daughter became more intense after a series of losses—including close friends and both his parents—over the space of just a few years. The result was that he became both overprotective and inappropriately involved in his daughter's everyday life. Her first year of college was complicated tremendously by Mr. Y's overreaction to every one of the normal stresses and upsets that college freshmen typically experience. (The child was oblivious to the fact that her father was overinvolved; all she knew was that she was under stress and Dad seemed to be willing to help. In her misfortune, she accepted his "help.") Mr. Y visited the campus too often. He made a nuisance of himself with his daughter's roommate, her dorm residential advisor, her teachers, and even the college administration. This inappropriate level of involvement was a clear sign of his overly intense attachment. In therapy he learned that he was overreacting to the symbolic loss of his daughter that he experienced when she went off to college. When he realized this and saw its connection to his grief over his many losses, he was able to direct his energies toward resolving his own intense sadness while allowing his daughter to manage her own life as a student and a young woman.

Effects on Future Generations

Sometimes the consequences of the failure to grieve echo down through many generations. I know of more than one case in which a mother, depressed following the loss of one of her parents, has been unable to give her children the warmth and love that make for a healthy and well-adjusted adult. Tortured by her own pain and unresolved grief, she is unattuned to the needs of her youngsters. The result is that they become maladjusted, craving love and warmth wherever they might find it. Many youngsters raised under such circumstances make unfortunate choices of relationship partners; unwanted pregnancies or premature entanglements are not unusual. Children born as a result of such relationships enter the world with two strikes against them. Even if the young parent tries to do his or her best to raise the child in a loving home, many factors work against the child. They include parental immaturity and financial stress. Just as important, a child born of parents who have themselves been parented inadequately may receive the same kind of inadequate parenting—knowing only poor parenting, the young parents in turn may be unattuned to their own children.

Unresolved grief can also result in major, lingering discomfort over issues of abandonment and separation that carries over from one generation to the next. The case of Mr. Y, who overreacted when his daughter went off to college, is a case in point. Left uncorrected, his unresolved grief might have had that sort of impact, echoing down through generations. I have known families in which the normal separations that are part of every family's life became major issues. A child's entering kindergarten becomes traumatic for both parents and child and results in the child developing a school phobia. An adolescent's age-appropriate efforts to separate from his or her parents become the occasion of huge battles. Going away to college results in emotional chaos. And so on. In almost all such cases, the family's difficulty with these transitions can be traced back to an unresolved grief that made every separation feel like a new death, a new abandonment.

NORMAL AND ABNORMAL MOURNING

For many years, researchers attempted unsuccessfully to distinguish between normal and abnormal mourning by looking for specific characteristics of each. Their untested belief was that there are qualitative differences between the two—that certain symptoms are characteristic of abnormal grief, whereas no such symptoms occur in normal grieving. For example, some speculated that in abnormal mourning there is *anger*, whereas in normal mourning there is *sadness*. Their research failed to confirm that view, and they were forced to conclude that no distinct characteristics define normal grief or distinguish it from abnormal grief—the same symptoms may occur in each, with a few minor variations. Instead, research has shown that normal and abnormal mourning can be distinguished not by the presence or absence of certain symptoms but by their intensity and duration. Thus, abnormal and normal grieving can be seen as falling along a continuum (Figure 8.1) from grief that is insufficiently intense or too short-lived at one extreme, to abnormally intense or protracted at the other extreme.

Figure 8.1 Continuum of Grief

ABNORMALLY NONINTENSE GRIEF	NORMAL GRIEF	ABNORMALLY INTENSE GRIEF
few or no outward signs of distress		many extremely intense and long-lasting signs of distress
few or no physical symptoms		many extremely intense and long-lasting physical symptoms
few or no disturbances of thought and behavior		many extremely intense and long-lasting disturbances of thought and behavior

The continuum is a useful device for conceptualizing the relationship between normal and abnormal grief. The more inappropriate the length or intensity of a person's reactions to a loss, the greater the likelihood that the grieving process has gone awry and that help is in order.

Therapists use several criteria to measure whether or not grieving has proceeded normally and has ended successfully. These criteria are both direct and indirect. Below is a questionnaire that addresses several signs relied on by therapists in assessing whether a person is satisfactorily grieving. The occurrence of *any* of these symptoms is an indication that professional help is almost certainly needed. If more than one of these symptoms occurs, then no time should be wasted in seeking help.

The feelings and behaviors catalogued in the "Grief Questionnaire" are not exhaustive, but they are suggestive of the most common signs of abnormal or unresolved grieving. In all cases, the intensity and duration of the symptoms are what distinguish normal grieving from abnormal grieving.

GRIEF QUESTIONNAIRE

Instructions: Circle *y* or *n* in response to each question. The questions are formulated as though you were assessing the success of your own grieving. By substituting *he* or *she* for *I*, and by making the necessary grammatical adjustments, you can use similar questions to assess whether another person's grieving is proceeding successfully.

y n 1. I am working very hard to keep unwanted thoughts about my dead parent out of my mind, even though a relatively long time has passed since she died.

y n 2. I do not feel anything about my parent's death.

y n 3. Even though most of my relatives have come to terms with my parent's death, I still am unable to control my feelings when I see a picture of her or think of her at all.

y n 4. I find myself unable to go to work, or to concentrate when I am there, because of thoughts of my parent.

y n 5. I find myself drinking or relying on other substances in an attempt to cope with my loss.

y n 6. Since the death of my parent, I have lost patience and have had outbursts of anger that are uncharacteristic of me.

y n 7. I feel as though I should die.

y n 8. Since my parent's death I have had constant nightmares that do not make much sense but from which I awaken in a state of terror.

y n 9. When I see a sad movie or TV show, or read a sad book, I cry uncontrollably and it takes many hours for me to regain my composure.

y n 10. I am extremely overprotective of my children since my loss, even though I realize it is not good.

y n 11. I am unable to dispose of any of the personal effects of my dead parent and become furious with anyone who tries to do so.

The more *y*'s you circled, the more important it is to seek professional help immediately.

Depression and Grief

In an attempt to distinguish between depression and bereavement, researchers have discovered rather subtle differences. Most of what is commonly called *grief* is very similar to what is usually called *depression*. Symptoms shared by both include sadness, lack of motivation, loss of interest in things that are usually pleasurable, loss of appetite, sleep disturbances, and feelings of hopelessness, emptiness, pointlessness, even lack of self worth, summarized in the phrase, "I am bad and worthless and deserve to die." Once again, the intensity and duration of these symptoms is a valid basis for drawing distinctions.

PART TWO: The Impact of Death on the Individual

What can you expect to experience after a parent dies? For the purpose of discussion, it is possible to create four classes of reactions: emotional reactions, physical sensations, intellectual reactions, and behaviors. Let us look at each of these in turn.

Emotional reactions can vary widely. They include feelings of sadness, loss, emotional paralysis, anger, resentment, self-pity, and relief. While these reactions may vary in their social acceptability (generally, it is not considered acceptable to experience relief when a parent dies), they are, in fact, all appropriate. No one can prescribe "correct" emotional reactions. The first step in healing is to accept them all. Only then can one express them, work them through, and get beyond them.

While your emotional reactions will be acute initially, you can expect that they will become less intense over time. However, you may well reexperience them in all their original intensity under certain circumstances. Special occasions and major life transitions frequently reactivate feelings of loss. That is why holidays are so difficult for so many people. Memories from the past color one's present experiences. Feelings of missing someone keenly can spur melancholy feelings on such occasions ("I wish Dad were here to see the children's happy faces on Christmas morning").

The same is true of formative events in one's life. One client whose father died when she was in her teens had coped well with his absence for many years. But when she married, she reexperienced the loss most acutely. Similarly, when she became pregnant, she found herself quite depressed. In the safety of the treatment relationship, she raved at her deceased father because he had not been around to see her married and now would not be able to see his grandchild.

Many physical sensations are components of grief, including an empty feeling in the pit of the stomach, dry mouth, lack of appetite, tightness in the throat, nausea, sleep disturbance, and extreme fatigue. Any one of these can be a frightening and disorienting experience. Taken together, these many physical sensations can be terrifying. Yet they are perfectly normal reactions, ways in which the body copes with the physiological and emotional shock that death occasions.

You can expect to experience mental confusion and disbelief. You may have the feeling that you are living in a dream, that what you are experiencing is not really happening. Quite often, people report that after the death of a parent they have only vague recollections of the funeral services. "I know I was at my father's wake," said one of my clients recently. "I even remember talking with people. But everything is in a cloud of some kind. I feel as though my body was there but the rest of me was someplace else." His reaction is not at all unusual.

Your mind may play other tricks on you. You may experience for-getfulness—not only generally, but you may actually forget your parent is dead. Unexpectedly, in unguarded moments, you may find yourself thinking, "I'm going to call Mother" or "Mother will enjoy wearing this." For many weeks after her mother's death, one woman reported that whenever she was in a crowd, she used to think she saw her. Difficulty concentrating is not unusual; neither are flashbacks—vivid recollections of past experiences with your parent.

VARIABLES THAT AFFECT INDIVIDUAL MOURNING

As noted earlier, the nature, duration, and intensity of your reactions are dependent on several variables, including the intensity of your relation-ship with your deceased parent. Were you unusually close? Did you have mixed feelings about her? Was she a warm person by temperament, or a cold and unpleasant personality?

Emotional preparation for the loss is another variable. Was the death expected? The death of an elderly person, especially one who has been ill, is easier to accept because we can see it coming. Other circumstances make coping with loss more difficult. For example, death in an accident, even if the victim is elderly, is very difficult.

Previous losses experienced by the survivor also play a role. Multiple losses in a relatively short time are a particular challenge. Similarly, if you are under stress for other reasons—for example, job or marital problems, or struggles with a teen at home—you may find it particularly difficult to cope with your parent's death.

Family, social, ethnic, and cultural factors play a role as well. Your cultural heritage shapes the way your family copes with losses. The way your parents mourned the death of their parents will likely influence the way you grieve now. You may recall from Chapter Three the story of a client of mine who lost her mother as a young girl. My client came from a family in which the expression of feelings was discouraged. When her mother grew ill and ultimately died, the family maintained a quiet composure, which compounded her loneliness and panic. My client recalled attending her mother's wake and crying next to the casket; the person who consoled her was not a family member, but a neighbor.

Before turning to the effects of a parent's death on the family as a whole, let me anticipate three questions I often hear from my clients: What should I tell my children about their grandparent's death? Should I allow my children to attend their wake and funeral? Should I tell my elderly parent that his sibling (or a dear, lifelong friend) has died?

CHILDREN

There is no definitive right way to handle the matter of death. However, experience and common sense suggest that it is advisable to keep the following six guidelines in mind.

Whether they show it in obvious ways or not, children are affected by death and loss. When a family is upset by a death, even though very young children may not fully understand what is happening, they feel it, and they often are frightened. It is never advisable to pretend that nothing is happening. Special support, reassurance, and attention are always warranted.

Each child is different. A child's age can be a general guide as to how much information you should provide. The *kind* of information you share should also be influenced by the youngster's age. (Be aware, however, that chronological age is only a rough guide, because levels of cognitive, emotional, and social maturity differ from child to child.) Furthermore, the intensity of the child's tie with the dead person can make a difference.

Usually, children will let you know how much information they want and how much they can tolerate. I recommend to clients that they answer all questions in an honest but age-appropriate manner. In fact, it is often desirable to encourage questions. If a child cannot formulate meaningful questions, due either to youth or to a lack of the needed words, explain why you and the other adults are upset. When talking about what it means to die, draw on the child's own experiences—the death of a pet, for example, or the departure of a friend who moved away. Provide reassurance. Make certain your youngster understands that he did not cause the death, and that one family member's death does not mean that *everyone* will soon die.

Many excellent books exist that can help children work through loss. Consult a school librarian or local children's librarian for help in finding books appropriate to your child's age. I often make use of books in my work with youngsters, sometimes reading to them or allowing them to read to me. Just listening quietly, sharing a touching word or phrase, or experiencing a moment of shared awareness can be very healing.

Accept a wide range of behaviors. Do not become alarmed if your child speaks about a favorite doll or imaginary friend who has died, or if the child plays at being dead herself. Acting out feelings—whether through misbehavior or play—is not at all uncommon among youngsters. Sometimes puppets and other projective toys and activities can allow the child to say things that would otherwise not be possible for them to verbalize. Mutual storytelling, for example, in which parent and child cooperate in fashioning a tale about a death, can provide opportunities for ventilation and healing. For older children, writing letters or and keeping a journal can be helpful.

Attendance at funerals and wakes should be the child's choice. I recommend explaining to children what will happen—whom they will see, what they will experience, what will happen, and how long it will take. Then let the child decide. Be prepared for the possibility that your youngster, having decided to attend, may change his mind at the last minute out of fear or uneasiness, and that he may need special support. Avoid forcing any issue. Provide understanding and acceptance. Do not make the mistake of using the child either as a pillar for yourself or to prove anything to anyone else.

If, after a reasonable length of time, a child fails to accept the death or to recover from it and resume normal functioning, seek help. Children often lack the skills required to cope with death. An experienced therapist can help you determine whether your child needs assistance and can provide the safe, supportive, and understanding environment your youngster may need. One 12-year-old client, who had witnessed his grandfather's death, seemed to handle the trauma adequately at first. Two years later, however, shortly after his mother was involved in a minor traffic accident, he began becoming anxious about his parents' safety. From school, he called home two or three times a day, just to ensure that they were all right.

Usually an active student and a fine athlete, he dropped out of after-school sports so that he could be home to ensure that all was well. He became extremely anxious any time either or both parents went out. Fortunately, they made the connection between his anxiety, his witnessing his grandfather's death, and Mother's auto accident. They sought treatment for the youngster. A short course of medication and an opportunity to talk through his fears enabled him to resume a normal life.

THE ELDERLY

I can think of few circumstances under which a normally functioning older person should be "protected" from the news of a death. To with-hold information, in my view, is arrogant, patronizing, and cruel. Seniors are entitled to the respect implied by keeping them informed of events in their world. I have never failed to be impressed with the aware-ness and resiliency of older people when they learn of the death of loved ones. (If, of course, an elderly person is severely demented and incapable of understanding what you are saying, there seems little point in shar-ing substantive news of any sort.)

You can often help older people work through a loss by simply lis-tening, empathizing, and encouraging reminiscence. Appropriate touching, hugging, and other acts of tenderness are also helpful.

Keeping in mind the variables discussed previously can help you prepare yourself for a person's reaction to the news of a death. How close was the survivor to the dead person? The closer they were, the more difficult the adjustment is likely to be. How many losses has the person experienced in the past few weeks? months? years? Expect that the older person's sense of her own mortality will be heightened when she hears of the death of a peer. Older bereaved people need company and support. They cannot simply be left alone and expected to cope after being informed of a death. You must commit to keeping in touch through visits, calls, and letters.

There is compelling research suggesting the elderly can become seriously depressed as a result of losses they experience and may become at risk for suicide. For example, it has been reported that in the United States people over age 65 account for more than 20 percent of the suicides, although they make up less than 13 percent of the population. Men above age 85 are particularly at risk. It is therefore crucial for adult children to be aware of warning signs that indicate inadequate grieving and depression among older people. These include sleep and appetite problems; a hopeless, despairing attitude; the development of physical symptoms without an organic cause; lack of interest in other people; inadequate self-care; failure to keep up one's home; and lack of food in the refrigerator. If you have any suspicions whatever in your mind that your surviving parent has failed to grieve adequately, be certain to consult a professional for an evaluation. As reported in Chapter Two, even very elderly people can profit from therapy and antidepressant medications.

PART THREE: The Impact of Death on the Family

You may recall from Chapter Three the definition of a *system* as a complex unit made up of parts that work together to accomplish a purpose. Whether you are talking about an automobile's fuel system, your body's respiratory system, or a family system, the definition applies. The family is made up of interrelated and interdependent individuals who must work together to accomplish a purpose.

You may also recall that every human system strives to maintain a balance or harmony that ensures its survival and effective functioning. A death threatens that balance. Consequently, when a family member dies, the family must reorder or restructure itself. Roles and relationships change, and these changes reverberate throughout the entire family. Dependencies may be transferred, and different levels of closeness or distance may develop.

The R family is a good case in point. Mrs. R was the family matriarch who had ruled the family quite sternly since her husband's death nearly two decades earlier. It was she who established trust funds for the grandchildren. She managed the lives of her adult daughters. She decided what would be done by whom under what circumstances. As a result of her tight control, significant dependencies developed. These were shattered when Mrs. R died after a brief illness.

With her passing, the family was jolted. As a result, much work was required to restructure and reorder the family, working toward a healthier and more equal distribution of power and prerogatives.

VARIABLES AFFECTING A FAMILY'S REACTION TO A DEATH

Two sets of variables affect the way a family copes with a death and grieves. The nature, intensity, and outward signs of a family's reactions are affected by (1) the characteristics of the person who died, including roles played by that person, and (2) the family's own characteristics.

Characteristics of the Person Who Died

How pivotal was he or she? The more central the person was to the family's functioning, the more disruptive will be the death, and the larger and more serious will be the number of adjustments required. Here are a few questions to help you estimate how pivotal a member has been in a family. The more frequently the answer is *yes* to these questions, the greater are the demands placed on the family after the person's death.

- Did others depend on him for many day-to-day needs necessary for survival and functioning?

- Did he overfunction while allowing others to avoid doing their fair share?

- Did he provide a key link (or the only link) between the family and the larger community?

- Was he viewed by others as the "heart and soul" of the family?

■ Did the family have difficulty coping with his absence (due to business responsibilities, health problems, or for other reasons) at times in the past?

When a pivotal family member dies, major role redefinitions are required. This process involves many subtle steps, most of which are followed without anyone's being fully aware of it. For example, suppose the person who died was one upon whom many family members were dependent. Before the family can reorder itself, many things must happen. For convenience, I will focus on four steps: selection, testing and proof, boundary setting, and maintaining the new balance.

1. *Who will be selected?* Surviving members must first select a replacement to pick up the slack left by the person's absence. (I am simplifying for purposes of brevity and clarity here. Many replacements may be selected, and tasks may be divided up among them.) The selection can be made by default—when, for example, there simply is no one else to perform the task. In addition, accidents of birth order or gender may influence the choice, as when the oldest son becomes the family patriarch after an elderly father dies. An individual may volunteer. Or, the survivor may be ordered by some outside authority figure to take on tasks formerly fulfilled by the dead person.

2. *Will the replacement person measure up?* Almost invariably, when a person takes up the task, she will be given responsibility, and then her behavior observed. Will she be up to it? If she must garner the cooperation of others, they may test her to see whether she can enlist their cooperation in her efforts. All this is done without any full awareness on anyone's part; yet it occurs with startling regularity.

    For example, in one family with whom I worked, holiday dinners had traditionally been held at the mother's house. The year she died, Ms. D, the oldest surviving daughter, took on the task. Chosen because she had been groomed for it during the elderly parent's declining years, Ms. D had acquired special skills and knowledge. Moreover, she possessed the temperament, intelligence, organizational skills, and emotional maturity required. Although family members cooperated graciously, on the day of the holiday dinner most commented in a sad-humorous way that they were going to watch carefully to see whether things were "up to their usual standards."

Sometimes, of course, the person chosen to fill the shoes of the dead parent may not be capable. Due to lack of innate ability, requirements of a job and family, or a difference in values, she may simply be unsuited. In these cases, the family must rethink the choice. Unfortunate compromises result—as in the case of one family whose traditional holiday dinners simply came to an end when the mother died. However, creative and refreshing solutions are also possible. In one family, for instance, because each sibling had demanding schedules and business obligations, three sisters agreed that the traditional holiday dinner would be replaced with a weekend getaway at a favorite local resort, where everyone could relax and enjoy each other's company while professionals did the preparation, cooking, and cleanup.

3. *What boundaries will be set?* Once a person has demonstrated that she can fulfill the tasks assigned her, the question of how much responsibility she will take on—or should be allowed to take on— arises next. "Yes, Betty *can* take over the job of caring for Dad, but does she want to? And is it fair to ask her to take on the entire responsibility?" Similarly, it might be true that John *can* rent the summer cottages for the family vacation, but should he be asked to do so?

4. *Can the new balance be maintained?* If the person selected fulfills the role adequately and if she and the family are able to establish realistic expectations and boundaries, then over time the family will establish and maintain a new balance. If not, it may be necessary to tolerate imbalance until a satisfactory resolution can be arrived at.

What roles did he or she play? A strife-ridden, or potentially strife-ridden, family may have been barely held together by the person who died. In one case, Mrs. K, widowed for many years, managed to keep the peace among her three strong-willed daughters and their families. To external observers, the large family appeared to be amicable and cooperative. As Mrs. K aged, she spent time with each of her three children. Each opened her home to Mrs. K. Each provided services and shared responsibility for her welfare. All the while, the entire family shared special occasions, vacationed together, and frequented each other's homes.

Within days after Mrs. K's death, the family began coming apart at the seams. The situation was so volatile that two of the sisters almost came to blows over some matter pertaining to Mrs. K's funeral. Recriminations about the uneven distribution of responsibilities during Mrs. K's declining years and about alleged wrongs perpetrated on her by one sibling or another resulted in alliances being formed, broken, and re-formed. After many months of arguing, two of the sisters wound up establishing an uneasy alliance; the third went to her grave several years later without ever saying another word to either of her siblings. Mrs. K had played the role of peacekeeper. When she died, the hostility and resentments that had boiled beneath the surface erupted.

Other key roles include the nurturer and the stabilizer. The more pivotal the role, the more important that someone pick up the mantle. Consider these examples:

- Shortly after his elderly father died, Robert immediately responded to a brewing feud between two of his siblings. Following in his father's footsteps, he arranged a meeting and facilitated a discussion that restored the harmony valued so highly by this family.

- After her mother's death, Shirley made it a point to record the birth dates of each niece and nephew. Every year thereafter she sent cards and other presents, as her mother had done for many, many years.

- A CPA, it was easy for Peter to take on the job of handling the family's finances, a task his elderly father had performed for most of his life.

In all these cases, key responsibilities were capably taken up by surviving adult children. These situations, far from being atypical, are the norm in most families.

What secret or conspiratory relationships did he or she have with other family members? In several families with whom I have worked, the deceased parent had maintained a special, even secret relationship with a privileged child. In some cases, the deceased parent had conspired with the privileged one to keep secrets from other siblings. Sometimes the secrets were trivial, although the mere fact that secrets were kept proved to be disruptive to the harmony among siblings. At other times, the secrets were anything but trivial. In one case, a father actually disinherited certain siblings while leading all of them to believe they would share equally in his modest estate. In all such cases, the parent's legacy is discord. Secrets and deceit have done more to destroy families after a death than almost anything I have observed in my professional experience.

Characteristics of the Family

To assess or predict the impact of a death on a family, it is useful to consider several variables. Let us look at three: the family's tendency to facilitate or hinder emotional expression (often tied to cultural influences), the kinds of relationships among family members, and life-cycle considerations.

Can the family tolerate and talk about feelings? Families may facilitate or hinder emotional expression. In some families, crying is actively discouraged because it is seen as a sign of craziness or weakness. More often than not, the inability to talk about feelings leads to acting-out behavior, in which people usually express their feelings by such self-defeating actions as drinking, arguing, and so on.

What kinds of relationships existed among family members prior to the death? Were they supportive of one another? Often, when family members are disconnected emotionally, they can do little to help each other. They may not be able to grieve at the time of death or contribute to each other's healing in any way.

Through what stage in its life cycle are the family and its individual members passing when the loss occurs? An elderly parent's death always occurs at a particular moment in time, which necessarily coincides with many other moments. An awareness of the point in the life-cycle at which survivors find themselves at the time of death can help anticipate likely responses. For example, when a parent dies, a surviving adult child may be going through a period of individual vulnerability occasioned by the birth of a child. The family of a surviving adult child may be in the midst of a crisis occasioned by an extramarital affair or the acting out of a rebellious teen. On the other hand, the death may coincide with a marriage, a college graduation, or the launching of a career. All such factors affect the feelings and reactions occasioned by the parent's death.

SIGNS THAT A FAMILY IS HAVING TROUBLE COPING WITH A DEATH

With a little knowledge, it is easy to tell if your family needs help in coping with the death of a parent. Here are several signs of problems:

- not grieving (always a sign that something is amiss)
- displaced emotions (scapegoating, blaming, misdirected anger)
- intergenerational issues (new conflicts with children, especially teens, over issues of separation and control)
- acting-out behavior (drinking, job problems, infidelity, failure to fulfill responsibilities—for youngsters, that means behaviors such as truancy, not doing homework, etc.)

- destructive alliances, withdrawal and indifference among family members (backfighting, fracturing of the family)

If any of these signs are noted, consulting a competent therapist—sensitive to issues of aging and death and skilled in working with families—is recommended.

How a Therapist Can Help a Family

A therapist skilled in working with families can help in several ways. Perhaps most importantly, a therapist can facilitate grieving and help the family successfully accomplish—or at least begin accomplishing—the four tasks of grieving mentioned earlier: accepting the reality of the loss, working through the pain and grief, adjusting to an environment from which the deceased is missing, and relocating the deceased person emotionally and moving on with life. If youngsters attend sessions, which I strongly recommend, they can learn—by seeing adults express sadness and cry openly—that it is normal and healthy to grieve.

Secondly, a mental health professional can help the family take stock of its situation, formulate goals for the future (what needs to be done, by whom, in what order?), and monitor progress toward those goals. This is especially important when there is a surviving elderly parent or other family member who was especially dependent on the deceased.

What methods is a therapist likely to use? One is to facilitate discussion of such topics as the meaning of the loss and its impact. A therapist may help the family articulate some of the ways the family has changed, and will need to change, following the death. The family may be encouraged to examine the roles that had been played by the dead person and to ask such questions as: Who is taking on those roles now? Was that person selected by default, by an accident of either birth order or gender, or by choice? Do others accept the new person in that role? In addition, family therapy provides an opportunity and a safe environment in which to explore new and changed alliances within the family. Once again, if any blaming, scapegoating, or other unhealthy behavior is occurring, the therapist can help the family see it, label it, and take steps to remedy it.

When a death occurs, conditions are ripe for the development of family pathology. As I noted previously in the chapter, if grieving is not completed, the failure to grieve adequately may affect future generations. Once unhealthy patterns develop, it is likely they will persist far into the future. As in the case of Mr. Y (page 248), unresolved issues of separation and loss may make it difficult for parents of subsequent generations to let go of their own children as they grow up and begin to make their own lives.

SUMMARY

The months following the death of a parent are critical to the process of successful readjustment. This chapter examined the nature of grief as well as some of the feelings, physical reactions, and mental responses a person is likely to experience when an elderly parent dies. Grief serves four critically important functions, and a distinction can be made between normal and abnormal grief. Variables that affect bereavement include the nature of the relationship between the deceased parent and family members, the roles the parent played, and the centrality of the deceased parent's position in the family. There are warning signs of inadequate grieving—direct and indirect indications that an individual or a family needs help in coping with a loss. A therapist can help both individuals and families with the grieving process.

Armed with this knowledge, and with an increased sensitivity to the issues involved, you are now in a position to anticipate and respond to the demands placed on individuals and families after the death of a parent. Perhaps no better example of successful grieving exists than the story of Dawn Smith, former Miss South Carolina and second runner-up in the Miss USA contest several years ago. The movie *Nightmare in Columbia County* recounts the terrible tragedy that befell her and her family when her older sister, Chris, was kidnapped and killed. Dawn played a very important role in apprehending her sister's murderer, at one point even putting her own life on the line.

Despite the horror through which she lived, Dawn has managed to make something meaningful of her sister's life and death. After accepting the reality of her sister's loss and working through her pain and grief, Dawn has gone on with her life. However, Chris is not forgotten. She plays a key role in the work Dawn now does as a minister and advocate on behalf of families who have survived tragedy. The experience of Dawn Smith serves as a model of what can happen, even under the most tragic circumstances, when grieving comes to a successful end.

SELECTED RESOURCES

ORGANIZATIONS AND AGENCIES

Note that in listing the following organizations, I have categorized them according to their main activity. However, the categories are less than airtight. For example, *all* organizations described as "Organizations That Advocate and Lobby" *also* provide information on request. No matter what your question is, if it seems that an agency may be of help, call or write to it.

Organizations That Advocate and Lobby

American Association of Homes
and Services for the Aging
901 E Street NW, Suite 500
Washington, DC 20004
1-202-783-2242

American Association of Retired
Persons (AARP)
Resource Services Group
Department QB
601 E Street NW

Washington, DC 20049
1-202-434-2277
*Alternate Address and Phone
for AARP:*
3200 East Carson Street
Lakewood, CA 90712
1-800-424-3410

American Health Care
Association
1201 L Street NW
Washington, DC 20005
1-800-321-0343
1-202-842-4444

Center to Improve Care of the
Dying
George Washington University
1001 Twenty-second Street NW,
Suite 700
Washington, DC 20037
1-202-467-2222

National Citizens' Coalition for
Nursing Home Reform
1424 Sixteenth Street NW,
Suite 202
Washington, DC 20036
1-202-332-2275

National Council of Senior
Citizens
8403 Colesville Road, Suite 1200

Silver Spring, MD 20910
1-301-578-8800

National Senior Citizens
  Law Center
1101 Fourteenth Street NW
Washington, DC 20005
1-202-289-6976

United Seniors Health
  Cooperative
1331 H Street NW, Suite 500
Washington, DC 20005
1-202-393-6222

Government and Government-Related Agencies

National Council on the Aging
409 Third Street SW,
  Second Floor
Washington, DC 20024
1-800-424-9046
1-202-479-1200

National Health Information
  Center (NHIC)
U.S. Department of Health and
  Human Services
P.O. Box 1133
Washington, DC 20013
1-800-336-4797

National Institute on Aging
9000 Rockville Pike
Bethesda, MD 20892
1-301-496-1752

U.S. Administration on Aging—
  Public Inquiry Line
330 Independence Avenue SW
Washington, DC 20201
1-202-619-0724

Organizations Providing Information and Support

Alzheimer's Association
919 North Michigan Avenue,
  Suite 1000
Chicago, IL 60611
1-800-272-3900

American Psychiatric Association
1400 K Street NW
Washington, DC 20005
1-202-682-6000

American Psychological
  Association
750 First Street NE
Washington, DC 20002
1-800-374-2723
1-202-336-5500

American Society on Aging
833 Market Street, Suite 511
San Francisco, CA 94103
1-415-974-9600

Children of Aging Parents
1609 Woodbourne Road #302A
Levittown, PA 19057
1-800-227-7294

Choice in Dying
1035 Thirty-ninth Street
Washington, DC 20007
1-800-989-9455

Eldercare Locator Service
1-800-677-1116

Family Service America, Inc.
11700 West Lake Park Drive
Milwaukee, WI 53224
1-414-359-1040

Hospice Helpline
1-800-658-8898

National Academy of Elder Law
    Attorneys
1604 North Country Club Road
Tucson, AZ 85716
1-520-881-4005

National Association of Area
    Agencies on Aging
1112 Sixteenth Street NW,
    Suite 100
Washington, DC 20036
1-202-296-8130

National Association for Home
    Care
228 Seventh Street SE
Washington, DC 20003
1-202-547-7424

National Association of
    Professional Geriatric Care
    Managers
1604 North Country Club Road
Tucson, AZ 85716
1-520-881-8008

National Association of Social
    Workers
750 First Street NE, Suite 700
Washington, DC 20002
1-800-638-8799

National Family Caregivers
    Association
10605 Concord Street, Suite 501
Kensington, MD 20895
1-800-896-3650
1-301-942-6430

National Hospice Organization
1901 North Moore Street,
   Suite 901
Arlington, VA 22209
1-800-658-8898
1-703-243-5900

National Institute on Adult Day
   Care (a division of National
   Council of the Aging)
409 Third Street SW,
   Second Floor
Washington, DC 20024
1-800-424-9046
1-202-479-1200

National Respite Locator Service
800 Eastowne Drive, Suite 105
Chapel Hill, NC 27514
1-800-773-5433

Visiting Nurse Association of
   America
11 Beacon Street, Suite 910
Boston, MA 02108
1-888-866-8773
1-617-426-5555

Retailers Offering Specialized Products

Bruce Medical Supply
P.O. Box 9166

411 Waverly Oaks Road
Waltham, MA 02254
1-800-225-8446

Sears Health Care Catalog
3737 Grader Street, Suite 110
Garland, TX 75041
1-800-326-1750
1-214-348-3600

BOOKS AND OTHER RESOURCES

Caring for Your Aging Parents by Donna Cohen and Carl Eisendorfer (NY: Putnam, 1993).

The Complete Elder Care Planner by Joy Loverde (NY: Hyperion, 1997).

Counting on Kindness: The Dilemmas of Dependency by W. Lustbader (New York: Free Press, 1991). This noteworthy and thoughtful book offers philo-sophical yet practical guidance for caregivers, and insights into the thoughts and feelings of care recipients.

Dictionary of Eldercare Terminology by Walter Feldesman (Washington, DC: United Seniors Health Cooperative, 1997). This book contains few medical terms (the author is an attorney), but emphasizes legal terminology, including home care, housing, insurance, managed care, Medicare, pensions and annuities, Social Security, taxes, and trusts.

How and Why We Age by Leonard Hayflick, Ph.D. (New York: Ballantine Books, 1994). This comprehensive and fascinating work, by a gerontologist of national repute, offers a detailed account of the biology and physiology of aging and its effects on elderly care recipients, as well as highly informative discussions of research underway to prolong life span. It is must reading for anyone caring for an elderly person.

How to Care for Aging Parents by Virginia Morris (New York: Workman Publishing, 1996). This informative book is well researched and contains many lists of resources for caregivers.

Life Worth Living: How Someone You Love Can Still Enjoy Life in a Nursing Home by William H. Thomas, M.D. (Acton, MA: VanderWyk & Burnham, 1996). This work provides a fresh perspective on life in a nursing home and recounts the origins of a movement toward "Edenization" of long-term care facilities.

Long Distance Caregiving by Angela Heath (San Luis Obispo, CA: Impact Publishers, 1993).

The Resourceful Caregiver by National Family Caregiving Association (Mosby-Lifeline, 1996). A *must buy* for any conscientious caregiver, this book provides information on organizations devoted to helping caregivers, as well as sources of information about specific disorders. It includes a state-by-state listing of respite services and a very detailed list of hotlines, helplines, online resources, and directories.

The 36 Hour Day: Family Guide to Caring for Persons with Alzheimer's Disease and Related Dementing Illnesses and Memory

Loss in Later Life, second ed., rev., by Nancy L. Mace and Peter V. Rabins (Baltimore, MD: Johns Hopkins Press, 1991). This minor classic contains many useful suggestions for *all* caregivers.

Today's Caregiver (magazine)
P.O. Box 800616
Aventura, FL 33180
1-954-962-2734

ONLINE RESOURCES

http://www.aarp.org (American Association of Retired Persons)

http://www.ama-assn.org (American Medical Asssociation)

http://www.caregiver.com (*Today's Caregiver* magazine)

http://www.healthnet.com

http://www.nfcacares.org

http://www.nhic-nt.health.org (National Health Information Center)

http://www.nih.gov (National Institutes of Health)

http://www.nih.gov/nia/ (National Institute on Aging)

http://www.senior.com

http://www.seniornet.com

GLOSSARY

This glossary is intended to provide brief definitions of several terms you are likely to encounter in the course of providing care for an elderly parent. It is not a definitive or an in-depth dictionary of medical or legal terminology. Consult an expert for guidance in answering specific questions pertinent to your parent's unique circumstances or condition.

activities of daily living (ADLs) Essential and basic requirements for self-care, including eating, bathing, dressing, and using the toilet.

advance directive Any legal instrument that enables an individual to specify what he or she wants (and does *not* want) done to prolong life as death approaches. The living will, the health-care proxy, and the durable power of attorney for health care are all types of advance directives.

adult day care Arrangements and facilities created to provide care for the elderly and infirm, including meals and supportive and therapeutic services.

aging network The network of agencies that provide services for the elderly. The network includes government agencies (federal, state, local, regional) as well as nonprofit and for-fee organizations and service providers.

apraxia One of the symptoms of Alzheimer's disease—inability to carry out motor tasks, despite the fact that the motor system is intact. The person may possess all the faculties necessary to pick up a fork, for example, but be unable to do so.

Area Agency on Aging A regional, government-supported agency that acts as a clearing house for services and programs for the elderly. There are local Area Agencies on Aging throughout the country. See the Selected Resources appendix for information on how to contact the National Association of Area Agencies on Aging.

arrhythmia Irregular heartbeat.

caregiving Performing tasks to maintain the well-being of a person who needs assistance. Caregiving can mean providing services such as shopping, light housekeeping, and help with finances, as well as personal care, which may include more difficult tasks such as administering medications and managing incontinence. Caregiving can also mean total supervision of a severely impaired person.

care plan A coordinated and carefully thought-out program of services, usually approved by a physician, for maintaining the health and well-being of a person requiring assistance. If Medicare is to pay for medical services, equipment, and other expenses, the components of the care plan must be ordered by a physician and approved by Medicare.

care management, case management The processes of determining a person's need for services (physical, psychological, or other), arranging for them, and monitoring their delivery. Private, professional care managers can be hired to oversee the care of an elderly relative who lives far away.

CVA (cardiovascular accident) Stroke.

dementia A progressive mental disorder that may be a disease in itself or a consequence of other conditions, such as stroke. Dementia results in increased difficulty remembering and performing everyday tasks. Alzheimer's disease is one of the many kinds of dementia.

durable power of attorney See **power of attorney**.

durable power of attorney for health care A legal instrument or document that gives the holder authority to make decisions about the medical care of a person when that person can no longer do so. It does not provide the authority to discontinue life support but *does* provide authority to make all other medical decisions, including decisions about elective surgery.

elderlaw The specialty within law that focuses on the legal and financial needs of the elderly, including estate planning (wills, trusts, etc.), Medicare and Medicaid eligibility and advocacy, and issues of competence. See **guardianship** and **power of attorney**.

executor, executrix Individual appointed before death by a person to manage the estate of the deceased person.

geriatrics The branch of medicine specializing in caring for elderly people.

gerontology The field of study that focuses on the well-being of elderly people. It includes the study of the medical problems unique to the elderly and of emotional and social matters of special relevance to the elderly and their families.

guardian A person appointed to manage another person's financial and personal affairs when that person can no longer do so. Guardians are appointed by the courts as a result of formal legal action.

health-care agent A person appointed by an individual to make end-of-life decisions when that individual can no longer do so and to see to it that the dying person's wishes are carried out.

instrumental activities of daily living (IADLs) Activities required to live independently, such as shopping, cooking, paying bills. IADLs are less crucial than and ancillary to **activities of daily living**.

levels of care A phrase used to categorize and distinguish among the kinds and intensity of care required by an elderly or ill person. There are three levels of care: **(1) Custodial care** consists of assistance with activities of daily living such as dressing, bathing, and eating. Custodial services are usually provided by licensed practical nurses (LPNs) and others, some of whom (for example, home-health aides) are not licensed medical professionals. **(2) Intermediate care** consists of not only assistance with activities of daily living but also rehabilitation services required as a result of a stroke or a broken hip. Intermediate care services are provided by licensed therapists and registered nurses (RNs) as well as by licensed practical nurses (LPNs). **(3) Skilled nursing care** consists of extensive and overall management of all life functions provided for individuals who are bedridden and cannot care for themselves at all. Skilled nursing care is provided by licensed medical personnel, such as RNs, under the direction of an attending physician.

living will A document that specifies which life-sustaining services an individual wants and does not want as he or she approaches death. A living will is one of a number of **advance directives**.

Medicare A federal program administered nationally by the Health Care Financing Administration. As of this writing, Medicare has no income or asset restrictions. (It is not "means tested," which means beneficiaries do not have to be impoverished or to meet other requirements to be eligible for benefits.) Procedures for application as well as extent of coverage do not vary significantly from one state or locality to another. Medicare does *not* cover long-term custodial care in a person's community or in a nursing home. Medicare will not cover services, supplies, medical equipment, or other items unless they are prescribed by a physician as part of a formal care plan.

Medicaid An insurance program funded by a combination of federal and state funds but administered by individual states. The administering agencies vary from state to state—for example, in Connecticut, the Medicaid program, called the Title IX ("Title 9") Program, is administered by the Department of Social Services.

Medicaid eligibility and benefits rules are quite complex and they also change periodically. Because of these complexities, expert consultation is advised if you are making care arrangements that involve Medicaid reimbursement. The following

Medicaid guidelines are generally true as of this writing.

Medicaid is a "needs based" medical assistance program for people who are at least 65 years of age and disabled, blind, or receiving public assistance. Recipients must have limited savings and low incomes. In other words, there is a "means test" for Medicaid beneficiaries, who must document their impoverishment in order to qualify. The value of a person's home is not counted in determining eligibility, nor is any life insurance or prepaid burial contract. However, the amount of income earned *is* considered. The income amount allowed for Medicaid applicants, whether individuals or couples, varies depending on the community in which the applicants live. Thus, among the various states, allowable income limits vary widely. Medicaid pays for most medical services, including the cost of care in a long-term care facility.

medigap insurance Private insurance that pays part of medical expenses approved by Medicare as medically necessary, but not covered by Medicare.

mental status exam A series of questions and instructions administered by a health-care provider to determine a person's level of mental functioning. Questions such as "What day is this? What year is this?" and instructions such as "Pick up the paper, unfold it, and read the number inside" are typical.

nutrition site A location, often a Senior Center or community facility, where meals are provided for seniors who qualify for the program.

ombudsman A person whose job it is to investigate complaints about long-term care facilities in which older people live.

polypharmacy The excessive and inappropriate use of medications, resulting in duplicate prescriptions and adverse drug interactions. Polypharmacy is often a result of lack of coordination among health-care providers.

power of attorney A document that authorizes one person to act on behalf of another in legal matters such as entering into contracts, transacting business, and paying bills. A power of attorney document may be unrestricted, in which case the attorney-in-fact (or agent) is given broad powers for an unlimited period of time. Or, it may be time limited and restricted, in which case specific powers *and only those powers* are granted to the agent, and for only limited periods of time. A **durable power of attorney** survives the incompetence or incapacity of the person authorizing another to act on his or her behalf. For most elderly people, it is wise to arrange for a durable power of attorney.

probate A legal proceeding as a result of which an estate is divided after death. The rules of probate vary widely from state to state.

respite care Short-term care arrangements, sometimes available through community agencies and long-term care facilities, that provide temporary relief from caregiving responsibilities.

INDEX

Dementia, 12, 85–86, 98
versus delirium, 98–99
Denial, as a response to parental aging, 28–29
Depression
biological basis for, 89
and bipolar disorder (checklist for), 99–100
and grief, 252–253
due to lack of adjustment, 200
due to loss of control, 16
and suicide among the elderly, 259
tests for, 111
Diagnosis of mental problems. *See* Mental problems, diagnosis of
Dialectical model, 56–58
Digestive system, age-related changes in, 9
Disappointment
with one's own life, 34–35
as a response to parental aging, 30
Distrust and disbelief, as a response to parental aging, 29
DNR (Do Not Resuscitate) order, 224
Durable power of attorney for health care, 228–229. *See also* Advance directives
Dying, 211–221. *See also* Advance directives; Death and dying; End-of-life decisions
death scenario, 208–210
defined, 216
"good death," 211
role of family in, 209–210
role of hospital administration in, 208
role of nurse in, 209
role of physician in, 208–209
staying in control of one's, benefits of, 211–214

E

EAP (Employee Assistance Program), 40
ECHO housing, 167. *See also* Housing options
Eden Alternative, 16–17, 189–190
Elderly. *See also* Aging; Safety in the home
classification of, 3–4
concerns of, 13–17, 173–175
developing sensitivity to the needs of (inventory), 17–23
Emergency personal response systems, 129–130
Emotional disorders, 84–85, 86–88. *See also* Mental problems
Emotional reactions
appropriate versus extreme, 36–38
to parental aging
as adult-child caregiver, 25–35, 44–48, 63–66, 122, 144
identifying and coping with, 35–41
to a parent's death, 253–255. *See also* Death and dying
Empathy, developing, 14, 17–23. *See also* Communication
EMS (Emergency Medical Service), 224
End-of-life decisions, 207–237
Erikson, Erik, 17
Euthanasia Society of America, 218
Exercise, effects of, on the elderly, 6, 10
Extended care facilities. *See* Nursing homes

F

Falls
avoiding, 123–129
effects of, 15

Living will, 222–226. See also
   Advance directives
Living with an elderly parent,
   159–164. *See also* Housing
   options
Long-term care facilities. *See* Nursing
   homes
Long-term care insurance, 191–194
Loss, 91–92. *See also* Mourning

M

Medical directives, defined, 229–230.
   See also Advance directives
Medicare and Medicaid, 145,
   146–147, 190–191, 195
   institutional standards and,
      185–186
   limited benefits, 150
Medications
   administration of, safety tips for, 128
   as a compounding factor in mental
      illness, 94–95
   history of an individual's, 108
   for mental problems, 89
   and polypharmacy, 205
Memory, 12–13
Mental problems, 81–115
   attitudes toward, 88–90
   checklist for, 98–101
   cognitive versus emotional, 85–88,
      98–101
   diagnosis of, 97–104, 107–113
   evaluating help for (checklist),
      111–113
   getting help for, 105–113
   how adult children can help the
      diagnostician of, 101–103
   how adult children can support
      their parent during treatment
      for, 113–114

inadequate treatment of, among the
      elderly, 88
   reasons the elderly are at risk for,
      90–95
   symptoms and warning signs of,
      96–101
Mental status exam, 109–111
Mourning
   children in, 255–258
   defined, 240
   importance of, 239–249
   normal versus abnormal, 249–253
   process of, and function of stages
      in, 242–249
   variables that affect the personal
      impact of, 253–255
Murphy's Law, 78
Muscles, age-related changes in, 5–6

N

National Citizens' Coalition for
      Nursing Home Reform, 187
Neglect, 93–94
Nonprofit agencies, 145, 147
Normal, defined, 83–84
Nurses
   role of, in death scenario, 209
   visiting, 146, 147
Nursing homes. 182–205. *See also*
      Institutionalization, pathways
      to and planning for
   adjusting to, 197–205
   categories of, 182–185
   costs of, and paying for, 190–194
   criteria for selecting, 188–190,
      195–197
   Edenized, 16–17, 189–190
   movement for reform of, 187
   statistics on number of people in,
      171

O

Office of the Aging, 187
Older Americans Act, 187
Ombudsman, long-term care, 187, 195
Overinvolvement and uneven distribution of responsibility, 63–66
Over-the-counter medications, 108. *See also* Medications

P

Passive-aggression, in response to parental aging, 32
Patient advocate, 105
Patient Self-Determination Act, 220–221
Patients' rights, concept of, 217–219. *See also* Advance Directives
Payment arrangements, and long-term care facilities, 190–197. *See also* Medicare and Medicaid
Personal possessions, importance of, 198–199
Personality changes
in the caregiving adult child, 37
due to cognitive or emotional disorders, 85–86, 97
PET-scan, 10
Physician, role of, in death scenarios, 208–209, 213–214, 216
Physician-assisted suicide, 219
Physiological changes due to aging, 2–13, 90
Polypharmacy, 205
Population, changing demographics of, 171
Poverty, 92–93
Power of attorney, 228–229
Private-pay agencies, 147
Problem management, 141–143, 156

Problem solving
by the Creative Problem-Solving Sequence, 70–72
by the Criterion Method, 72–79
identifying and discussing the problem, 63–70
variables that affect the quality of a family's solutions, 58–62
Projection, as a response to parental aging, 31–32
Publicly funded agencies, 147

Q

Quality of life, 207–213. *See also* Advance directives; Aging in place; Right to Die movement
Quinlan, Karen Ann, 218

R

Religious assistance, 40
Resentment, as a response to parental aging, 30
Resistance
to discussing end-of-life decisions, 232–237
to in-home care, 157–158
to institutionalization, 179
Respite care, 131–132
Rest homes, 184
Retirement communities, continuing-care, 173–175. *See also* Housing options
Reverse mortgage, 194
Right to Die movement, 214–220. *See also* Dying; Patient Self-Determination Act; Quality of life
Role changes in family, 259–265
Rollin, Betty, 219

S

Safety in the home, 123–129
"Sandwich generation," 55
Self-determination
    by parent, 119, 122, 174, 178
    by patient, 220–221
Self-oriented grief, 34
Senior housing, 167–168. *See also* Housing options
Senses, age-related diminishment of, 6–8
Sensitivity, developing, to needs of the elderly (Inventory), 17–23
Shared housing. *See also* Housing options
    with adult child(ren), 159–164
    with roommate(s), 166–167
Shock and surprise, as a response to parental aging, 27–28
Siblings
    consultation among, 123
    cooperation and competition among, 44–50
    relationships among, 56–60, 62, 63–66
    and resistance to discussions, 234
Skilled-nursing care institutions, 183
Sleep disturbance, 90
Smell, losing ability to, 8
Smith, Dawn, 267–268
"Stranger medicine," 208–209
Stressors and mental problems, 107–108. *See also* Mental problems, diagnosis of
Subsidized housing, 168
Suicide
    among the elderly, 259
    feelings of, in adult child, 40

T

System
    defined, 44
    family as a, 44–50
    life cycle of the family, 50–79

T

Taste, losing ability to, 7–8
Teenagers, grieving and, 247
Telephone
    enhancements, 128
    reassurance ("telecare"), 130
Trophic factors, 5–6

U, V, W

Vascular dementia, 12
Viatical settlements, 194
Vision loss, 6, 127–128
Visiting nurse associations, 146–147. *See also* Home care
Visits with parent, maximizing, 203–205
Water temperature, 124. *See also* Safety in the home
Weight training, benefits of, 6

X, Y, Z

Zung Self-Rating Depression Scale, 111